P9-DTQ-603

KiTCHEN COACH
WEEKNIGHT COOKING

Life is short! Join me in the Kitchen!

John Bushnell

KiTCHEN COACH

WEEKNIGHT COOKING

JENNIFER BUSHMAN
and Sallie Y. Williams

WILEY

Wiley Publishing, Inc.

Copyright © 2004 by Wiley Publishing, Inc., Hoboken, New Jersey. All rights reserved.

No part of this publication may be reproduced, stored in a retrieval system or transmitted in any form or by any means, electronic, mechanical, photocopying, recording, scanning or otherwise, except as permitted under Sections 107 or 108 of the 1976 United States Copyright Act, without either the prior written permission of the Publisher, or authorization through payment of the appropriate per-copy fee to the Copyright Clearance Center, 222 Rosewood Drive, Danvers, MA 01923, (978) 750-8400, fax (978) 750-4744. Requests to the Publisher for permission should be addressed to the Legal Department, Wiley Publishing, Inc., 10475 Crosspoint Blvd., Indianapolis, IN 46256, (317) 572-3447, fax (317) 572-4447, E-Mail: permcoordinator@wiley.com.

Trademarks: Wiley and the Wiley Publishing logo are trademarks or registered trademarks of Wiley Publishing, Inc., in the United States and other countries, and may not be used without written permission. All other trademarks are the property of their respective owners. Wiley Publishing, Inc., is not associated with any product or vendor mentioned in this book.

Limit of Liability/Disclaimer of Warranty: While the publisher and author have used their best efforts in preparing this book, they make no representations or warranties with respect to the accuracy or completeness of the contents of this book and specifically disclaim any implied warranties of merchantability or fitness for a particular purpose. No warranty may be created or extended by sales representatives or written sales materials. The advice and strategies contained herein may not be suitable for your situation. You should consult with a professional where appropriate. Neither the publisher nor author shall be liable for any loss of profit or any other commercial damages, including but not limited to special, incidental, consequential, or other damages.

For general information on our other products and services or to obtain technical support please contact our Customer Care Department within the U.S. at 800-762-2974, outside the U.S. at 317-572-3993 or fax 317-572-4002.

Wiley also publishes its books in a variety of electronic formats. Some content that appears in print may not be available in electronic books.

Library of Congress Cataloging-in-Publication Data:

Bushman, Jennifer, 1967-
    Kitchen coach weeknight cooking / Jennifer Bushman and Sallie Williams.—1st ed.
        p. cm.
Includes index.
    ISBN 0-7645-4314-8 (Paperback : alk. paper)
  1. Cookery. I. Williams, Sallie Y. II. Title.
    TX714.B88 2004
    641.5—dc22

                                2003020229

Manufactured in the United States of America
10 9 8 7 6 5 4 3 2 1

Contents

Acknowledgments

So many people have played such a vital role in the creation of this book that it is impossible to thank them all here. I would first like to thank Linda Ingroia, my editor, who had the confidence to allow me to undertake this project. Thanks also to Jennifer Mazurkie, who helped whip this book into shape, and to Jeff Dow for his terrific photos. My thanks and appreciation go out to the entire staff and all the investors of Nothing to It! Culinary Center, who have spent hours poring over my recipes to help me make this book sound and look its best. I also want to express my thanks to the students of Nothing to It! Culinary Center, who have been motivated by my passion for cooking, and who, in turn, motivate me to greater goals. Thanks to Stacey Glick, my agent, who never gave up on the idea of a Kitchen Coach cookbook. To Craig and Charlotte Haase, profound thanks for your continuing patience and support. Thank you, Lila Gault, for believing in me from the very beginning. Very special thanks must go to my parents, Larry and LaNae Gralla, who have supported me throughout my cooking journey and my life in countless ways. To my husband Jay and my son Matthew, our life together gives me the love, passion, and energy I need to pursue my dreams. Finally, to my dear "Gram," whose spirit in her life and in her kitchen lives on in me every day of my life.

Jennifer Bushman

Introduction

Here's the truth: I love to cook, but I, too, juggle a busy schedule with the demands of feeding my family good food every night. Of course, it's very simple to pick up some ready-cooked foods or go out to eat, but instead, I remind myself of why I love to cook (and why it sometimes just makes sense to cook).

The sights, smells, and sounds of cooking really are a source of true pleasure, and the methodical rituals of cooking—chopping tomatoes, stirring pasta—are a way to unwind. Cooking also offers a creative challenge: I may start by thinking, what can I create with what's already in my kitchen? What's seasonal or fresh that will be simple to turn into dinner? When it turns out that I've actually outdone my own expectations, I get a kick out of how simply roasting super-fresh fish in olive oil or tossing together a sizzling stir-fry can make me feel as accomplished as a four-star chef—and so glad I cooked at all.

I bring my love for—and sense of fun with—food to all the cooking classes I teach. My students have found that mastering some versatile techniques and adaptable recipes can make anyone a comfortable, efficient, confident cook. As my students' "kitchen coach," I go one step further and inspire and motivate them to want to cook, to enjoy the process of cooking, not just the results. In *Kitchen Coach: Weeknight Cooking*, I aim to get you in on the fun, too, even for the trickiest, sometimes most challenging kind of cooking: the Monday through Friday meals.

One of the key goals of this book is to help you downshift your brain from autopilot to manual in order to appreciate cooking for both its up-front and its less tangible benefits. There's no getting around the fact that preparing a meal usually takes more time than you spend eating it. And the usual focus is on getting the food on the plate, and on the table. But developing a sense of pleasure and fulfillment while working in the kitchen takes out the "chore" factor you may often feel.

I have found that people usually don't hate cooking; they hate wasting time in the kitchen. You'll see that I emphasize time management and organization. Even though this sounds as if you'll have to follow unpleasantly rigid practices, in fact, this just boils down to some simple principles, starting with the French culinary concept of *"mise en place,"* or "everything in its place," which actually simplifies preparing a meal. Simpler means less stressful, which means more enjoyable. By organizing your ingredients, equipment, and utensils, and by properly anticipating the time a task will take, you set the mental boundaries needed to focus on the experience to its fullest.

Cooking can also be more manageable and fun when you target your cooking to your specific needs of the day. Sometimes you're tired; other times your family wants a favorite dish, like pizza, again; sometimes your kids and spouse have crazy schedules and you need food that can travel, or that will keep, or that can be easily reheated.

In the chapter "Why Cook?" you'll find a chart to help you decide what to prepare for dinner or at least help you kick-start your thinking about dinner. I'll give you several suggestions for types of dishes or meals—like stir-fries, sandwiches, tacos, or chicken—and you decide what will work for your family, and, quite frankly, what you're in the mood to cook. (And isn't that truly what happens? Sometimes you really love the idea of a quick but delicious steak dinner; sometimes instead you want to make something a little special, a little exotic, like Mediterranean food.) You might refer to this chart a few times, but soon it will become an automatic trigger, an easy mental checklist, to think about before you plan any meal. It takes the pressure off and gets you on the right path.

Kitchen Coach: Weeknight Cooking will be your guide to weeknight/work-night cooking success. Success might mean you get a round of applause from the family because you outdid yourself, or maybe it just means that everybody's fed and you've stopped thinking about the work you need to do back at the office. Cooking isn't magic, but it is true that if you make a little effort, at the end of it, everyone's hunger will be sated and you will have had an opportunity to exercise your creativity and exorcise your stress along the way. I'll give you the tools and the ideas you need to get the most out of cooking no matter what your weeknight reality is from day to day. Enjoy!

Why Cook?

Any day of the week, especially weeknights, cooking is an option, not a necessity. Go to a restaurant, get takeout, or pick up a prepackaged heat-and-serve "meal" at the market and you can get by just fine, giving your body adequate nutrition without dirtying a dish or breaking the bank. So why go to the trouble and time to cook anymore when it can be done for you so conveniently?

Why? Because cooking even just a couple of times a week will make you happier. I don't have a double-blind placebo-controlled study to prove it, but I see the proof every day during the course of my work teaching people how to cook, and in cooking for my own family.

Ask yourself a few questions:

1. Do you feel you are spending too much time and money eating out?

2. Do you come home from a busy day and think you are too exhausted to cook something good for your family?

3. Do you feel you and your family could be eating better-quality food than you are, and more healthful food as well?

4. Would your family benefit from sitting down together for dinner a bit more often?

5. Do you find yourself dreading the time spent in the kitchen?

If you answered yes to any of these questions, this book is for you. Cooking can give you a bigger return for your time invested than any other nonjob activity I know. Bottom line—you'll be happier that you cooked. (Unless, of course, you set the kitchen on fire. But read the section on kitchen safety, and you'll be fine.) Sounds simple, possibly even the equivalent of a campaign promise, but, with all the amazing variety of activities you could do in the modern world, the age-old activity of cooking, regardless of your background or lot in life, fulfills many basic human requirements: the need to be fed (actually the need to be well-fed), the need for sensory stimulation, and the grander goals that you may not think about all the time—the needs to learn, achieve, and contribute.

How? Here's a scenario: It's dinnertime and you decide to make pasta with tomato sauce, again, but you're bored or irritated by the idea. Stop. Now think about it in a different way: It's the peak of summer tomato season, and the tomatoes are beautifully smooth and red and juicy, so they barely need to be cooked. As you cook the sauce, the sizzling garlic perks up your ears, the garlic aroma stops you for a minute; you take a deeper breath. You decide on a whim to add a little oregano instead of basil. You remember you bought a package of a new pasta shape—maybe cavatappi (corkscrews), instead of penne—so you use that, and you decide to puree the tomatoes to see if the sauce coats the pasta better. (It does, you discover, and the flavors blend together nicely, too.) Your result is something simple yet different, terrifically flavored, filling, and fairly cheap to make—quite an achievement. In fact, it's a small but personal triumph. To top it off, your family hasn't seen you all day and they are so happy you cooked a homemade meal that they finish off all the pasta. That's a lot of good stuff happening and it's just for making a simple dinner.

Okay, so maybe dinner at your house won't be like that every night, but it's worth striving for. Take some satisfaction that in accomplishing the smaller, mostly unacknowledged, steps of cooking, you benefit. A tasty pasta dish one night, a perfectly cooked steak another night, these are little perks in your life—and they add up to keep you going.

For many people, including me, cooking is also part of "the good life." The time we put into cooking is valuable time, not wasted time. Many cooking and eating experiences last well beyond the food and flavors of the moment. Every time you cook, what you bought, how you cooked it, and how you and your family responded register in your mind and add up, giving you a bank of ideas for future reference—about how to cook more efficiently, more creatively, and more precisely, just for starters.

Also, good food, good meals—even weeknight meals—can become lasting memories. Even if your family didn't cook much, you may still be nostalgic for the fried-eggs-on-Sunday ritual, or the s'mores your mom made. For me, there are plenty of great memories: My grandmother's latkes, my grandfather (who took his pancake griddle everywhere) making buttermilk pancakes, my mother's melt-in-your-mouth peanut butter cookies. Our life experience is the sum of all the good and bad we take in. Cooking allows us to stack the deck in our favor. Knowing there's something to look forward to at the end of the day makes life's ride a little easier, whether you are thinking about the grilled chicken you're going to make for dinner at 3 PM because your stomach is grumbling or anticipating your child's reaction when you make her favorite treat. To me, the good life is about pleasurable experiences. The more of these experiences you create in the kitchen, the happier you and your family will be.

Enjoying the Journey

You have likely heard the expression, "Life is about the journey, not the destination." In the same way, you could also say, "Cooking is about the process, not what's on the plate." My guess is, if you've picked up this book and are still reading, you probably do love food, or can imagine that you might, if only . . . To help you enjoy the process of cooking, first you have to switch your brain from autopilot (often needed to handle your busy day) to manual, in order to appreciate what's happening when you cook. Going back to the example of cooking pasta with tomato sauce, there was the sound and aroma of the garlic cooking in the pan. Making

other sensory connections to food and cooking means paying attention, being curious, and being adventurous: sort through the lettuce bin to pick the freshest, brightest greens; rub herbs to release their aroma; taste cheese before adding it to a dish. Actually, tasting, in particular, is an essential thing to do all through your cooking (except with potentially unsafe foods, like raw poultry, of course). Tasting tells you if your cooking is going in a direction you like or if alternative action is needed. And if it is good, you'll be quite pleased with yourself!

Fitting Cooking into Your Life

In my years of working with home cooks, I've heard just about every reason for not cooking, including no time, hectic schedules, the ease of having restaurants on every street corner, and the availability of takeout and delivered meals.

First, let me be clear that I am not a proponent of cooking every single night of the week. It's fun to get out and try new restaurants, or frequent old favorites. And if you want or need to bring home takeout on occasion, or to have something delivered to the door, do it. But because there are so many benefits from cooking, the scale should be tipped well in favor of cooking at home.

I've found that teaching someone how to cook is not the tricky part. It's helping them fit cooking into their daily lives that isn't easy, especially on busy weeknights. That often takes a little outside-the-box thinking and creativity. Fitting cooking into your life is really no different from fitting in other things that you want and need to do. You just have to make the time.

I don't mean to be one of those rah-rah time-management proponents, but advance planning really does work. I mentioned in my introduction the French concept of *mise en place*, the everything-in-its-place strategy of cooking preparation. This concept holds true from the easiest aspect of cooking—organizing your ingredients to have them ready—to the most challenging (sometimes)—organizing your life so you can cook.

Try not to fall into a rut of thinking that you have "no time" every week. Obviously, each week, your schedule will vary. Some weeks you might not have any time at all to cook. Other weeks you might be able to squeeze in an extra night. Looking at the upcoming weeknights, which nights might you have an hour or so to cook? Most of the people of whom I ask that question are surprised when they realize they have more nights available than they thought. If cooking is a priority, typically, the time appears somehow. So take a good look at your calendar.

Once you find the time, think about planning the details. Spend 10 to 15 minutes planning the shopping and cooking in advance, visualizing how you are going to get it done. Which store has what you need? What's the first thing you need to do when you get home? Just a little bit of forethought will make things go more smoothly when you are home and ready to cook. It's okay to wing it now and then, but cooking almost always turns out better when you put a bit of thought into it. As great athletes will attest, visualizing (or at least thinking through) before doing really improves performance.

Another reason people don't cook, and this is usually for people who rarely cook, is that they feel uneasy and apprehensive with even the idea of cooking. Very few want to admit it, but they are a bit scared of cooking because they never really learned how. Part of it may be because the traditions and legacy of cooking stopped in their parents' generation; their mothers (the family cooks for the most part) weren't in the kitchen sharing their culinary skills. So, today, they may know how to get by in the kitchen—to program the microwave, turn on the stove, and follow the directions on the back of a box—but there's no comfort or confidence in cooking. (So, keep in mind that your cooking in your own kitchen will help you develop more self-reliant children.)

If this represents your situation and you do want to get past rudimentary skills and the fear of failure, first you have to tell yourself two things: "I can be a good cook," and "I can enjoy this, mistakes and all." Remember, it's just food. If it doesn't turn out the way you want, you'll have another chance. You have to eat every day, don't you? My goal in this book is to help you address what your cooking issues are—fear of cooking, lack of skills, lack of time, lack of ideas—and help you cook foods that work within your world. I'll also help you shore up your cooking ability and confidence so that weeknight cooking doesn't feel like a chore, a bother, or an insurmountable challenge. (Be sure to read the introductions to each chapter that detail basics on preparing each type of food, and read the tips, too, to achieve precise results.)

The key to good cooking lies in a simple equation: Good Ingredients + Good Techniques = Good Food. It's really that simple.

So, let's get started.

Dealing with Cooking Challenges

There are 150 recipes and lots of cooking information in this book, and you can use it any way you like. Pick your three favorite recipes and make only those until they are your specialties. Or, look in the index for an ingredient you have in the kitchen to make a spur-of-the-moment meal. Or, try all the recipes—one at a time. They are all simple to make and tasty, and the majority of the recipes can be made in 30 minutes, some in even less time, especially after you have made them once or twice. (There are a few recipes that take longer but they are such family pleasers, you'll want to have them as options.)

Here's another way to get yourself in gear for weeknight cooking:

Make a list of things you and your family like to eat. If you like, make a computer file with the list, so you can print it out and use it as a shopping list, adding to it the things you might need for particular recipes.

Add a line that says "Foods to Try" and on a regular basis jot down one or two items—like arugula or panko bread crumbs—so you remember to look for them in the supermarket or figure out where there's a specialty food store nearby that might have them. Trying a new food from time to time will keep cooking interesting and creative.

Next, and most important, make a list of things that you consider challenges to your making dinner on a regular basis. I've done this for myself and with cooking students, and we have found it helpful in making cooking regularly more manageable.

Maybe you are stressed from work, or too tired to cook, or your kids are picky eaters. It's possible that there are several challenges at the same time. But try to identify what the primary issue is for you on a given day, then look for recipes on the following chart that will satisfy your needs. Keep checking back here to figure out where to start, then just keep the categories in mind when thinking about dinner or food shopping. Here is a chart of situations you might recognize and some of my suggestions.

The Situation	Type of Recipe Needed	Recipe Suggestions
1. You don't know how to cook	You need to try one new, simple dish at a time	Try reviewing the "Is Your Kitchen Ready?" chapter (page 6), then test the recipes in "Comfort Foods," like Quick-and-Easy Shepherd's Pie (page 139), and the "Mix-and-Match Pastas and Sauces" chapter (page 82), especially Angel Hair with 10-Minute Tomato-Basil Sauce (page 83). Also, try the Vegetable Skewers with Louis Dressing (page 71) and Grilled Portobello Stacks (page 130).
2. You are too tired to cook	You need something simple, requiring little effort	Try delicious updated sandwiches from "The Sandwich Board" chapter (page 30), or the simple Hot Roast Chicken and Monterey Jack Wrap (page 41), or Mom's Chutney Chicken Salad (page 21), Panzanella (page 131), Cold Roast Pork with Spicy Coconut Sauce (page 119), or Bacon, Lettuce, and Tomato Soft Tacos (page 52).
3. You are running really late tonight	You need something requiring little or no preparation or cooking time, made ahead to reheat, or supplements to store-bought food	Try Chicken, Avocado, and Bacon Wrap (page 40), anything from the "Sensational Salads" chapter (page 14), or think about how quick and easy eggs are in the "Breakfast for Dinner" chapter (page 154). Also, try Fresh Crab Tacos (page 49) or Classic Caesar Salad with Mustard Grilled Chicken (page 26).
4. You didn't eat much today or feel wiped out	You need something substantial	Try Cumin-Glazed Pork Filet with Apples and Pears (page 118), or Moroccan-Spiced Grilled Strip Steaks with Couscous (page 115), or Roasted Herb-Crusted Salmon with Extra-Virgin Olive Oil (page 109), or healthy but satisfying Game Hens with Wild Rice and Grape Stuffing (page 150), or, of course, Quick Macaroni and Cheese (page 137).
5. It's time for chicken—again	You need to experiment, try some new flavors	Try Oven-Barbecued Chicken (page 97), or any of the other recipes in the "It's Chicken, Tonight!" chapter (page 95), or Pesto Chicken and Vegetables (page 76), Eastern Braised Chicken Over Noodle Pillows (page 127), Lemon Roasted Chicken (page 134), Pasta Salad with Chicken and Grapes (page 22), or Cold Sesame Noodles with Pulled Chicken (page 94).
6. Your family really wants fast food	You need something that looks and tastes like their favorites but is fresher and (likely) healthier	Try taco recipes from the "Tacos and Enchiladas for Everyone" chapter (page 45), or a couple of the pizzas from the "Midweek Pizza Party" chapter (page 55), or one of the deli-type wraps from the "Wrap It!" chapter (page 36). Also, try Classic Caesar Salad with Mustard Grilled Chicken (page 26) or Fried Buttermilk Chicken Drummettes (page 138).
7. No one is home at the same time to eat together	You need foods that can be served warm or cold or can be reheated, or need only a little extra preparation	Try Bacon, Lettuce, and Tomato Soft Tacos (page 52), or Baked Penne with Basil, Tomatoes, and Sausage (page 92), or Roast Beef and Roasted Potato Salad (page 28), or Cajun Meatloaf Patties (page 117). Also, try Game Hens with Wild Rice and Grape Stuffing (page 150), Cold Roast Pork with Spicy Coconut Sauce (page 119), or Quick-and-Easy Shepherd's Pie (page 139).
8. You're on a budget	You need pantry-ready recipes or those requiring few ingredients	Try Linguine with White Clam Sauce (page 84), Roasted Vegetable Hero (page 33), Mock Eggs Benedict (page 158), Oven-Barbecued Chicken (page 77), Vegetable Skewers with Louis Dressing (page 71), Roasted Tilapia with Garlic and Parsley (page 112), or Lemon Roasted Chicken (page 134).

The Situation	Type of Recipe Needed	Recipe Suggestions
9. You want to eat healthfully but you don't want to suffer for it	You need nutritious, flavorful, and creative recipes	Try the dishes in the "Spa Cooking" chapter (page 147), like Linguine with Tomato-Fennel Sauce (page 152) or Mustard-Crusted Chicken with a Trio of Peppers and Couscous (page 149); or check out the recipes in the "Sensational Salads" chapter (page 14), like Pasta Salad with Chicken and Grapes (page 22); or try Provençal Grilled Halibut (page 111) or Shrimp and Cucumber Sticks with Spicy Tomato Sauce (page 68).
10. Your kids are finicky	You need to make something fun	Quick Macaroni and Cheese (page 137) almost always hits the spot, but also try foods from the "On a Stick–Skewered Foods" chapter (page 64), or the "Wrap It!" chapter (page 36), and Cream Cheese French Toast Sandwiches (page 162) or Banana Pancakes with Honey Butter Spread (page 160) from the "Breakfast for Dinner" chapter (page 154), which will make everyone smile.
11. Your kids want to "cook"	You need something really simple and safe to make that they will like to eat	Try Bumps on a Log (page 193), or any of the recipes in the "Kids in the Kitchen" chapter (page 192). Also, try Bacon, Lettuce, and Tomato Soft Tacos (page 52), Banana Pancakes with Honey Butter Spread (page 160), Off the Shelf Mud Pie (page 117), or Shrimp and Cucumber Sticks with Spicy Tomato Sauce (page 68).
12. Your children aren't eating their lunches	You need peanut butter and more peanut butter (I'm only half kidding)	Try the "No-Trade Lunches" chapter (page 183) for that and other options. Also, try Pasta Salad with Chicken and Grapes (page 22) or Fried Buttermilk Chicken Drummettes (page 138).
13. You have snack duty for your child's class	You need flavor and presentation the kids will love	Try Peanut Butter and Jelly Mini-Muffins (page 200) or Chicken and Fruit Salad Cups (page 202) from the "Classroom Snacks" chapter (page 199). Also, try Fruit Sticks with Strawberry–Cream Cheese Dip (page 189) or Cut Vegetable Medley with Ranch Dipping Sauce (page 190).

Other tools you might find useful in choosing recipes are the phrases below the recipe titles, highlighting dishes that offer certain benefits, such as Easy Preparation (for when you don't have the energy to do chopping and washing and the like); Make-Ahead (so you can finish it off right before you need to eat); No Cooking Needed (for time-strapped or just plain hot nights); Take-Along (for foods you and your family can take with you on busy nights); and Something Special (for when you want to make a little extra effort for yourself, family, or guests).

This isn't a cooking bible with thousands of recipes, but a source of ideas based on situations I know many cooks are faced with. Some days you want to cook like a chef on TV; other days your kids only want to eat peanut butter. Cooking regularly naturally ebbs and flows this way. Refined chefs have secret fetishes for junk food; I sometimes use prepared seasonings and bottled condiments or ready-cooked foods in my meals one night, then feel inspired to bake a quiche from scratch.

I know some people might think it is sacrilegious to serve pancakes for dinner or wouldn't call making sandwiches cooking, but you know that the demands and challenges you face every day could keep you out of the kitchen altogether if you let them. If you are the cook, you make the call about what's right for you and your family. As long as you keep an eye on nutrition, and aim for variety, go with the type of cooking that your family will eat, enjoy, and make you glad you cooked.

Is Your Kitchen Ready?

In order to enjoy cooking regularly and not find it a bore or a chore, get yourself and your kitchen into gear—literally and figuratively. Put your mind toward organizing your kitchen so that it is well stocked and arranged in a way that makes it a comfortable, safe, and inspiring place to work. Clean out your pantry and refrigerator, make sure you have the right cooking equipment and pans, and plan food shopping that will provide a balance of fresh, seasonal foods.

A Well-Stocked Pantry

To keep shopping time to a minimum, you will need to keep a properly stocked pantry. And properly stocked may mean different things to different cooks. There is a set list of items well worth everyone having on hand, but then your supplies will also be based on what you like to cook and what your family eats. Before you take a look into your cupboards, look at my suggested pantry list and, from it, make a list of what you think should be on hand. Then, go have a look at what you actually have on the shelves, decide what you need, and start getting your kitchen into shape.

A Trip Through Your Pantry

Setting the Scene
Put your work clothes on and plan to spend some time. Get a few trash bags out, and be ready to fill them. It's quite possible you have been shopping for food for years, but have never thought to clean out stuff that you might not even remember you have and is probably out of date anyway. Some things have just been taking up space and cluttering your cabinets since the day you bought them. There is no telling how long the job will take, especially if you are a serious saver, so let's begin with a few guidelines.

A Guide to Organizing Your Pantry

1. If you don't use it, lose it. Stop waiting for those "just in case" moments that never happen and get rid of it.

2. Dried herbs last 1 year, dried spices last 1½ years. That is all! So if you still have grandma's spices from when you cleaned out her kitchen 5 years ago, throw them away! The natural oils dry up when they get much older. P.S. If you just can't bear to part with them, before using them, heat them in a dry skillet over medium heat, just until you can smell their aroma. This activates whatever oils remain.

3. Beans and grains are best used within 1½ years. Once a box or package is opened, maintain the food's shelf life by storing it in a tightly sealed container.

4. Oils, such as vegetable, canola, and olive oil, last about 1 year; vinegar, vanilla, and other extracts last 2 years. Some oils have a shorter shelf life, such as walnut oil or other nut oils. Flavored oils have a very short shelf life once opened because of the additional organic elements such as garlic or chiles—they usually do not last more than a few days stored in the refrigerator.

5. If you have kitchen equipment that you use infrequently, like an ice cream machine, try to find an out-of-the-way spot for it.

6. Make a map of your kitchen. What are your cooking and food preparation patterns? If you have your pans stored more than 5 feet away from the stove, that is too far. Consider that you need to be able to reach the cabinets where you store the glasses and plates while standing close to the dishwasher. What about your spices? They should be near your food preparation area (but not near the heat or the quality will deteriorate).

7. In general, keep foods—fresh or dry—away from heat, light, air, and moisture and they should stay fresher longer. The elements help grow food but can also decrease their usable life.

Here's my suggested list of what to have on hand:

Dried Herbs and Spices

_____ Basil

_____ Bay leaves

_____ Cayenne pepper

_____ Chile powder

_____ Cinnamon, ground and sticks

_____ Coriander, whole seeds and ground

_____ Cumin, ground

_____ Curry powder

_____ Ginger, ground

_____ Marjoram, dried

_____ Mustard, dried powder

_____ Nutmeg, seeds and ground

_____ Old Bay Seasoning (spicy seasoning with great pepper flavor)

_____ Oregano, dried

_____ Paprika, sweet Hungarian

_____ Peppercorns, black and white (and a grinder)

_____ Poppy seeds

_____ Dried red pepper flakes

_____ Rosemary, dried

_____ Sage, dried

_____ Salt (if possible, sea salt, ground and coarse)

_____ Seasoned pepper (such as Mrs. Dash, for quick effective seasoning of everyday foods)

_____ Sesame seeds

_____ Tarragon, dried

_____ Thyme, dried

_____ Turmeric

Other Seasonings and Flavorings

_____ Anchovy fillets in olive oil

_____ Double-acting baking powder

_____ Baking soda

_____ Bouillon: cubes and powder (to use in a pinch if you have no broth or stock)

_____ Beans: white, great northern, and black, in cans

_____ Brandy

_____ Bread crumbs, unseasoned (and Italian seasoned, if you like)

_____ Low-sodium chicken broth: canned or boxed

_____ Chocolate: unsweetened and semisweet morsels

_____ Cocoa, unsweetened baking

_____ Cornmeal, yellow

_____ Cornstarch

_____ Cream of tartar

_____ Flour, unbleached all-purpose

_____ Gelatin, powdered and unflavored

_____ Honey

_____ Horseradish, jarred

_____ Ketchup

_____ Mustard: Dijon and yellow

_____ Nuts: one or more packages of pecans, walnuts, almonds, peanuts, or pine nuts

_____ Oil: olive (regular and extra-virgin), vegetable, peanut, Asian sesame, and walnut

_____ Dry sherry

_____ Sugar: white granulated and dark brown

_____ Soy sauce: light and, possibly, low sodium

_____ Tabasco sauce

_____ Tomatoes: whole plum, tomato paste, tomato puree, and sun-dried

_____ Vanilla extract

_____ Vinegar: white wine, red wine (If you like vinegars, add: balsamic, cider, rice wine)

_____ Wine: Chardonnay, Sauvignon Blanc, Cabernet, Madeira, and Port (optional)

_____ Worcestershire sauce

_____ Yeast, dry active

Fresh Basics

_____ Butter: unsalted (or salted if you prefer, except for baking)

_____ Eggs, large grade A

_____ Garlic: fresh cloves or finely chopped in oil to use in a pinch

_____ Lemons

_____ Margarine

_____ Mayonnaise

_____ Milk

_____ Yogurt, plain nonfat

Pasta and Grains

_____ Bulgur

_____ Couscous

_____ Lentils

_____ Thin pastas: i.e. linguine, spaghettini, or angel hair

_____ Rice: white and basmati

_____ Risotto

_____ Small shells and other shapes

Kitchen Equipment

Do you have the kitchen equipment you need? From sharp knives to good pans, quality equipment makes your job easier and more enjoyable. Just like when you have new or high-quality running shoes or sports gear, good equipment makes you want to jump right in and see what you can do.

How to Outfit a Working Kitchen

Knives

Knives are your most important kitchen tools. If you can, invest in high-quality knives. I prefer nonserrated knives. Although serrated don't need to be sharpened, their edges aren't suitable for all foods and can make your work more difficult. Keep all knives sharp (read directions and talk with a knife seller) and carefully stored in a butcher block, on a magnetic rack, or with the blades covered. Remember that dull knives are dangerous—more so than very sharp ones.

Knives should be professionally sharpened every six months or at least once a year. Ask the meat cutter in your supermarket where you can get your knives sharpened. If you bought a knife set, sharpen the knife with the sharpening steel rod that came with it every two or three times you use it. (You can buy the sharpening steel on its own too. Review the instructions or ask for a demonstration to understand the technique.) Never put knives in the sink. Wash them separately, dry them, and put them away as you use them. Here's the set I recommend:

_____ 3-inch paring knife: for all those small cutting jobs; very useful for people with small hands

_____ 8- or 9-inch chef's knife: the workhorse knife; for slicing, dicing, and most other cutting jobs

_____ Bread knife

_____ Tomato knife (long knife with a scalloped edge): not essential but very useful tool for slicing tomatoes, cheese, and foods that tend to stick to flat knives

_____ 10-inch slicing/carving knife: this is very useful for slicing roast meats, ham, etc., or for carving poultry

_____ Sharpening steel/rod, diamond edge: an everyday tool used for bringing back a fine edge; cannot sharpen a very dull knife

Equipment and Utensils

_____ Set of 11 glass nesting mixing bowls

_____ Set of measuring spoons consisting of ¼ teaspoon, ½ teaspoon, 1 teaspoon, and 1 tablespoon measures

_____ Two sets of measuring cups, one for dry foods, one for liquid. Liquid measures are glass or plastic and are available in 1-, 2-, and 4-cup sizes. Dry measures come in sets of four sizes, ¼ cup, ⅓ cup, ½ cup, and 1 cup.

_____ An instant-read meat thermometer and a frying thermometer

_____ Oven thermometer: oven temperature controls are not always accurate

_____ Several wooden spoons for stirring foods or serving

_____ Stainless steel slotted spoon: a long-handled spoon useful for removing foods from liquids

_____ Stainless steel cook's spoon: the same as the slotted spoon without holes, used for basting, mixing liquids and removing foods from pots and pans

_____ Large strainer/colander

_____ Fine-mesh strainer

_____ Whisk

_____ Two rubber spatulas

_____ Flat metal spatula: for transferring and serving food

_____ Ladle

_____ Cook's fork: a three-tined or two-tined fork used for moving foods around while cooking, and for holding meats and poultry steady while carving

_____ Tongs: spring action are extremely useful for moving meat and poultry in and out of pans, off and on the grill, or for turning without piercing the exterior and releasing essential juices

_____ Grater

_____ Bulb baster: essential in the kitchen

_____ Heavy can opener with bottle opener

_____ Vegetable peeler

_____ Citrus zester (my favorite is the Microplane zester)

Pots and Pans

_____ 1-quart and 2½-quart saucepans, both with lids

_____ 8-quart stockpot with lid

_____ 10- or 12-inch slope-sided skillet with ovenproof handle

_____ 12-inch straight-sided skillet with ovenproof handle (sauté pan)

_____ 8-inch skillet, nonstick preferred, with ovenproof handle

_____ Roasting pan with rack

Baking Equipment

_____ Rolling pin

_____ 10-inch springform pan

_____ 8- or 9-inch removable-bottom tart tin

_____ Two cookie sheets: heavy stainless steel

_____ Two baking (half-) sheets with raised edges

_____ Two 8-inch cake pans

_____ Two 9- × 5- × 3-inch loaf pans

_____ 9-inch glass pie plate

_____ 12-cup muffin tin

_____ 9- × 13- × 2-inch ovenproof glass dish

_____ Flour sifter

_____ Wire cooling rack

_____ Pastry brush

Machines

These items are expensive but worth every penny. With proper care they will last a lifetime. Because these are big purchases, I offer my favorite brands, which have stood the tests of use and time.

_____ Food processor: preferably one with a large capacity. My preference is for the 11-cup Kitchen Aid for versatility and power. It has a mini chopper built in, which is so convenient.

_____ Stand mixer: I prefer the 5- or 6-quart Kitchen Aid, as smaller models are not as durable. My grandmother's big Kitchen Aid has been working since 1943. Now that's a great investment.

_____ Heavy-duty blender: 40-ounce capacity. My preference is Waring, though Oster is another good one. I have Gram's Waring from 1942 and it works better than most new ones.

_____ Digital kitchen scale: a spring-action scale with a digital readout useful for weighing ingredients and for portion control.

_____ Immersion blender: a very useful appliance for mixing and pureeing in the container in which the food is being prepared. Wonderful for pureeing soups, for quickly beating eggs, for making homemade mayonnaise, and for whipped drinks such as milk shakes. Saves cleanup and the mess of transferring food from one container to another.

Kitchen Safety

Safety in the kitchen is mostly common sense, though there are definitely things to remember. Here are just a few.

Utensils

Knives

_____ Keep out of reach of children. If possible, always store them with blades covered. If using one of the magnetic racks, store with the sharp edge away from you.

_____ Never let a knife sit in the sink, leaving yourself open to accidental contact.

_____ Never cut with the sharp edge pointed at your other hand or your body.

Pots and pans

_____ Always turn handles away from the front edge of the stove so children cannot reach them, and so you don't accidentally hit a handle and spill the contents.

_____ Always use dry cloths or pot holders to take hot pans from the oven; a wet or damp cloth will transfer the heat quickly to your hand and burn you.

_____ Always drain liquids away from you so the steam will not burn your face.

_____ Be very careful of noninsulated pot and skillet handles. While it is wonderful that they can go from stovetop into the oven, they become quite hot. One chef I know sprinkled the handle with flour the minute he took a pan out of the oven to remind himself that the handle was extremely hot.

_____ Do not wear dangling jewelry or extremely long or loose sleeves when cooking as they may catch on pot handles and lead to spills or burns from the hot stove or pots.

Appliances

_____ Check all cords to be sure they are not frayed and are plugged in correctly, without too many appliances on one circuit.

_____ Be sure appliance cords are not tangled; this could make the appliance fall when cords are moved.

_____ Hold the covers on blenders and food processors with your hand to keep them from splashing liquid—especially hot liquid. Use a pot holder or folded towel to prevent accidental burns if a hot liquid should leak.

_____ Always have a small kitchen fire extinguisher readily available—not in the broom closet or under the sink—just in case there is a flare-up in a pan or in the oven. Learn how to use it.

_____ Anchor any mats or rugs to the floor so you do not slip while holding a knife or a pot full of hot food. Wipe all spills as soon as they happen for the same reason, and take particular care if you spill oil or fat of any kind.

Basic Food Safety

Shopping

_____ Buy the freshest foods possible. Check expiration dates and buy the freshest of the lot. And don't buy anything you don't think you can use before the expiration date—it is a waste of money.

_____ Do not buy dented cans, or cans that have a bulge in the top or bottom.

_____ Do not buy meat if the wrapping has been cut or torn.

_____ Do not buy food in plastic bottles or packages if they are dented or cracked.

_____ Arrange your trip around the supermarket to buy the most perishable things last. Dairy products, juice, eggs, and frozen food products should go in last and come out first at home.

_____ Do not refreeze ice cream or frozen products that have melted on your way home.

_____ If the weather is warm, keep a cooler in the back of your car or truck and transfer the refrigerated and frozen foods to it for the trip home.

_____ Go through the refrigerator regularly and discard anything that is past its expiration date, or has been cooked and then left for more than 2 to 3 days. It's best to throw it away in a tightly closed container, so pets and animals outside cannot get to it.

Safety in Preparation

_____ Wash your hands frequently before, during, and after food preparation and cooking—especially after handling anything raw, such as meat, poultry, and fish.

_____ Use plastic cutting boards for meat, poultry, and fish and wash the boards thoroughly between uses. Do not cut meat on a board that has been used for poultry or fish without thoroughly washing it with hot soapy water first.

_____ A good rule of thumb, if you can follow it, is to cut fruit first, then vegetables, then the meat, poultry, or fish you will be using. That isn't always practical, so:

_____ Wash cutting boards that have been used for meat, poultry, or fish with hot soapy water before using them to cut up fruits and vegetables, especially if the produce will be eaten raw.

_____ A good idea is to buy several cutting boards in order to be sure you will have a clean one at hand. Reserve one for meats, poultry, and fish, and one for other foods.

_____ Don't leave raw eggs, meat, poultry, or fish out of the refrigerator for more than about 20 minutes—or the length of time to warm to room temperature—before cooking or re-refrigerating.

_____ Throw away marinades that have been used on raw meat, poultry, or fish. If you want to use some for basting, reserve a quantity in a separate container before you add the rest to the food to be marinated. The only exception is if you boil the marinade for a few minutes to make it into a sauce.

_____ Don't put cooked food on the same plate that has held raw food without washing the plate in hot soapy water first.

Making the Most of the Market

In addition to organizing your pantry and kitchen, it is important to make the most of every trip to the food market. The core of good cooking is: use the best available ingredients. I don't mean excessively expensive or exotic vegetables and condiments. I mean search local markets for the most vibrantly fresh, brightly colored fruits and vegetables, quality condiments, freshly butchered meats and poultry, and just-out-of-the-water fish and shellfish.

Today, the range of foods accessible to us across the country is truly incredible. While cities and sophisticated urban areas may offer a wider selection than smaller communities do, never before have Americans had such a variety of fruits, vegetables, and other fine edibles within reach.

Supply is a question of demand. Restaurant chefs and experienced home cooks are demanding more choice and better quality in fresh foods. Gradually supply has begun to catch up with demand.

At farmers' markets, green markets, and well-stocked supermarkets everywhere, you may likely see a new fruit or vegetable nearly every week. Old, familiar vegetables are reappearing in new guises. Tiny yellow pear-shaped tomatoes are offered as well as several varieties of the customary cherry tomatoes. More familiar red and green bell peppers are seen in company with varieties of orange, purple, black, and white ones.

Even sizes are changing. Petite culinary gems are pushing out the old bigger-is-better prizewinners. Small and toothsome seem to be watchwords in today's world of vegetables. Tiny, crisp carrots, pencil-slim leeks, and miniature ears of corn are just a few of the varieties available.

It shouldn't be long before eating well does not mean eating expensively, but instead, knowing how to buy fresh foods at the peak of their quality, how to store them, how to prepare them, and, ultimately, how to cook them appropriately so that they retain the best of their flavor. And that is where I come in.

Fine food does not have to be exotic, complex, or complicated. A perfectly fresh piece of white cod, roasted with olive oil and garlic, alongside freshly steamed or perhaps grilled vegetables, is both nutritionally and gastronomically superior to a heavily sauced portion of Fettuccine Alfredo.

Convenience has become the working family's mantra. In stores you will find cleaned and pared vegetables, washed and dried greens, even boned meats and fishes, portioned and often already marinated or stuffed. Everything seems ready to pop into the pot or oven, or toss onto the grill. You can take advantage of the fact that some of the kitchen work has already been done, enabling you to put more interesting food on the table in a short period of time. The convenience does come at a cost, though: the price still remains low enough that very little home effort can produce an excellent meal less expensively than even a low-end restaurant.

Here are a few tips for a successful trip to the market :

_____ Choose ingredients that are in full season—while they are at the peak of quality, full of flavor, and capable of being prepared with a minimum of effort.

_____ Leafy vegetables should be bright or richly green—no yellow patches. Leaves must be crisp and sound, not limp, slimy, brown, or full of holes.

_____ Root vegetables must be plump and firm, not floppy or limp, with no shiny, soft or damp patches, or other surface damage such as nicks and cuts. Look for potatoes with few if any eyes and no greenish tint.

_____ Tomatoes and peppers should have taut, shiny skins full of bright color—no bruises or soft spots.

_____ Herbs must be vibrantly colored, with strong scent and flavor. Avoid any that are wilted, yellowed, or showing signs of rot. Trim the stems and store them, stem down, in a jar of water in the refrigerator. If you like, cover with a plastic bag to protect other foods from their strong scents.

_____ Plan to use items from the farmers' market within two days of purchase at the very most. Almost all vegetables (some potatoes and other tubers are an exception) are more nutritious if they are at their freshest when you use them—ideally the same day picked or purchased. In fact, most fresh produce, with a few notable exceptions, is best within hours of being harvested. This just maintains a smart tradition long followed on farms. There is an old adage that says you should have the kettle boiling before you pick the corn for dinner. Now that's last-minute freshness!

_____ Ask local growers or purveyors about the foods they are selling. Usually they take great pride in what they produce, and often they can and will provide a wealth of information on how to prepare what they sell. Ask to sample things you haven't tried before (or at least smell, touch, or discuss raw foods to best determine quality). Often, you will enjoy the new flavor or food, and may decide to introduce it to your family.

_____ While bringing a list helps you to shop efficiently, don't consider it written in stone when you are in fresh food markets or aisles of the supermarket selling produce, meats, and fish. Decide what appeals to you and looks freshest, then form your menus around what you have bought, just as many great chefs do. This may take a little more time, but is really sometimes more rewarding than following your list or a recipe which calls for food not at the peak of quality, or even in season. Good food choices will make you a better cook even before you step in the kitchen.

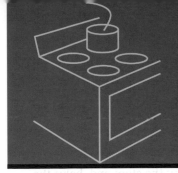

Sensational Salads

I love salads, and you may too, but do you think about them as an important part of dinner? Salads should be more than just a humdrum side dish or simple first course. When made well, salads offer flavor, crunch, color, and nutrients to your meal and come together easily once you clean and prepare the ingredients. Many nights you may want a light meal—light on effort and good for your health—and salad hits the spot. With the right ingredients—such as avocado, nuts, cheese, or bacon—flavorful greens, and a great dressing made in a flash, you have a satisfying meal. Or you can make the simplest salad of fresh greens and ripe tomatoes, then add cooked meat, chicken, or even good-quality tuna to make it more substantial. Salads are also so easy to vary—add jarred marinated artichokes or peppers, cured olives, fruit, or whatever you may have in your pantry or can pick up in a quick stop at the store. The same with the dressing—add a little lemon juice, mustard, or soy sauce, or experiment with other ingredients, all to make dinner simple, tasty, and possibly even fun to create. Here are some practical tips.

Basic Salad Tips

1. If you are in a hurry, rinse the salad in a clean sink full of cold water, then spin the greens dry in a salad spinner.

2. If you have more time to prepare: When using a whole head of lettuce or greens from a bag, soak them for at least 20 minutes in icy cold water. (The water needs to be very cold to prevent the greens from absorbing too much and becoming limp instead of crisp.). Wrap the lettuce in paper towels and store it in the refrigerator for several hours. This will remove the excess moisture and crisp up the salad.

3. Always tear lettuce for tossed salads. Cutting the greens will give the lettuce a wilted look and leave a bitter taste.

4. If your greens are wilted or old, douse them with hot, but not boiling, water, then immediately immerse them in cold water with a little bit of vinegar added to it. However, this will not work with seriously flabby greens. Those can only be rinsed, dried, and stirred into your next stir-fry or vegetable soup.

5. Before adding dressing, lightly season your salad greens with salt and pepper to enhance the flavor.

6. To make your own simple vinaigrette, the perfect proportion is two parts oil to one part vinegar. Don't add the oil to the vinegar and other seasonings until you are ready to serve the salad. Add the oil in a thin stream, whisking as you add it. Then add the dressing to the salad and toss it to combine.

7. Use salad dressing sparingly. A thin coat of dressing will flavor the greens without overpowering them or making them wilt.

8. If your dressing seems too thick, dilute it by whisking in a little oil, vinegar, wine, or even water.

9. Add tomatoes after you toss the salad once, then toss again. Otherwise, the water in tomatoes tends to thin out the salad dressing.

10. Serve salads on a platter or individual plates instead of in a bowl. The flavorful ingredients will be more evenly distributed and accessible, rather than at the bottom.

Preparing Raw Vegetables

Prepare your vegetables just before you are ready to use them. Make sure they are dry and in an open plastic bag when you store them in the crisper. Here are some tips for handling common salad vegetables:

Celery: Remove the leafy ends and save them for soup stock. Remove the tough ends and peel off any tough strings. Chop or dice the celery according to the recipe. If not using right away, store in ice water.

Cucumber: Peel the cucumber, halve it lengthwise, and remove the seeds with the tip of a spoon. With the exception of the hothouse English-style cucumber, which comes wrapped in plastic, most store-bought cucumbers are heavily waxed, so they need to be peeled. The seeds are bitter and should be removed. Cut the cucumber in the shape of your choice—thick slices or sticks, then chunks.

Garlic: Peel garlic cloves by placing them one at a time on the cutting board and, using the side of your knife, pressing down with your palm firmly and sharply until it's slightly crushed. Pull off and discard the loosened skin. Chop the garlic finely, adding a pinch of salt. Use as is, or for better blending, mash the garlic with the edge of a heavy knife several times to form a creamy garlic paste.

Green onions (sometimes labeled scallions, although they are technically not the same onion variety): Cut off the ends and all but two inches of the green tops. Chop once into thin slices. Do not chop green onions until just before you use them, or they will become limp.

Mushrooms: When choosing mushrooms, look for firm ones with no bruises or moldy spots, and store them in your refrigerator in a paper bag. Brush them clean or rinse quickly with just a little bit of water; do not let them soak, or they will end up soggy and without flavor and texture. Chop or dice according to your recipe.

Onions: Look for firm onions with paper-thin skins and no bruises. Store them in a cool, dark place. To chop: Cut in half through the root from top to bottom (the root will keep the onion intact while you cut). Then place the halves flat side down on the cutting board. Cut in vertical strips with your knife without cutting all of the way through the root end of the onion. Then cut a series of horizontal slices. Finally, chop across the onion vertically to produce finely chopped onion. The most important thing to remember with the onion is not to over-chop it or to chop it in the food processor. This causes the onion to give off its juices and become stronger in flavor. To mellow an onion's flavor and make the slices crisper, chill the slices in ice water several hours before using them.

Bell peppers (green, yellow, or red): Cut out the stem end, halve the peppers, and remove and discard the seeds and ribs. Remove the round ends and cut into julienne (long, thin) strips. Dice or chop the peppers according to the recipe.

Tomatoes: Vine-ripened tomatoes are the best choice for all salads. They have the best flavor and cannot be beat for their juiciness and texture. In my mind these are the only type of tomatoes you should use, but they may be difficult to find. Grow them yourself, ask your supermarket to carry them if they don't, take a trip to a specialty food store, go to the farmers' markets and farm stands in season, ask your gardening neighbors to be kind and share—but use these tomatoes!

The best time of year to use fresh local tomatoes is in the late summer and early fall, when they are at the peak of their season. During the rest of the year, the vine-ripened variety that comes from hothouses or countries where it is hot all year are a close second.

To prepare tomatoes for salads, begin by rinsing the tomatoes and blotting them dry with a paper towel. Cut tomatoes in half and squeeze out any excess juice and seeds. (Cherry and grape-size tomatoes do not need to be cut.) Cut the halves into strips and blot the strips dry. Remove any visible seeds and then chop according to the recipe. Do not add tomato wedges to your salad too soon, because the juices will water it down. If you like tomato wedges, toss them in at the very last moment, just before serving.

To prepare a tomato in order to stuff it with salad, begin by cutting a thick slice off the top of the tomato. With a small spoon, scoop out the juices, seeds, and pulp. Salt the inside of the tomato and place the tomato upside down on a paper towel. Allow it to drain 15 minutes, or until ready to stuff. Rinse the inside and dry with a paper towel.

Lemon Vinaigrette

✓ EASY PREPARATION   ✓ MAKE-AHEAD   ✓ NO COOKING NEEDED   ✓ TAKE-ALONG

When I was younger, it was my job to make the salads before dinner. If there was a lemon in the house, I always made this dressing. You can keep this vinaigrette in a tightly sealed glass container in the refrigerator for at least a week.

2/3 cup fresh lemon juice
(about 4 medium lemons)

2 tablespoons finely chopped
shallots (2 to 3 medium bulbs)

1/4 cup (4 tablespoons)
good-quality Dijon mustard

Salt and freshly ground pepper,
to taste

1 cup olive oil (use extra-virgin for
a fruity taste)

In a medium bowl, combine the lemon juice, shallots, mustard, salt, and pepper. Add the olive oil in a slow stream, whisking constantly, until the dressing thickens. Serve immediately. *

*TIP: Here are basic **guidelines for preparing a vinaigrette:** Choose an oil and vinegar that complement each other as well as the foods that they will dress. Combine the vinegar, seasonings, and any other flavorings. (By adding herbs, spices, shallots, garlic, mustard, or other flavorings to your vinaigrette, you can enhance its simple flavor.) Whisk in the oil. Taste, and adjust seasoning. Allow the finished dressing to rest a few hours at room temperature before using so the flavors will blend. Re-whisk before using.

Simple Mustard Vinaigrette

MAKES ABOUT 2/3 CUP

✓ EASY PREPARATION   ✓ MAKE-AHEAD   ✓ NO COOKING NEEDED   ✓ TAKE-ALONG

This recipe is my friend Elizabeth Barry's favorite dressing. You can make it ahead, keep it in a tightly closed jar, and use it as needed.

1 tablespoon good-quality Dijon
mustard

1/4 cup (4 tablespoons) cabernet red
wine vinegar, or other good red wine
vinegar

1 teaspoon sea salt

1/2 teaspoon freshly ground pepper

1 tablespoon finely chopped fresh
Italian flat-leaf parsley

1/2 cup extra-virgin olive oil

1. Put the mustard in a small bowl. Whisk in the vinegar, salt, pepper, and parsley.

2. Add the olive oil in a slow stream, whisking constantly, until the dressing thickens. Adjust the seasonings. Serve immediately.

Baby Greens with Sugared Almonds

✓ *EASY PREPARATION*   ✓ *SOMETHING SPECIAL*

A surefire crowd pleaser, this salad uses fresh summer greens and strawberries. The dressing and sugared almonds add a sweet surprise. Change the fruit depending on the time of year—sliced apples in autumn, or thin wedges of peaches and pears in late summer, or even citrus fruit in winter. The almonds can be made several days ahead.

SALAD

¼ cup sugar

½ cup slivered almonds
(about 2 ounces)

10 cups baby greens, washed and
well dried (about 1 pound)

DRESSING

2 tablespoons sugar

1 tablespoon chopped fresh Italian
flat-leaf parsley

2 tablespoons champagne vinegar
or white wine vinegar

½ teaspoon salt

Freshly ground pepper, to taste

¼ cup extra-virgin olive oil

2 tablespoons finely chopped green
onions (2 whole green onions)

1 pint strawberries, cleaned, hulled,
and sliced ∗

1. In a small skillet, heat the sugar over medium-high heat until it begins to melt. Add the almonds to the pan and toss rapidly until the sugar coats all of the almonds and they are lightly browned, about 3 to 4 minutes, watching carefully so the sugar does not burn. Pour them out onto a Pyrex or other heat-proof dish and separate the almonds with a fork. Cool until hardened, and break into pieces.

2. To prepare the salad greens, begin by soaking them in icy cold water for 20 minutes as soon as you bring them home. Do not tear the leaves. Just remove them from the head or bag and soak them. Next, dry the greens thoroughly. Layer the dried greens in a heavy-duty resealable plastic bag, separating each layer of greens with a paper towel to absorb the extra water. Close the bag, leaving a 2-inch opening to allow the greens to breathe. No more than 6 hours before serving, tear the greens and place them in a bowl. Put a damp towel over the top, and place the bowl in the refrigerator to keep them crisp and moist until you are ready to dress them.

3. To prepare the dressing: In a small bowl, combine all of the dressing ingredients except the olive oil. Add the oil in a slow stream, whisking constantly, until the dressing thickens.

4. In a large bowl, pile the greens, green onions, and strawberries—or whatever other fruit you are using. Toss them with the dressing. Add the almonds, toss lightly, and serve.

SERVING SUGGESTION

To make this a main dish salad, serve it topped with sliced grilled chicken or steak that has been basted in the dressing during grilling.

∗**TIP:** Strawberries and raspberries are very fragile fruit and should be treated with care. Just before using, rinse them quickly in very cold water and drain on paper towels. Don't let them sit in water, as they will soak it up and become bland and mushy.

Pear and Cheese Salad with Honey Vinaigrette

✓ *NO COOKING NEEDED*   ✓ *SOMETHING SPECIAL*

Keep some of your favorite cheeses on hand to make a simple salad elegant. Blue cheese, Parmigiano-Reggiano, or even a hard, aged cheddar can work well. I also keep canned fruit, such as pears and mandarin oranges, in the pantry for garnishing a salad when there hasn't been time to stop at the supermarket.

HONEY VINAIGRETTE

3 tablespoons white wine vinegar

1/2 teaspoon honey mustard (or 1/2 teaspoon Dijon mustard)

1 teaspoon finely chopped green onion

Pinch salt

Freshly ground pepper, to taste

2 tablespoons honey

1/2 cup canola oil

SALAD

3 cups mixed greens (such as baby greens, mesclun, and leaf lettuce), washed and well dried (about 4 1/2 ounces)

2 large ripe pears, peeled, quartered, and cored (or use one 15-ounce can pears, drained)

1 teaspoon fresh lemon juice

2 ounces Parmigiano-Reggiano, shaved into thin sheets *

1. To prepare the vinaigrette: In a small bowl, beat together the vinegar, mustard, onion, salt, and pepper. Beat in the honey until dissolved. Add the oil in a slow stream, beating constantly, until the dressing thickens.

2. In a large bowl, toss the greens with a small amount of the vinaigrette.

3. Divide dressed greens among four chilled salad plates. Gently toss pears with the lemon juice and then with the greens. Garnish each salad with cheese shavings. Pass remaining dressing on the side.

★ TIP: Use a vegetable peeler to cut **very thin shavings** from a piece of good Parmigiano-Reggiano cheese.

Endive Salad with Bacon, Pecans, and Blue Cheese Vinaigrette

✓ *EASY PREPARATION*   ✓ *SOMETHING SPECIAL*

The sharp flavor of endive is perfect for cutting the richness of the blue cheese and bacon in this recipe.

VINAIGRETTE

¼ cup white wine vinegar

1 tablespoon finely chopped shallots (about 2 medium bulbs)

2 tablespoons Dijon mustard

2 teaspoons chopped fresh mint

¼ cup crumbled blue cheese, about 1 ounce ✱

⅓ cup extra-virgin olive oil

Salt and freshly ground pepper, to taste

SALAD

6 slices smoked bacon, cut into 1-inch pieces

4 cups small curly endive, leaves separated, washed, and well dried (about half a small head of endive)

Salt and freshly ground pepper, to taste

½ cup crumbled blue cheese (about 2 ounces)

½ cup pecans, toasted and chopped (about 2 ounces)

1. To prepare the vinaigrette: In a medium bowl, combine the vinegar, shallots, mustard, mint, and cheese. Add the oil in a slow stream, whisking constantly, until the dressing thickens. Season with salt and pepper. Set aside.

2. In a medium frying pan, fry the bacon over medium-high heat until crisp, about 10 minutes. Pour off the fat into a heatproof container periodically as you fry the bacon. Drain the bacon on a paper towel. (Reserve the fat for later frying, or discard it.)

3. Place the endive in a large bowl, and season with salt and pepper. Toss with the vinaigrette.

4. Arrange the dressed endive on four individual salad plates—chilled if you like—and garnish with the bacon, blue cheese, and pecans.

✱TIP: Substitute Stilton or Gorgonzola for the blue cheese if you like a more pronounced blue cheese flavor.

Apple, Cabbage, and Cashew Slaw

✓ *MAKE-AHEAD*   ✓ *NO COOKING NEEDED*

This salad actually improves an hour or two after it is made. Put it all together before leaving home, and it will be perfect by mealtime.

SALAD

1 cup peeled quartered cored and very thinly sliced Granny Smith apple (about 1 large apple)

1 tablespoon fresh lime juice

1/2 cup very thinly sliced sweet onion, such as Vidalia or Texas Sweet (about 1/2 medium onion)

3 cups finely shredded savoy or napa cabbage (about half a small head of cabbage) or 3 cups commercially prepared cole slaw mix *

1/2 cup dried cranberries, plumped in boiling water and drained

DRESSING

2 tablespoons fresh lime juice

1 teaspoon Dijon mustard

1 teaspoon sugar

2 tablespoons chopped fresh Italian flat-leaf parsley or cilantro

Salt and freshly ground pepper, to taste

1/3 cup extra-virgin olive oil

1/2 cup salted cashews (about 2 ounces)

1. In a medium bowl, toss the apple slices with the lime juice to keep them from turning brown. Toss with the onion, cabbage, and cranberries. Mix well.

2. For the dressing, beat together the lime juice, mustard, sugar, parsley, salt, and pepper. Add the olive oil in a slow stream, whisking constantly, until the dressing thickens.

3. Toss the dressing with the salad. Just before serving, toss the salad with the cashews.

∗TIP: The easiest way to **shred** this small amount of cabbage is with a large chef's knife or cleaver. Slice the head of cabbage in half or quarters, then very thinly across the grain.

Mom's Chutney Chicken Salad

✓ *SOMETHING SPECIAL*

Some traditions are surely worth honoring. When I was a little girl, this salad was my favorite. It is relaxing and comforting to prepare because it's so easy to make, it's filling and flavorful, and it can make a meal if served on a bed of greens, along with some crusty bread. I have even served it in warm pita bread with lettuce, or on a toasted croissant.

DRESSING

1 cup mayonnaise

¼ cup mango chutney

2 teaspoons mild curry powder (use more, or a hot curry powder, if desired)

2 teaspoons lime zest

¼ cup fresh lime juice (from about 2 medium limes)

½ teaspoon salt

SALAD

2 large boneless skinless chicken breast halves

3 cups low-sodium chicken broth

Two 13½-ounce cans pineapple chunks, drained

2 cups diced celery (about 5 or 6 ribs)

1 cup thinly sliced green onion (about 15 onions)

¼ cup slivered almonds, toasted (about 1 ounce)

3 cups mixed greens, washed and well dried (about 4½ ounces)

1. To prepare the dressing: In a small bowl, combine the dressing ingredients and stir until blended.

2. To prepare the salad: In a medium-size saucepan, bring the chicken and chicken broth to a simmer over medium-low heat. Simmer gently, uncovered, until the chicken reaches a temperature of 160°F on an instant-read thermometer when inserted into the thickest part of the breast, about 15 minutes. Remove the chicken from the broth and let cool completely. Reserve the broth for soup or other uses.

3. Cut the cooled chicken into bite-sized cubes.

4. In a large bowl, combine the chicken cubes, pineapple, celery, green onion, and almonds. Pour about one quarter of the dressing over the chicken mixture and toss until everything is nicely, but thinly, coated. (Better to add a little more dressing later than to drown the salad with too much at the beginning.)

5. Serve the salad on a bed of mixed greens, and pass the remaining dressing alongside.

Pasta Salad with Chicken and Grapes

✓ *MAKE-AHEAD*   ✓ *SOMETHING SPECIAL*

I can't tell you how often I have served this salad for a quick, refreshing summer supper. The sweet crispness of the grapes is perfect with chicken. All you need are some good greens to serve as a bed for the salad, and a crusty loaf of French or Italian bread to go along with it.

2 small boneless skinless chicken breast halves

3 cups low-sodium chicken broth or water ✱

SALAD

8 ounces rotelli pasta

Salt, for the pasta

One 8-ounce can pineapple chunks, drained, juice reserved for the dressing

1/2 cup chopped celery (about 1 1/2 large ribs)

3/4 cup stemmed seeded deveined and chopped red or yellow bell pepper (about 1 small pepper)

1/4 cup trimmed and chopped green onions (about 4 or 5 thin onions, or one bunch)

1/2 cup sliced almonds, toasted (about 2 ounces)

1 cup seedless white grapes

1/2 cup seedless red grapes

1/2 cup peeled and chopped Granny Smith apple

DRESSING

1 cup mayonnaise

1/4 cup pineapple juice, reserved from the can

1 1/2 teaspoons fresh lemon juice

1 teaspoon ground cumin

1/2 teaspoon salt

1/4 teaspoon freshly ground pepper

1/2 cup chopped fresh Italian flat-leaf parsley

1. To prepare the salad: In a medium-size saucepan, bring the chicken and chicken broth to a simmer over medium-low heat. Simmer gently, uncovered, until the chicken reaches a temperature of 160°F on an instant-read thermometer when inserted into the thickest part of the breast, about 15 minutes. Remove the chicken from the broth and let cool completely. Reserve the broth for soup or other uses. When the chicken is cool, cube it to the size of the pineapple chunks.

2. Cook the rotelli in 6 quarts of boiling salted water until just tender, about 9 minutes, and drain.

3. While the pasta is cooking, in a large bowl, combine the pineapple, chicken, celery, bell pepper, onion, almonds, grapes, and apple.

4. To prepare the dressing: In a small bowl, combine all of the dressing ingredients, and beat with a fork until smooth. Add the drained pasta to the large bowl with the chicken mixture. Pour the dressing over the salad, starting with half of it and adding more as needed.

5. Toss to mix. Taste and season with salt and pepper, if necessary, then serve, or refrigerate for 30 minutes or more before serving. Serve remaining dressing alongside.

SERVING SUGGESTION

Arrange a bed of crisp leaf lettuce on a chilled round serving platter or in a large chilled serving bowl. Mound the salad on the platter or in the bowl and garnish with a little more chopped parsley. Serve chilled.

✱ TIP: As an alternative to poaching chicken on top of the stove, you can use your oven. Poach the chicken by preheating the oven to 350°F. Lay the chicken breasts in a small roasting pan. Sprinkle them with salt and pepper, and then pour enough dry white wine or chicken broth over them to cover them half way. Cover the pan with aluminum foil and place it in the oven. Poach for about 30 minutes, or until cooked through. Pour off the broth and reserve for use as a soup base.

Pasta Salad with Tuna

✓ *EASY PREPARATION*   ✓ *MAKE-AHEAD*

I love this main dish salad. The tuna becomes part of the dressing and flavors the entire salad. Serve with crunchy bread sticks.

One 7½-ounce can water-packed tuna, drained (or use the vacuum-pack bag of tuna that requires little or no draining)

⅓ cup olive oil

¼ cup red wine vinegar

1 tablespoon whole-grain mustard

⅓ cup mayonnaise

1 teaspoon salt, plus more for cooking pasta

Freshly ground pepper, to taste

8 ounces small penne pasta

8 ounces green beans, tipped, tailed, and steamed until crisply tender *

½ cup chopped celery

1 cup stemmed seeded and thinly sliced red bell pepper (about 1 medium pepper)

1 tablespoon capers

¼ cup chopped fresh Italian flat-leaf parsley

1. In a large bowl, combine the tuna and olive oil with a fork until it is a coarse paste. Add the vinegar, mustard, mayonnaise, salt, and pepper. Combine the mixture with a fork until smooth.

2. Meanwhile, cook the pasta in 6 quarts of boiling salted water until just tender, 9 or 10 minutes. Drain the pasta well and cool.

3. Cut the beans into ½-inch pieces and add to the tuna mixture. Toss in the celery, bell pepper, capers, and parsley. Add the cooked pasta, and toss lightly.

4. Serve immediately at room temperature.

SERVING SUGGESTION

To make this salad ahead, be sure to reserve some of the dressing, as the salad will absorb dressing over time. To serve, remove the salad from the refrigerator, bring it to room temperature, and then toss it with the remaining dressing.

★ TIP: The best way to prepare vegetables like broccoli, carrots, or green beans for salads **is to steam or blanch them**. (Blanching means cooking briefly—only 1 to 2 minutes—in boiling water then immersing immediately in cold water.) You should salt the water if the vegetables are colored, but not if white, like cauliflower, because the salt will make the white vegetables mushy. Quickly steam or blanch the vegetables of your choice and then place them in an ice-water bath as soon as they are tender. This will keep the chlorophyll from dissipating so the vegetables stay brightly colored for the salad. The ice bath also stops the vegetables from cooking further so that they don't become overcooked and too soft.

Grilled Pita Salad with Spicy Grilled Shrimp

This is my version of a Greek salad mixed with an Italian bread salad. By grilling or broiling the pita you will give it a toasted, freshly made taste. Then, after sitting with the dressing for a little while, it absorbs some of the delicious flavor and tastes even better. Even though it is unusual, give it a try.

One 12-ounce package white, wheat, or sourdough pita

Spicy Grilled Shrimp (below)

3 cups peeled seeded and diced cucumbers (about 3 medium cucumbers)

3 cups seeded and diced vine-ripened tomatoes (about 3 large or 4 medium tomatoes) ∗

½ cup thinly sliced red onion

½ cup (3 ounces) whole Kalamata olives, pitted, rinsed, and sliced

⅓ cup red wine vinegar

1½ tablespoons grainy Dijon mustard

¾ cup fruity extra-virgin olive oil

¾ cup fresh oregano leaves, or 1½ tablespoons dried oregano

1 cup (4 ounces) crumbled feta cheese

1. Preheat the grill for 10 minutes on high, or the broiler for 3 to 4 minutes. Toast the whole pitas on the grill or under the broiler for 2 to 3 minutes, watching carefully so they do not burn—which can happen in an instant. When they are cool, cut them into triangles.

2. While the grill is hot, prepare the shrimp.

3. In a large bowl, combine the pita wedges, cucumbers, tomatoes, onion, and olives.

4. In a small bowl, mix the vinegar and mustard together. Add the olive oil in a slow stream, whisking constantly, until the dressing thickens. Pour the dressing over the salad, add the oregano and the feta cheese, and toss lightly. Cover, let stand about 20 minutes, and then serve, topped with the grilled shrimp.

SERVING SUGGESTION

This salad has great texture when served about 20 minutes after it has been tossed. If you wait much longer than that, the pita will get mushy. If you need to make it ahead, prepare the pita and vegetables, make the dressing, and keep them refrigerated separately; then just toss everything together when you are ready to serve.

∗**TIP:** The juice from **tomatoes** can water down a salad. To avoid that, trim the tomato around the outside with your knife, cutting deeply to remove the flesh and leave the pulp and seeds. Or, use a spoon to remove most of the juicy pulp along with the seeds, leaving just firm flesh. Pat the tomato pieces with a paper towel to dry them, then slice and add to the salad. Throw out the pulp or, better yet, reserve the pulp in a resealable freezer bag and freeze it to use in a sauce at a later date.

Spicy Grilled Shrimp

✓ *EASY PREPARATION*

This shrimp can be made on the outdoor grill, on a grill pan, or even in the oven. It is a great pairing for the Pita Salad or even as the final touch on a Classic Caesar Salad (page 26).

3 tablespoons butter

3 tablespoons olive oil

2 tablespoons fresh lemon juice

2 teaspoons paprika

1/2 teaspoon dried oregano

1 teaspoon chili powder

1/2 teaspoon garlic powder

1/2 teaspoon salt

1/2 teaspoon freshly ground pepper

2 pounds large (21 to 30 per pound) shrimp, in the shell

1. In a small saucepan, melt the butter and oil together over medium heat. Remove from the heat and add all the remaining ingredients except the shrimp. Stir well and set aside to cool to room temperature.

2. Place the shrimp in a large, resealable plastic bag and pour in the marinade. Press the air out of the bag and seal tightly. Marinate, refrigerated, for 30 minutes. ✱

3. Remove the shrimp from the bag and discard the marinade. Grill the shrimp on a seafood screen or tray over high heat until they are just opaque in the center and firm to the touch, 2 to 4 minutes altogether, turning once halfway through grilling time. Remove from the grill. If you prefer, broil the shrimp on a broiler pan, about 4 inches from the hot element, 2 to 4 minutes, turning halfway through the broiling time. ✱

SERVING SUGGESTION

Arrange the hot grilled shrimp around the edge of a serving platter, and fill the center with Pita Salad (above). Serve quickly, while the shrimp are still warm. Everyone gets to shell his own.

✱ TIP: Although you can easily buy the shrimp with the shells removed, **grilling the shrimp in the shell** helps to preserve their flavor and texture by protecting them from the high heat. To clean the shrimp without removing the shell, use a sharp knife, and split open the back of each shrimp and remove the black vein. Rinse the cleaned shrimp and pat them dry.

✱ TIP: The **seafood screen or tray**, a grill accessory that is placed directly on top of the grill, has smaller openings than the regular grill and prevents the shrimp from falling onto the fire or coals.

Classic Caesar Salad with Mustard Grilled Chicken

✓ SOMETHING SPECIAL

The Caesar salad has become an American classic, and adding chicken makes it a hearty meal. Because the egg in it is uncooked, I use Eggbeaters or another refrigerated egg substitute instead of fresh one-minute eggs. This eliminates any chance of salmonella in the final dressing while still giving it enough consistency to fully coat the romaine. If you're in a hurry, you don't have to make homemade croutons, but boy, are they good and worth the effort when you do have a little extra time. Just imagine the luscious smell of the toasting garlic!

Mustard Grilled Chicken (below)

Garlic Croutons (below, optional)

DRESSING

1/2 cup olive oil

One 2-ounce can flat anchovy fillets, drained and chopped to a paste *

3 teaspoons finely chopped garlic (about 3 large cloves)

1 tablespoon Dijon mustard

1 1/2 teaspoons Worcestershire sauce

1/4 cup refrigerated egg substitute, such as Eggbeaters

3 tablespoons lemon juice (from about 1 1/2 lemons)

SALAD

2 heads romaine lettuce, washed, well dried, and torn into bite-sized pieces *

1/4 cup (1 ounce) grated Parmigiano-Reggiano cheese

Freshly ground pepper, to taste

1. Prepare the chicken. Then prepare the croutons.

2. To prepare the dressing: In a medium bowl, combine the olive oil, anchovies, garlic, mustard, and Worcestershire sauce. Add the Eggbeaters on top of the ingredients. Pour the lemon juice over the egg. Beat with a fork until the dressing is thick and evenly blended.

3. In a large bowl, toss the dressing with the romaine lettuce, and then add the croutons; sprinkle with Parmigiano-Reggiano cheese and season with freshly ground pepper. Toss lightly.

4. Divide the salad among chilled salad plates. Slice the grilled chicken on the diagonal and arrange on top of each salad.

*TIP: If you are not keen on **anchovies**, which by the way were not an original ingredient of the salad, simply leave them out (although they do add good flavor).

*TIP: The original Caesar salad also featured only the smaller leaves from the heart of the **romaine**, left whole, and piled up on the plate like logs. A bit difficult to eat, but very attractive. Try it if you like.

Mustard Grilled Chicken

MAKES 6 SERVINGS

✓ SOMETHING SPECIAL

Chicken is a versatile meat that can be grilled whole, in halves, in quarters, or in parts. It combines well with many different flavors. Use free-range chickens, if you can find them, for the best possible flavor.

1/2 cup Dijon mustard

1/4 cup whole-grain mustard

1/4 cup white wine vinegar

1 teaspoon cayenne

1 tablespoon fresh lemon juice

Freshly ground pepper, to taste

1/4 cup olive oil

1 pound chicken breasts, with skin on

1. In a small bowl, combine the mustards, vinegar, cayenne, and lemon juice, and season with pepper. Add the oil in a slow stream, whisking constantly, until the marinade thickens and emulsifies.

2. Place the chicken in a resealable plastic bag and pour in the mustard marinade. Press the air out of the bag and seal it. Massage gently to distribute the marinade evenly around the chicken. Set in a large bowl and refrigerate until ready to use, at least ½ hour if you can.

3. Preheat the grill or grill pan to indirect medium-high heat. ✷

4. Place the chicken skin side down on the hot side of the grill.

5. Once the chicken is nicely browned on the bottom, about 15 minutes, turn it and brown the other side, about 5 minutes more. Once it is browned on both sides, move the chicken to the cool side of the grill (if using a grill pan, reduce the heat to low, or put the whole pan in the oven at 300°F) and cook until the

chicken reaches a temperature of 160°F on an instant-read thermometer when inserted into the thickest part of the breast, about 10 minutes more.

6. Remove the chicken from the grill and set aside on a plate. Cover with foil and allow the chicken to rest for 10 minutes.

✷ **TIP:** When **grilling chicken breasts,** set up the grill for indirect heat. With charcoal, bank the charcoal on one side so that it gets hot and the other side stays cool. On a gas grill, have one or two burners set on medium-high and the other burners off. If you are using a ridged grill pan on top of the stove, preheat for 5 to 8 minutes, until very hot. Then start with the skin side down. Don't forget to turn on the exhaust fan.

Garlic Croutons

MAKES ABOUT 4 CUPS OF CROUTONS

✓ SOMETHING SPECIAL

These croutons can be made ahead of time and kept crisp in an airtight container. Toss them into any salad to make it a more festive dish.

⅓ cup olive oil

1½ tablespoons sliced garlic (about 4 large cloves)

4 thick slices coarse sourdough bread, crust removed, and cut into ¾-inch cubes ✷

1. In a large frying pan, combine the oil and the garlic; fry the garlic over medium-high heat until brown, but not burned, about 1 minute. Remove the garlic from the oil and discard. Add the bread cubes to the pan and fry over

high heat, stirring or tossing often, until browned, for 4 to 5 minutes.

2. Transfer to paper towels to drain. Let cool completely.

✷ **TIP:** Day-old bread works best for croutons; if the bread is fresh, lightly toast the slices before continuing.

Roast Beef and Roasted Potato Salad

✓ *MAKE-AHEAD*   ✓ *TAKE-ALONG*

Meat and potatoes have come to symbolize the ultimate traditional Midwestern meal. Try this combination in a salad, and even men who don't think a salad makes a meal will be convinced!

2 pounds small baby red potatoes

1 tablespoon olive oil

3 large eggs, at room temperature

½ cup chopped red onion,

1 cup chopped celery (about 2 to 3 ribs)

1 cup stemmed seeded deveined and chopped green bell pepper (about 1 medium pepper)

¼ cup chopped fresh Italian flat-leaf parsley

1 pound cooked roast beef, cut into thin strips *

1 tablespoon Dijon mustard

¼ cup red wine vinegar

½ cup olive oil

½ cup mayonnaise

½ teaspoon Tabasco sauce

1 teaspoon salt

½ teaspoon freshly ground pepper

1. To prepare the salad: Preheat the oven to 425°F. Toss the potatoes in the 1 tablespoon of olive oil. Arrange the potatoes on a rimmed baking sheet and roast until tender, about 1 hour.

2. In a small saucepan, place the eggs and cover with cold water. Bring to a boil and boil for 2 minutes. Remove from the heat, cover, and let stand for 12 minutes. Chill the eggs under cold running water. Remove the shells. Separate the yolks from the whites. Set the yolks aside. Chop the whites and reserve.

3. When the potatoes are cooked, slice them about ¼ inch thick and place in a large bowl. Add the onion, celery, bell pepper, parsley, and roast beef. Toss lightly and set aside.

4. To prepare the dressing: In a small bowl, use a fork to combine the hard-boiled egg yolks with the mustard until smooth. Stir in the vinegar, and then add the oil in a slow stream, stirring constantly, until the dressing thickens. Add the mayonnaise, Tabasco, salt, and pepper. Beat with a fork until thick and smooth.

5. Gently toss the reserved egg whites with the salad ingredients. Pour the dressing over the salad and toss until combined.

SERVING SUGGESTION

Arrange a bed of your favorite greens on a chilled serving platter. Mound the salad on the greens, and serve at room temperature. Serve crisply toasted slices of Parsley and Herb Garlic Bread (page 87) with this salad. A plate of thinly sliced cantaloupe makes a nice accompaniment.

*TIP: Don't wait until you have leftover **roast beef** to make this salad. Buy the roast beef from your favorite deli and have them give it to you in one large, thick piece (to keep it moist). Then all you need to do is cut it into thin strips and add it to the salad.

Fresh Tropical Fruit Salad

✓ *EASY PREPARATION*   ✓ *MAKE-AHEAD*   ✓ *NO COOKING NEEDED*   ✓ *TAKE-ALONG*

Fruit salads can be a great accompaniment to many main dishes. This fruit salad is really wonderful by itself for post-holiday meals or on hot summer nights, or when served with a piece of grilled or broiled fish. Have some crisp crackers or slices of crusty raisin-nut bread, to pass with it.

1 large ripe mango, peeled, stoned, and sliced ∗

1 large ripe papaya, peeled, halved, seeded, and sliced

2 ripe kiwi, peeled and sliced

1 large banana, thickly sliced

1 cup fresh pineapple chunks (about 1/3 whole pineapple)

2 cups low-fat small-curd cottage cheese

1/2 cup fresh orange juice

1/3 cup grated unsweetened coconut (optional)

Arrange the fruit on individual dinner plates or on a large serving platter. Top with a scoop of cottage cheese. Drizzle with fresh orange juice and garnish with coconut. Chill at least 1 hour.

SERVING SUGGESTION

For dessert, serve this salad without the cottage cheese and substitute your favorite cookie or brownie as an accompaniment.

∗TIP: The **mango** is one of the finest of the tropical fruits. To cut one you must first cut the flesh away from the long plank-like pit. With the mango lying on a cutting board, find the pit with a serrated knife. Moving the knife slightly away from the pit, cut lengthwise sections or "cheeks" from either side of the pit, then cut the fleshy portions at the top and bottom of the pit. Next, remove the skin from the fruit and slice the fruit.

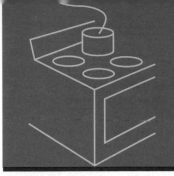

The Sandwich Board

They're hearty, tasty, and fast. Some nights, sandwiches are just what you and your family want to eat.

My sandwich memories began with my grandparents in Los Angeles, California. My parents and I would fly across the country to visit them, and as soon as we hit California soil we made a beeline to Art's Delicatessen. It was at Art's that as a child I ventured past my comfortable peanut butter and jelly. His sandwiches weren't fancy, but he featured wonderful combinations that I crave even today. As he said, "Every sandwich is a work of Art."

Art made his sandwiches special, and even without a deli meat slicer, you can make sandwiches more inspired and satisfying than bologna on white bread. Today, sandwiches have kept up with the times, incorporating trendy ingredients (think of the Italian pressed sandwiches called panini sold everywhere these days), while retaining their down-home appeal. You can opt for a classic but ever-satisfying grilled cheese, or go for a more sophisticated version with fontina, prosciutto, and garlic bread. Or, make familiar sandwiches like heroes heartier with roasted vegetables or meat.

The only rule is to make your sandwiches—no matter what kind they are—with the highest-quality ingredients you can afford. Use the best bread, seasonal produce, fresh herbs, top cheeses and meats, and tasty condiments. If you need to, round out the meal with a salad or a side of vegetables. Sandwiches are great for busy nights, too—if you have evening activities like school meetings and sports events, take sandwiches with you and have something delicious when you get there.

My Classic Grilled Cheese Sandwich

✓ *EASY PREPARATION*　　✓ *TAKE-ALONG*

No matter what your age, you can always enjoy a grilled cheese sandwich. This recipe gives you the basics; add your own favorites to jazz it up.

16 slices artisan or rustic bread, egg bread, or country-style white bread

8 ounces Monterey Jack cheese, cut into ¼-inch slices

8 ounces medium-sharp cheddar cheese, cut into ¼-inch slices

4 tablespoons butter, at room temperature

1. Heat a large heavy skillet or griddle over medium-high heat.

2. Place eight of the slices of bread on a work surface and cover each with a slice of Monterey Jack cheese and a slice of cheddar cheese. Top with the remaining slices of bread.

3. Spread the butter in a very thin layer on the top surface of each sandwich.

4. In batches, place the sandwiches in the skillet or on the griddle buttered-side down. Spread a thin layer of butter on the top of each sandwich. Cook until golden brown, 2 to 3 minutes, depending on the heat of the pan. Turn the sandwiches, pressing down slightly with a spatula; cook 2 to 3 minutes more, until the bread has browned and the cheese is completely melted. (Watch carefully, as timing is hard to pinpoint, though it will take only a few minutes.) Remove the sandwiches from the pan. Cut each in half on the diagonal, and serve. ✳

✳ TIP: Try these other **grilled cheese combinations:** cheddar cheese, tomato, bacon, and avocado; fresh mozzarella, tomato, and basil; Monterey Jack cheese and chopped green chiles; or turkey, Swiss cheese, and Dijon mustard.

Fontina, Prosciutto, and Tomato on Roasted Garlic Bread

✓ *EASY PREPARATION*

Fontina is a mild, slightly nutty-tasting cheese from Italy that is especially good for melting. Prosciutto is an Italian cured ham. The very specific way the pigs are raised and the meat is cured give it a unique flavor and texture. When included in a grilled cheese sandwich it warms slightly and gives off an incredible sweet flavor.

8 thin slices crusty roasted garlic bread

8 thin slices fontina cheese

8 very thin slices prosciutto *

1 large tomato, thinly sliced

Salt and freshly ground pepper, to taste

2 tablespoons of butter

1. Heat a heavy skillet or grill over medium-high heat.

2. Arrange 4 bread slices on a work surface. Place 2 slices of cheese on each of the bread slices. For each, arrange 2 slices prosciutto on top of the cheese, folding if necessary. Top with tomato slices. Season well with salt and pepper.

3. Cover with remaining bread slices.

4. Spread the butter in a very thin layer on the top surface of the sandwiches.

5. In batches, place the sandwiches in the skillet or on the griddle buttered-side down. Spread a thin layer of butter on the top of each sandwich. Cook until golden brown, 2 to 3 minutes, depending on the heat of the pan. Turn the sandwiches, pressing down slightly with a spatula, and cook 2 to 3 minutes more, until the bread has browned and the cheese is completely melted. (Watch carefully, as timing is hard to pinpoint, though it will only take a few minutes.) Remove the sandwiches from the pan. Cut each in half on the diagonal and serve.

SERVING SUGGESTION

Serve this with soup or a tossed salad, or accompany with cole slaw or oven-fried potatoes.

★TIP: When buying **prosciutto**, make sure it is sliced paper-thin. The slices should be separated between layers of wax paper. This will ensure that the prosciutto doesn't dry out or stick together and tear.

Roasted Vegetable Hero

✓ *TAKE-ALONG*

There is something so enticing about a crusty roll filled with colorful, roasted vegetables. Add a thin slice or two of fresh mozzarella if you like a heartier sandwich.

2 medium zucchini, ends trimmed, sliced lengthwise

1 medium eggplant, ends trimmed, sliced lengthwise

2 large sweet onions, thickly sliced

2 large green bell peppers, stemmed, seeded, and quartered

3 tablespoons olive oil

2 cloves garlic, finely chopped

1 tablespoon fresh thyme leaves

1 tablespoon chopped fresh oregano

Salt and freshly ground pepper, to taste

4 hero rolls

Hero Dressing (below)

1. Preheat the oven to 400°F.

2. Toss the vegetables with the olive oil. Spread the vegetables in one layer in a large shallow roasting pan. *

3. Sprinkle with garlic, thyme, and oregano. Season with salt and pepper.

4. Roast the vegetables in the oven until tender and lightly browned, about 30 minutes, turning from time to time.

5. While the vegetables are cooking, prepare the dressing. Remove the roasted vegetables from the oven and cool slightly.

6. Layer the vegetables on split hero rolls. Drizzle with the dressing. Close and cut in half on an angle. Serve while still warm.

TIP: Alternate the **vegetables** in these sandwiches to include seasonal changes and any special requests from your family. I like to add thick slices of tomato or slices of fennel bulb, or fresh asparagus—or even slices of potato to the roasting pan.

Hero Dressing

✓ *EASY PREPARATION*

Make a double batch of this dressing and keep it on hand in the refrigerator to drizzle over thickly sliced tomatoes and cucumbers, or other vegetable salads.

¼ teaspoon salt

1 teaspoon dried Italian herbs

Freshly ground pepper, to taste

3 tablespoons vinegar

½ cup olive oil

In a small bowl, combine salt, herbs, pepper, and vinegar. Add the olive oil in a slow stream, whisking constantly, until the dressing thickens slightly. Store in a sealable plastic or glass container in the refrigerator.

Brie, Avocado, and Scallion Sprouts on Baguette

✓ EASY PREPARATION   ✓ TAKE-ALONG

The foundation of this sandwich is a good-quality Brie. Brie is one of the most beloved soft French cheeses in the world. It is a soft-ripe cheese made from whole milk, and the mild flavor is the perfect backdrop for this creamy sandwich. The sprouts may be new to you but they add crunch and flavor, and are worth adding to an otherwise simple sandwich. This sandwich is great for quick dinners at home or for tailgate picnics.

1 narrow baguette-style loaf of French bread, split and lightly toasted

2 tablespoons butter, softened

4 ounces Brie cheese, sliced *

1/2 small ultra-sweet onion, such as Vidalia, Texas Sweet, or Walla Walla, very thinly sliced

1 ripe avocado, peeled, stoned, and sliced

1 container scallion sprouts *

Salt and freshly ground pepper, to taste

Cornichons or miniature dill pickles for garnish (optional)

1. Preheat the grill to medium-high, or preheat the oven to 475°F. Lightly butter one cut side of a French loaf. Arrange the slices of Brie down the length of the loaf.

2. Top the Brie with the avocado slices and the onion. Pile with sprouts. Season well with salt and pepper. Cut the loaf into 4 segments.

3. Wrap each segment in foil and cook on the grill or in the oven 5 to 7 minutes, turning once. Serve hot, in the foil, with cornichons or dill pickles on the side, if you like.

SERVING SUGGESTION

This sandwich is a perfect make-ahead, take-along sandwich as long as you sprinkle a small amount of lemon juice on the avocado before putting it on the sandwich. Wrap the sandwich in the foil up to 8 hours before serving. Leave in the refrigerator until ready to grill. Bring to room temperature in the foil before grilling.

✱ TIP: When **Brie** is fully ripened it is so soft that a slice will not even hold its shape. For this reason, it can be difficult to slice, so slice it when it is chilled and a little firmer—straight out of the refrigerator—and dip your knife into hot water between slices. Then, for the best flavor, allow the slices to come to room temperature before using.

✱ TIP: **Scallion sprouts** are available in containers in many supermarkets. If you have trouble finding these oniony sprouts, radish sprouts would be a nice spicy substitute. In Chinese groceries you might find more mature scallion sprouts, almost like very immature green onions, but these would be too strong for this mild, rich, and creamy sandwich.

Turkey-Onion Barbecue Sandwich

✓ *EASY PREPARATION*   ✓ *MAKE-AHEAD*

My favorite pizza combination is the barbecued smoked gouda–chicken pizza at Blue Moon pizza in Reno, Nevada. This sandwich was inspired by that combination.

1 tablespoon butter, softened

2 cups thinly sliced red onion (about 1 large)

2 tablespoons sugar

½ cup barbecue sauce

4 kaiser or French rolls

1 pound roasted deli turkey, thinly sliced, or slices from a whole deli-roasted chicken *

4 ounces smoked Gouda or cheddar cheese, thinly sliced

1. In a medium skillet, melt the butter over medium heat. Add the onions and begin to stir them only after they have begun to wilt and cook down. Lower the heat to medium-low, sprinkle the onions with the sugar, and continue to cook the onions slowly until they begin to turn golden, about 10 to 15 minutes. Let cool and store in the refrigerator for up to 1 week.

2. Spread some of the barbecue sauce on the rolls. Arrange a layer of turkey on the bottom half of each roll. Add the onions and the cheese. Place the tops of the rolls on the sandwiches and wrap each sandwich tightly in plastic wrap or foil until ready to eat.

SERVING SUGGESTION

Serve this with a side of can't-eat-just-one Old Bay Oven-Fried Potato Chips (page 170).

*TIP: Instead of relying on cooked turkey or chicken from the store, try grilling (even on a stove-top grill) large batches of boneless chicken or turkey to keep in the freezer and have on hand when you need it. After grilling, allow the turkey or chicken to cool, then freeze it in resealable plastic bags. The night before you want to use the meat, move it to the fridge.

Wrap It!

Wraps are not a sandwich, not a taco, and certainly not a burrito. They are a fun, full flavored, all-in-one meal. I make wraps in advance and keep them in the refrigerator to slice and serve for a quick dinner on schedule-packed nights, ready whenever each person in the family is ready to eat. You can also take wraps along with you to the soccer game, pack them for a quick lunch, or enjoy them for a post-workout snack.

Because there are variations of wraps served around the world, the wrappers you can use range from thin, crepe-like Armenian lavosh bread to corn or flour tortillas to rice paper. Fillings can be almost anything—from deli meats to seasoned cheese spreads, even curried lamb. A filling can incorporate your grilled vegetables or the remainders of last night's dinner. Your choices for fillings are limited only by your imagination.

The main point is that these savory little wraps will fit your busy lifestyle and they add fun to the mix of dishes you can serve your family in a hurry. They come together with minimum fuss and transport easily.

Tips for Making Perfect Wraps

- As you work, keep the wrappers covered with plastic wrap or a clean, damp cloth to prevent them from drying out while preparing the recipe.

- For lining the wraps, look for flat foods such as spinach, Bibb lettuce, fresh basil leaves, cold meats like roast beef, sliced cheeses, or jarred roasted peppers. These form an even first layer in the wrap, making them easy to roll and less likely to become soggy. Also avoid watery fillings such as tomato slices to prevent sogginess.

- If your wrappers aren't very fresh, or if they start to crack as you fold them, briefly heat them in a warm oven to soften, place them in a steamer you've set over a pot of boiling water, or wrap them in a damp towel and steam them in the microwave for a few seconds.

- Don't overfill the wraps. Adding too much filling makes them hard to roll up tightly, and can make the wrap unroll when you slice it rather than retain its shape.

Building a Perfect Cylinder Wrap

1. Spread a soft cheese, flavored butter, mustard, or mayonnaise on the wrapper, leaving a half-inch border around the edges.

2. Arrange meat, vegetables, or cheese on top of the spread.

3. Roll up tightly like a jelly roll.

4. Slice off the ends (which can be dry and unattractive) and discard, then slice the wrap on the diagonal into fourths and serve.

5. To store in the refrigerator, tightly wrap in plastic wrap and keep for up to three days.

Building a Perfect Burrito Wrap

1. Mound the filling slightly below the center of the tortilla.

2. Fold both sides in over the filling.

3. Starting at one of the unfolded sides, roll the wrap tightly.

4. To store in the refrigerator, place seam side down on plastic wrap and wrap securely until ready to eat, within a few hours.

Lavosh Roast Beef Wrap with Caramelized Onions

✓ *EASY PREPARATION*   ✓ *MAKE-AHEAD*   ✓ *TAKE-ALONG*

Armenian lavosh is very thin—almost paper-thin—and comes in large, nearly round sheets that can be folded in quarters. Some commercial lavosh is thick and spongy; if this type is all you can find, it would be better to use flour tortillas here. These can be made, wrapped in plastic wrap, and kept in the refrigerator for up to 24 hours. Use any combination of fillings that you want, making sure not to use too many watery vegetables, as they will make the lavosh soggy.

2 pieces of Armenian lavosh, each about 18 inches in diameter

¼ cup unsalted butter

4 white onions, thinly sliced

Salt and freshly ground pepper, to taste

Pinch sugar (optional)

1 cup mayonnaise

¼ cup grainy Dijon mustard

2 tablespoons creamy prepared horseradish

1 pound roast beef, thinly sliced

2 jarred, roasted, red bell peppers

2 cups (about 3 ounces) mixed greens, washed and well dried

1. Run the lavosh pieces quickly under cold water. Wrap them individually in a damp towel and place them in the refrigerator for at least 2 hours or up to 12.

2. Meanwhile, in a large, heavy skillet, melt the butter over medium heat. Add the onions and cook them, stirring slowly, until they start to soften and are beginning to brown, about 15 minutes. Season with salt and pepper, and maybe a pinch of sugar, if necessary, to bring out the sweetness. Cool the onions. This step can be done 2 days ahead. ＊

3. In a small bowl, combine the mayonnaise, mustard, and horseradish. Working with the lavosh one at a time, place one round on a cutting board. Spread half of the mayonnaise mixture evenly over the entire sheet of lavosh. Arrange half the roast beef on the lower third of the round in a straight line. Top it with half of the cooked onions, half of the peppers, and half of the greens. Season with salt and pepper.

4. Tightly roll the wrap into a cylinder, starting with the lower end nearest to you. Pull the lavosh and tighten as you roll it to remove any air pockets. Don't worry if the lavosh tears at the beginning, because the tear will be covered with the other layers. Repeat with the other lavosh.

5. Trim the ends of the wrap with a serrated knife and then cut into 1-inch slices—or larger if you like, up to 6 inches in length. Place the slices on a platter and serve immediately. You can also store the wrap, unsliced, tightly wrapped in plastic wrap, for up to 24 hours in the refrigerator.

＊TIP: For a unique twist on the **caramelized onions**, add ¼ cup of balsamic vinegar, 3 tablespoons Dijon mustard, and 2 teaspoons of sugar to the onions once they have softened. This makes a delicious onion relish for the wrap—or for any cold, sliced meats such as lamb or pork. The relish can be made up to three days ahead and stored, covered, in the refrigerator.

Onion, Pepper, and Goat Cheese in Spinach Wrap

✓ *EASY PREPARATION*   ✓ *MAKE-AHEAD*   ✓ *TAKE-ALONG*

You can find spinach wraps in the tortilla section of the supermarket. Try mixing the goat cheese with fresh herbs or pesto for a great base to this wrap.

2 Vidalia onions, other super-sweet onions such as Texas Sweet, or white onions, peeled and cut into 1/2-inch slices

1/4 cup olive oil

Four 12-inch spinach wraps or flour tortillas

6 ounces prosciutto or deli smoked ham, very thinly sliced (optional)

4 ounces fresh soft goat cheese, such as Montrachet

2 red peppers, roasted, peeled, and quartered (see Tip on page 60)

About 1 teaspoon balsamic vinegar

Salt and freshly ground pepper, to taste

1/4 cup fresh basil leaves, washed and well dried ✱

1. Preheat the oven to 450°F.

2. Brush the onion slices with oil and arrange them in one layer on a baking sheet lined with foil. ✱

3. Roast the onion slices in the hot oven, turning once with a spatula, until well browned, about 12 to 14 minutes. (This step can be done the evening before, the onions cooled, covered with foil, and refrigerated.)

4. Spread the wraps on a working surface. If using prosciutto, divide it among the wraps, covering most of the surface. Spread each with one-quarter of the cheese. Divide peppers and onions among the wraps. Drizzle each with a few drops of balsamic vinegar and season with salt and pepper.

5. Arrange basil leaves randomly over all. Roll up wraps, cut off the ends, and then cut the roll on the bias into halves or thirds. Arrange the sandwich pieces on a platter, and serve.

✱ **TIP:** When buying **fresh basil**, make sure the leaves are unblemished and have an intense aroma. To keep it fresh for about a week, take the basil out of the plastic and trim the bottom of the stems. Immerse the stems in a small glass, then pour cold water into the glass only to the top of the stems. Loosely cover the basil with plastic wrap or a plastic bag and store in the refrigerator until ready to use.

✱ **TIP:** Use the new **nonstick foil** on baking pans, for quick, easy cleanup.

Salmon–Scrambled Egg Wrap

✓ *EASY PREPARATION*   ✓ *SOMETHING SPECIAL*

Eggs don't have to be served with toast; they can be piled on English muffins, stuffed into pita bread, and even added to pasta. A quick and portable way to serve them is in a wrap. These smoked salmon and egg wraps will please a crowd without demanding much time from the cook. Each person gets two wraps for a meal, or serve one per person if you are preparing other dishes.

Eight 8-inch flour tortillas

1 tablespoon olive oil

3 tablespoons butter

¼ cup finely diced green bell pepper (about ¼ medium pepper)

1 bunch green onions (about 5 or 6 thin), white and light green parts thinly sliced

1 cup halved seeded and chopped ripe tomato (about 1 large tomato)

Salt and freshly ground pepper, to taste

8 large eggs, lightly beaten

¼ pound smoked salmon, coarsely chopped

1 tablespoon chopped fresh dill, plus sprigs for garnish

Sour cream for garnish

1. Preheat the oven to 200°F. Stack the tortillas and wrap them in a clean cloth towel, then heat in the oven for 15 minutes.

2. In a large, heavy skillet, heat the olive oil and 1 tablespoon butter over medium-high heat. Cook the peppers and green onions, stirring from time to time, until just tender, about 10 minutes. Stir in the tomato. Cook 2 minutes more. Season lightly with salt and pepper.

3. Transfer the vegetables to a bowl and wipe out the skillet.

4. Heat the remaining butter in the same skillet. Add the beaten eggs and cook, stirring, just until the curds begin to set, for 1 or 2 minutes. Stir in tomato mixture, chopped salmon, and dill. Stir until eggs are just cooked through but still soft, about 1 minute more. ✳

5. Spread warm wraps on a work surface. Spoon one-eighth of the egg mixture down the center of each of the tortillas. Fold bottom of wrap up about 2 inches and then roll loosely from one side into cylinders. Serve at once, garnished with dill, with sour cream on the side, counting on 2 wraps per serving.

SERVING SUGGESTION

To pack these to go, fill the tortillas with the egg mixture then wrap each one in foil, to keep it warm.

✳TIP: For the perfect **scrambled egg**, make sure you begin with large eggs at room temperature. Gently stir beaten eggs in the melted butter over medium heat until they are set. You can cook them until soft and creamy or firm, depending on your taste.

Chicken, Avocado, and Bacon Wrap

✓ *EASY PREPARATION* ✓ *TAKE-ALONG*

Say goodbye to the ho-hum old turkey club sandwich. In this recipe we start with delicious roasted chicken. The chicken can be leftover home roasted, or one you bought already roasted from the supermarket. Mix and match the ingredients for this chicken club and you will be able to produce more than one fantastic dinner.

⅓ cup Garlic Mayonnaise (below)

8 slices bacon

1 large ripe avocado, halved, stoned, peeled, and sliced ∗

1 teaspoon lemon juice

Four 12-inch wraps, any savory flavor, such as spinach or sun-dried tomato

6 ounces fresh leaf spinach, stemmed, washed, and well dried

½ pound smoked chicken breast or leftover cold roasted chicken or turkey, thinly sliced

2 small tomatoes, thinly sliced

Salt and freshly ground pepper, to taste

1. Make the mayonnaise. Then, in a large frying pan, fry the bacon slices over medium-high heat until crisp, about 6 to 8 minutes. Drain on paper towels. Discard the bacon fat.

2. Toss the avocado slices with the lemon juice.

3. Spread wraps or tortillas on a work surface. Spoon a little mayonnaise on each one and spread into a thin layer. Arrange a layer of fresh spinach over each wrap. Top with chicken slices, tomato, and avocado. Season with salt and pepper.

4. Arrange two slices of bacon on each sandwich. Roll up cylinder-style and slice in half or thirds on the diagonal. Serve at once.

SERVING SUGGESTION

You can make these wraps ahead and then wrap them in foil. I like to serve them warmed slightly in the oven. Just place them, still wrapped in the foil, in a preheated 375°F oven for 10 minutes before serving.

∗**TIP:** To speed up the ripening of an **avocado**, pop it into a paper bag, close the top, and set aside for 24 to 48 hours. To use the avocado, first cut around the seed lengthwise. Twist with both hands to separate into halves. To remove the seed, put the half with the seed on a work surface, then gently, but forcefully, strike the pit with the blade of a knife. Once the knife is secure in the pit, hold the bottom of the avocado in one hand and gently twist the knife to remove the seed. Tap the knife handle on the edge of the sink to release the seed.

Garlic Mayonnaise

✓ *EASY PREPARATION* ✓ *MAKE-AHEAD*

By mixing extra ingredients into mayonnaise you can create a somewhat fancy sauce that can go with just about anything. This garlic mayonnaise is perfect for the wraps, but try mixing mayonnaise with pesto, prepared horseradish, or even grainy mustard for a different version.

1 cup mayonnaise

1 teaspoon finely chopped garlic

2 tablespoons finely chopped fresh curly-leaf parsley

Beat together all ingredients in a small bowl. Refrigerate for at least 1 hour to blend the flavors.

This mayonnaise can be stored, covered, in the refrigerator for up to 5 days.

Hot Roast Chicken and Monterey Jack Wrap

✓ *EASY PREPARATION*   ✓ *TAKE-ALONG*

This is a great recipe for a make-your-own-wrap gathering for your family and friends. The microwave comes in very handy to speed up dinner preparation here. You could warm these wraps in a 350°F oven for about 10 minutes, but using the microwave is much quicker and more convenient.

Eight 8-inch sun-dried tomato wraps or flour tortillas

1/2 pound fresh roasted chicken breast, thinly sliced

2²/₃ cups (about 10 ounces) shredded Monterey Jack cheese ✱

1/2 cup Fresh Picante Salsa (page 54)

1/2 pint (8 ounces) sour cream

1. Spread wraps on a work surface.

2. Divide the chicken breast slices evenly among the wrappers. Spread each with 1/3 cup shredded cheese. Spoon a little salsa on the cheese. Roll up.

3. Microwave the wraps on high just until the cheese is melted, 30 seconds. Once cooled slightly, just trim off the ends of the wraps and slice into thirds on the diagonal. Serve hot with more salsa and sour cream on the side. ✱

✱**TIP:** The difference between shredded cheese and grated cheese is that shredded cheese is cut into longer and thinner pieces than grated, which makes it melt more quickly. Just use the smallest size hole on your box grater or food processor. But do grate it yourself. Pre-grated cheese doesn't have the same flavor or melting quality as cheese that is freshly grated. Microplane graters make this task simple and very fast. This culinary adaptation from the wood-working shop is a very sharp, easy-to-use rasp-like tool that has revolutionized grating and zesting.

✱**TIP:** Allow these **wraps** to sit for a few minutes after heating them in the microwave. They will slice more easily once the cheese has set a little. And cheese melted in the microwave can be deceptively hot.

Grilled Beef–Green Onion Wrap with Garlic-Soy Sauce

✓ *TAKE-ALONG*

You can use rice paper spring roll wrappers instead of tortillas to make these fantastic wraps. Soak the rice paper briefly in warm water, lightly blot with a towel, and then fill with the filling.

½ cup dry red wine

⅓ cup olive oil

1 tablespoon chopped fresh rosemary

2 tablespoons chopped fresh Italian flat-leaf parsley

Salt and coarsely ground pepper, to taste

1 pound flank steak or thick-cut chuck steak, scored diagonally across the grain in a crosshatch pattern

Garlic-Soy Dipping Sauce (below)

Eight 8-inch herbed wraps, flour tortillas, or rice paper rounds *

1 small head fresh leaf lettuce, leaves separated, washed and well dried

8 green onions (about 2 bunches) well washed, cut into 5-inch lengths, white end cut into brushes (brush effect optional) *

8 fresh mint sprigs

1. Combine wine, oil, herbs, salt, and pepper in a large resealable plastic bag. Add the steak, seal the bag, and let sit in the refrigerator to marinate, turning occasionally, for 15 minutes up to overnight.

2. Make the dipping sauce. Then, preheat the grill 10 minutes on medium-high heat.

3. Preheat the oven to 200°F. Stack the tortillas, wrap them in a cloth towel, and warm in the oven.

4. Remove the steak from the marinade and pat dry. Grill over medium-high heat about 4 minutes per side. Slice very thinly on the diagonal, across the grain.

5. Spread warm wraps on the work surface. On each wrap arrange fresh lettuce, a green onion brush, mint sprigs, and sliced beef. Fold up bottom third of wrap and then roll from left to right. Keep warm, covered with a slightly damp cloth, in the oven until all wraps are made and are ready to serve. Serve with dipping sauce.

＊TIP: If you are using **rice paper,** soak the sheets in warm water for about 2 minutes each until they are soft and pliable. Do not soak them all at once. Soak them as you need them or they will get soggy and fall apart.

＊TIP: **Green onion brushes** are a pretty way to serve green onions. Cut the well-washed onions into 5-inch lengths. Then slash the white part lengthwise into thin strips for about 1½ inches, leaving all the strips attached at the green end. Soak the onions in ice water for about 10 minutes and drain thoroughly. The slashed end will open up like a paintbrush.

Garlic-Soy Dipping Sauce

MAKES ABOUT ¾ CUP

Soy sauce is widely used throughout Asia and Hawaii, just as freely as Westerners use salt or ketchup. Soy sauce mixed with spices and vinegar makes a great dipping sauce. It can also be used as a salad dressing, as a marinade, and as a basting sauce to brush on grilled meats; just remember it can be super salty, so limit extra seasoning.

½ cup rice wine or dry white wine

3 tablespoons light soy sauce *

1 teaspoon sugar

1 tablespoon peanut or other vegetable oil

4 cloves garlic, finely chopped

2 tablespoons grated fresh ginger

¼ cup finely chopped green onions (the white and up to 1 inch of dark green from about 5 green onions)

1. In a small bowl, combine wine, soy sauce, and sugar.

2. In a heavy medium saucepan, heat the oil over medium heat. Add the garlic, ginger, and green onions and cook for 2 minutes, stirring. Add the wine mixture and cook 2 minutes more.

3. Remove from heat and cool to room temperature.

*TIP: Soy sauce is a fermented sauce most often made from soy beans, wheat, and salt, and is widely used all over Asia. Soy is available in many varieties, including light and dark, which refers to the color and not the salt or calorie content. Soy sauce is usually very salty, but low-sodium varieties are also available. Chinese soy sauce has a flavor that is slightly different from Japanese, and many people prefer Japanese varieties for cooking. Choose one that is naturally fermented.

Strawberry-Mascarpone Wrap with Chocolate-Mint Sauce

✓ *EASY PREPARATION*   ✓ *TAKE-ALONG*

If you're in wrap mode, finish the meal in-theme with these delicious dessert wraps. Or take these easy-to-make wraps to any gathering and they will be an instant hit. They are wonderful with whatever fruit is in season; so try using kiwi, mango, or even pineapple for a different version.

Chocolate-Mint Dipping Sauce (below)

1 pint fresh ripe strawberries, stemmed, rinsed, drained, and thinly sliced

1 tablespoon sugar

Four 8-inch honey and wheat flour tortillas, or cinnamon-sugar wraps

4 ounces mascarpone cheese, at room temperature *

4 sprigs fresh mint

1. Make the dipping sauce. Then, in a medium bowl, toss the strawberries with the sugar and let stand 10 minutes or more. *

2. Arrange the tortillas or wraps on a work surface. Spread each with one-quarter of the mascarpone cheese. Top with a layer of drained strawberries. Add the mint garnish and roll up.

3. Serve with small individual bowls of the dipping sauce alongside for dipping, or slice the wraps and drizzle the sauce over the top.

SERVING SUGGESTION

You can make these wraps up to 2 hours before you are ready to serve them, keeping them refrigerated. After that, the strawberries begin to lose their wonderful bright texture and flavor.

✱TIP: Mascarpone is a fresh Italian cheese made from cream. It has the consistency of sour cream, but is rich and slightly sweet, which makes it the perfect complement to fresh fruit. It is the principal ingredient in tiramisu—that lavish Italian version of a trifle.

✱TIP: Try changing this recipe by tossing the **strawberries** with sugar and herbs such as basil or some of the flavored mints, such as lemon mint, that are sometimes available in supermarkets, farmers' markets, or possibly your own or your neighbor's garden.

Chocolate-Mint Dipping Sauce

MAKES 1 CUP

Chocolate mint chips make this a quick and easy sauce. This sauce goes wonderfully with the wraps, or you can use it with chunks of fresh fruit and pound cake for a quick and easy fondue.

4 ounces chocolate mint chips

2 tablespoons unsalted butter

½ cup sugar

1 cup heavy cream

In a small saucepan, melt the chocolate over low heat. With a wooden spoon, beat in the butter and sugar. Beat in the cream.

Simmer over medium heat for 4 or 5 minutes. Remove from heat and serve warm. *

✱TIP: You can make the **sauce** in a small saucepan over low heat, over a double boiler, or in the microwave on a low setting.

Tacos and Enchiladas
for Everyone

Although originally Mexican, tacos evolved as they crossed the border and became part of what we call Southwestern (and sometimes Tex-Mex) cooking. This region features delicious foods based on the blending of Mexican and American Indian cuisines along with whatever hearty produce—such as chiles, corn, squash, and beans—was possible to cultivate on the area's challenging land. Mexican spices and other flavorings common to this area became so popular, they spread to Mexican food lovers throughout the country—even those who had never visited the region. No surprise, though, because the exciting and flavorful Mexican-Southwestern combinations are a nice change of pace for dinner.

Tacos and, similarly, enchiladas for dinner have been a long-standing tradition in many Southwestern households, and they are easy to incorporate into your own meals. With these great recipes and tips you can bring a taste of the Southwest into your home any day of the week.

Taco Tips

- Corn or flour tortillas—or both—are key to any Mexican meal. Obviously, it is preferable to buy tortillas from a Mexican market that makes them fresh daily, but you're more likely to buy tortillas at the supermarket. Because they are several days or even weeks old by the time you buy them, you will need to freshen up the flavor and texture. Here are a few ways:

Frying: Although you don't have to fry tortillas, traditional tacos and enchiladas are made with tortillas that are quickly fried before being filled. To make tacos this way, fry the tortillas in peanut oil at 350°F. Then drain on paper towels and fill as desired. For enchiladas, quickly drop the tortillas in the hot oil, then drain them. While they are still warm, fill them, then roll them and place them in a pan lined with sauce.

Steaming: I like to steam tortillas. Very fresh tortillas will have better flavor when steamed, and steaming will save you a lot of fat and calories over the fried version. I steam them in the microwave, wrapped in a damp towel, for just a minute or two. If the tortillas are a week or more old and beginning to dry out a bit, you can add some butter to them before steaming to make them extra pliable. Traditionally, the tortillas were steamed in a steamer basket over hot water.

- These days, fillings can be just about any roasted, grilled, or lightly fried vegetable or meat. Take inspiration from the fillings in the recipes I share here, but also feel free to experiment and create your own.

- Accompaniments can include shredded lettuce or cabbage, chopped tomato, grated cheese, salsa, sour cream or Mexican soft white cheese, guacamole, olives, and fresh cilantro. Again, serve what you like or your family prefers.

Chili Steak Tacos

✓ SOMETHING SPECIAL

A spicy, quickly fried mixture of steak and vegetables is used as a flavorful filling for these soft tacos. Any other type of freshly cooked tender meat—such as chicken, turkey, or pork—can be broken up or shredded into this mixture.

2 tablespoons olive oil

½ cup chopped green onions (about 8 onions)

1 teaspoon finely chopped garlic (1 medium clove)

1 cup stemmed seeded deveined and chopped red bell pepper (1 medium pepper)

½ pound flank steak, cut diagonally into thin strips

1 teaspoon ground cumin *

2 teaspoons chili powder

Salt and freshly ground pepper, to taste

1 tablespoon chopped fresh cilantro

Eight 8-inch corn tortillas

1 cup grated cheddar cheese (4 ounces)

1 cup chopped fresh tomatoes (1 large tomato)

1 cup shredded lettuce (about ¼ head iceberg lettuce)

1 cup (½ pint) sour cream

1. Heat the oil in a large, heavy skillet over medium heat. Add the onion, garlic, and chopped bell pepper and cook, stirring occasionally, until tender, about 10 minutes. Transfer to a warm plate.

2. Add the sliced steak to the skillet and stir until no longer pink, about 1 minute. Return the onion, garlic, and pepper to skillet. Add the cumin and chili powder, and stir until heated through, 2 to 3 minutes. Season with salt and freshly ground pepper. Remove the skillet from the heat and stir in the cilantro. Transfer the steak mixture to a bowl and cover to keep warm.

3. Wrap the tortillas in a damp towel and steam them in the microwave for 2 to 3 minutes. Transfer to a napkin-lined basket and cover with another napkin to keep warm. At the table, pass the tortillas, steak mixture, cheese, tomatoes, lettuce, and sour cream separately, so everyone can assemble his or her own special tacos.

✱ TIP: Cumin should be bought as whole seeds and ground fresh for the best flavor. Place the seeds in an inexpensive coffee grinder that you use only for grinding spices. If the ground cumin is going directly into the pan as in this dish, grind it raw and add it to the pan. If the cumin is going into a dish with liquid, such as a soup or a sauce, toast the seeds in a skillet over medium heat before grinding. Heat the spice just until you begin to smell the aroma. Allow to cool a little, then grind and use.

Chicken–Green Chile Enchilada Pie

✓ *EASY PREPARATION*

There is something really satisfying about a meal that comes together this quickly and results in a beautiful casserole-style pie. Make these enchiladas with leftover pork or steak, or just fill them with cheese for an easy main course. Serve the enchiladas with refried beans and packaged Mexican-style rice.

2 boneless skinless chicken breasts

Salt and freshly ground pepper, to taste

Twelve 8-inch fresh corn tortillas

2 tablespoons unsalted butter, softened

One 10-ounce can green chile enchilada sauce

One 4-ounce can chopped green chiles

2 cups grated Monterey Jack cheese (from 8 ounces)

Fresh Picante Salsa, for garnish (page 54)

2 cups grated cheddar cheese (from 8 ounces)

1 head iceberg lettuce, shredded

½ bunch fresh cilantro leaves, washed and well dried, chopped

1 cup (½ pint) sour cream, for garnish

½ cup black olives, for garnish

1. Preheat the oven to 375°F. Place the chicken breasts in a glass pie plate or shallow dish and season them with salt and pepper. Pour ¼ cup of water into the dish and cover with plastic wrap. Microwave the chicken on high for 5 minutes, or until it reaches a temperature of 160°F on an instant-read thermometer when inserted into the thickest part of the breast. Remove from the microwave and let cool.

2. Shred the chicken with two forks and set it aside. ∗

3. Place the corn tortillas in a buttered ceramic or glass pie plate and cover with plastic wrap (or wrap them in a damp cloth towel). Steam in the microwave on high for 1 to 2 minutes.

4. Butter a 9- × 13-inch glass baking dish. Pour the enchilada sauce into a shallow bowl. Spread a thin layer of the sauce on the bottom of the glass dish. Dip a tortilla in the sauce and lay it on the right half of the glass dish. Arrange two or three pieces of chicken on the tortilla, then some of the chopped green chiles and a sprinkling of each of the cheeses. Top with another tortilla that has been dipped in the sauce. Repeat the layering process until you reach the sixth tortilla. Finish with a layer of sauce and cheese. Make another enchilada pie in the same way on the left-hand side of the dish with the remaining ingredients.

5. Bake for 20 minutes, until heated through and the cheese is melted.

6. Make the salsa.

7. Combine the shredded lettuce with the cilantro in a medium bowl. Remove the enchilada pies from the oven and cut into wedges. Serve on heated plates, with the lettuce-cilantro combination, salsa, sour cream, and olives served alongside in separate bowls.

∗TIP: When the grill is hot, or the oven is on, think about cooking **extra chicken** to shred for quick future use. After the chicken is cooled and shredded, place it in a resealable freezer bag and freeze for up to 2 months. The next time you want to make this pie, take the chicken out of the freezer in the morning and place it in the refrigerator. It will be thawed by the time you are ready to make the pie in the evening.

Roasted Vegetable Tacos

✓ *EASY PREPARATION*

Filled with a wonderful mixture of vegetables and spices, these roasted vegetable tacos can be made with freshly roasted vegetables or even leftover ones.

1 medium red onion, cut into ¼-inch slices

3 large portobello mushrooms, cut into ¼-inch slices

2 small zucchini, halved lengthwise and cut across into ¼-inch slices

1 red bell pepper, stemmed, seeded, cut into ¼-inch strips

2 tablespoons olive oil

¾ tablespoon chili powder, or more to taste

1 cup Fresh Guacamole (page 53), or more, to taste

1 cup Fresh Picante Salsa (page 54), or more, to taste

Eight 8-inch crisp taco shells

1 cup sour cream

1 cup fresh cilantro leaves

1. Preheat the oven to 450°F.

2. Toss the cut vegetables with the olive oil in a large bowl. On a large rimmed baking sheet, arrange the vegetables in 1 layer. Sprinkle with chili powder. Roast 25 minutes. ∗

3. While vegetables are roasting, make the guacamole and salsa.

4. Heat the taco shells on a cookie sheet in the oven 2 to 3 minutes. Spoon the roasted vegetables into the hot, crisp taco shells. Top with the salsa, sour cream, and chopped cilantro. Serve the guacamole on the side.

SERVING SUGGESTION

Serve with a bowl of shredded Monterey Jack, cheddar, or traditional Mexican cheeses like queso añejo or queso blanco, or even good-quality Parmigiano-Reggiano or Romano cheese for garnishing the tacos. Pour tall glasses of ice-cold beer or Sangria for the adults, lemonade for the kids.

∗**TIP:** If you don't want to turn on the oven, or if you just prefer the flavor of grilled vegetables but don't want to heat the grill, use a sturdy **ridged grill pan**. Preheat the grill pan over high heat, then oil the vegetables and add them in a single layer to the heated pan. Cook them—in batches, if necessary—until they are caramelized and well browned, turning once. Remove each type of vegetable as it is cooked, and continue grilling the rest.

Fresh Crab Tacos

✓ NO COOKING NEEDED ✓ SOMETHING SPECIAL

Though not for every day, this is one of my favorite meals because it features simple, fresh, quality ingredients in a quickly made dish. The best taco provides a taste of every ingredient in each bite. It is the combination of the distinct flavors that really makes this work.

I use fresh citrus fruits, removing the zest for the salsa and squeezing the juice for the cucumber mixture. The cucumber, onion, tomato, and citrus fruits should all be at room temperature. (As soon as you walk in the door, even possibly before your coat comes off, take all of the ingredients, except the crab, out of the refrigerator.)

For the best blending of flavors, chop the salsa ingredients as evenly and finely as you can—but don't mash them; you do want a little texture. Buy fresh lump crabmeat, if you can find it, and look for good corn tortillas. Fresh corn tortillas that are a day old or less have a sweet flavor that beautifully complements the crab.

✱ TIP: The **crabmeat** should be mild and sweet, with no fishy odor. If it was previously frozen, it may have extra water. Drain off the water by putting the crab in a colander for 5 to 10 minutes and then blotting it with a paper towel to remove the excess moisture.

1 cup peeled seeded and finely chopped cucumber (from 1 large cucumber)

3/4 cup chopped red onion (1 small onion)

2 cups halved seeded and diced vine-ripened tomatoes (from 2 large tomatoes)

2 tablespoons chopped fresh cilantro

1 teaspoon ground cumin (see Tip on page 46)

1/3 cup fresh lime juice, plus 2 tablespoons for drizzling (from 4 medium limes)

1/3 cup fresh orange juice (from 1 medium orange)

2 tablespoons lemon juice

Salt and freshly ground pepper, to taste

Twelve 8-inch fresh corn tortillas

1 tablespoon unsalted butter, softened

1 head butter leaf lettuce, separated into leaves, washed and well dried

3 cups fresh lump crabmeat, picked over to remove any bits of shell, taking care not to break up the lumps (about 1 pound) ✱

2 avocados peeled stoned and thinly sliced

2 tablespoons extra-virgin olive oil

2 cups chopped tomatoes, for garnish (from 2 large tomatoes)

2 cups shredded iceberg lettuce, for garnish (about 1/2 medium head)

1. In a large bowl, mix the cucumber, onion, tomatoes, cilantro, cumin, and citrus juices (except 2 tablespoons lime juice) together. Season with salt and pepper. Let this salsa stand at room temperature while you prepare the tacos.

2. Place the corn tortillas in a buttered ceramic or glass pie plate and cover with plastic wrap (or wrap them in a damp cloth towel). Steam in the microwave on high for 1 to 2 minutes.

3. Working with several tortillas at a time, place a lettuce leaf on each tortilla and add some crabmeat and then 2 tablespoons of the cucumber salsa. Top each with an avocado slice. Season with salt and pepper. Drizzle with a little lime juice and olive oil. Fold each taco in half and serve. Pass bowls of freshly chopped tomato and shredded lettuce for garnish.

Fish Tacos with Spicy Picante Salsa and Herbed Mayonnaise

✓ *SOMETHING SPECIAL*

A great fish taco is a culinary joy. Some people think it's complicated, but here's the simple secret: Start out with fresh white fish fillets, bread them while cold, and fry them just before you are ready to place them in the taco shells.

1 cup Fresh Picante Salsa (page 54), or more, to taste

1 cup Herbed Mayonnaise (below)

1½ pounds fish fillets, cut into 1- × 2-inch or 1- × 3-inch sticks (shark, cod, pollock, catfish, or any white-fleshed fish)

1 cup spiced fish breading mix, such as House Autry or Lawry's

1 to 2 cups peanut oil

Eight 8-inch crisp corn taco shells

2 limes, cut into wedges

2 cups finely shredded cabbage, lettuce, (about 1/4 head), or your favorite cole slaw

1 cup grated Monterey Jack cheese or other cheese (optional)

1. Prepare the salsa. Then, prepare the mayonnaise.

2. Preheat the oven to 375°F. Be sure the fish pieces are very cold so the coating will stick. Toss the fish in a paper bag with the spiced fish breading mix until well coated. Place the breaded fish in the refrigerator while the oil is heating.

3. Pour the oil into a large, heavy, straight-sided skillet to a depth of 1 inch. Heat the oil to 375°F, using a frying thermometer to gauge the temperature. Add the cold breaded fish, a few pieces at a time. Do not overcrowd the pan, or the oil temperature will fall. Check the thermometer to make sure the oil stays above 350°F during the entire frying time; raise the heat gently, as needed. Once the fish is browned and crisp, 3 to 4 minutes per batch, remove it from the oil, drain on a paper towel and keep warm in the preheated oven. Repeat with the rest of the fish. Fried foods taste heavy and greasy only when the oil used dips below 350°F and too much of it is absorbed.

4. Heat the taco shells on a cookie sheet in the oven 3 to 4 minutes. Spoon a little of the mayonnaise into the bottom of the taco shells. Top with a piece or two of fish and sprinkle with a little squeeze of lime juice. Spread a little cabbage or lettuce on top. Serve while fish is very hot, with the salsa. (Even though it isn't common to serve fish and cheese together, you can serve this with a bowl of shredded Monterey Jack, cheddar, or a combination of Mexican cheeses for garnishing the tacos.)

Herbed Mayonnaise

✓ *EASY PREPARATION*   ✓ *NO COOKING NEEDED*

Similar to tartar sauce, this simple sauce—called "white sauce" by Baja Californians—is great on tacos, potatoes, sandwiches, and even grilled meats. The combination of cumin and cilantro seems to make it perfect for tacos.

½ cup mayonnaise

½ cup low-fat (not nonfat) sour cream

⅓ cup thinly sliced green onion, white and up to 1 inch dark green (1 full bunch)

½ teaspoon ground cumin

⅓ cup chopped fresh cilantro

Blend together all the ingredients with a whisk in a small bowl. Cover and chill.

Bacon, Lettuce, and Tomato Soft Tacos

✓ *EASY PREPARATION*

My 12-year-old son loves these "BLT" tacos for dinner or any time, even as a snack after school. I leave the ingredients ready in the refrigerator, and when he comes home he can make one for himself. The bacon is already cooked and can be quickly reheated in the microwave.

½ pound bacon, thinly sliced

½ cup mayonnaise

1 tablespoon mustard

Four 12-inch flour tortillas (such as garlic and herb), at room temperature

Leaf lettuce, washed, well dried, and crisped in the refrigerator

2½ cups seeded and coarsely chopped tomatoes (from 3 medium tomatoes)

Salt and freshly ground pepper, to taste

1 cup shredded Monterey Jack cheese (from 4 ounces)

1. Fry the bacon in a large, heavy skillet until crisp, 6 to 8 minutes. Drain well on paper towels, and discard bacon grease left in the skillet. *

2. Combine the mayonnaise and mustard in a small bowl.

3. Arrange the tortillas on a work surface. Arrange the lettuce on the tortillas. Divide the bacon among the tortillas. Sprinkle each liberally with chopped tomato. Top each with a tablespoon of the mayonnaise mix and season with salt and pepper. Sprinkle each with a little cheese.

4. Fold over the bottom quarter of the tortillas, and then wrap the sides, loosely overlapping them. Serve at once.

SERVING SUGGESTIONS

Add cooked turkey to these tacos to make them a little heartier. Serve them with a fresh green salad.

Also try these in crisp commercial taco shells that have been preheated in the oven or toaster oven 3 to 4 minutes.

*TIP: To avoid some of the mess of cooking the **bacon**, bake it in the oven or toaster oven at 400°F, spread in one layer on a rimmed baking sheet. The bacon will cook and crisp up in about 15 minutes. Remove the bacon from the cookie sheet and drain on paper towels before serving or storing.

Fresh Guacamole

✓ *EASY PREPARATION*   ✓ *NO COOKING NEEDED*   ✓ *SOMETHING SPECIAL*

Whether in a bowl with fresh chips, on top of tacos and enchiladas, or as part of a vinaigrette for salad, this quick guacamole will be part of any Mexican or Southwestern fiesta night from now on. My real time-savers for making homemade guacamole are the food processor and store-bought salsa (usually found in the refrigerator section) to season it.

*TIP: Once cut, **avocados** turn brown quickly. To prevent this, toss or brush gently with lemon or lime juice, or vinegar.

6 large ripe avocados, peeled and stoned *

¼ cup prepared salsa, as spicy as you like

¼ cup chopped white onion (from 1/4 medium onion)

2 tablespoons finely chopped fresh cilantro

2 tablespoons fresh lime juice

Salt and freshly ground pepper, to taste

Place all of the ingredients in the food processor or blender, and pulse to process until the mixture is just coarsely chopped. The guacamole should be chunky in texture, not smooth. Taste the guacamole to determine if the seasonings are correct; adjust the lime juice and salt if needed.

Fresh Picante Salsa

✓ *SOMETHING SPECIAL*

This cooked salsa will be a perfect addition to your Mexican favorites. It would be great mixed into rice, or served over enchiladas or grilled meat and fish.

6 medium-sized vine-ripened tomatoes, cut in large chunks

½ cup chopped white onion

1 serrano chile, finely chopped, or more to taste

2 tablespoons vegetable oil

1 teaspoon salt

1. In a food processor fitted with a metal blade, combine the tomatoes, onion, and chile and process until nearly smooth, but the mixture should retain some texture. ✱

2. Heat the oil in a small skillet over medium heat to warm it.

Add the tomato mixture and the salt. Cook until the mixture thickens, about 7 minutes. Remove the salsa from the heat. Transfer to a heatproof serving bowl, let cool completely, and serve.

✱ **TIP:** This Mexican **salsa** is usually cooked but I love it simply served fresh. So if you want a quick fresh salsa, just adjust the seasonings to taste at this point and serve.

Midweek Pizza Party

Pizzas baked in wood-burning brick ovens have a long, delicious history in Italy and are a much-beloved food in the United States. Although Italians pride themselves on traditional versions, in America, pizza has seen its share of spin-offs. We can now find pizza that ranges from old favorites like plain tomato and cheese or pepperoni to goat cheese and smoked salmon with dill. We are only held back by our own imaginations.

Whether you go the traditional route or try your own creative ideas, show your family and friends that truly great pizza can come from your oven, not a box.

Basic Ingredients

- **Flour**

  All-purpose flour: Make sure to use a good-quality brand of all-purpose flour, though my recipe works quite well with bread flour, too, if you have it on hand.

  Whole-wheat flour: For a more wholesome, hearty crust, use good-quality whole-wheat flour. If the recipe doesn't call for whole-wheat flour, but you would like to use it, replace only half of the all-purpose flour with the whole-wheat to create a hearty dough without it being too heavy.

  Semolina flour: Coarse-grained semolina flour made from hard durum wheat is great for sprinkling on your pizza board. It keeps the dough from sticking, makes it slide on and off of the paddle easily, and gives the crust a pleasant texture.

- **Yeast:** Always use the freshest yeast you can find. The expiration date is clearly marked on the package. When it approaches the use-by date, it may not be as active as when it was freshest, and may not rise as quickly. There are special pizza yeasts available at Williams-Sonoma. SAF yeast is also good, or Red Star active dry yeast. Whichever yeast you choose, make sure that it is fresh, and not quick rising.

- **Olive oil:** Use rich, fruity olive oil that enhances the flavor of the sauce you choose. I also love to drizzle a little infused oil, such as garlic oil, on pizza crusts before putting the toppings on for added flavor.

- **Tomatoes:** Summer is the best time for fresh vine-ripened tomatoes. Use them fresh over pizza while they are at the peak of their season. When the tomatoes are not at their best, use canned organic plum tomatoes. You can make wonderful sauces from these and even use them drained and sliced on top of the pizza just as you would use fresh. If a tomato is too acidic, try adding a pinch of sugar or fresh nutmeg to the sauce to mellow it out a little.

- **Herbs:** There are a number of good fresh and dried herbs for pizza. Among them are oregano, basil, Italian (flat-leaf) parsley, thyme, and rosemary. Make sure when using fresh herbs that they are very fragrant and blemish free. Dried herbs should be no more than one year old and stored in a cool dark place. A good rule of thumb for substituting dried herbs for fresh is to use one-third the amount of dried herbs as fresh. In other words, if a recipe calls for 3 tablespoons fresh herbs, use 1 tablespoon dried.

• Cheeses

Grating cheeses: These cheeses are the hard, aged cheeses. They have a sharp, intense flavor and are usually the top layer on the pizza. Parmigiano-Reggiano is the best-flavored Italian imported cheese. This tangy cow's milk cheese is aged at least two years. Also worth using are pecorino and Romano; both are made with sheep's milk. They have sharper flavor than Parmigiano-Reggiano. Do not buy these cheeses grated. They have the best flavor when freshly grated as you need them. Store the ungrated cheese in the refrigerator tightly wrapped and away from anything that is strong in flavor.

Fresh or melting cheeses: Fresh, soft mozzarella is much milder and creamier than most commercial mozzarella. While it used to be available only in specialty cheese stores or Italian groceries, it is now available packed in brine in many supermarket fancy cheese sections. It will not grate the same, but can be sliced or diced and sprinkled over the pizza.

There are many other wonderful melting cheeses that can be used for pizza. In combination with mozzarella, or alone, try using Swiss cheese, Gouda, fontina, Brie, and a variety of smoked cheeses.

Specialty cheeses: Many specialty cheeses are used to make pizzas more interesting. Most remarkable is goat, a soft, rich, tangy flavorful cheese that has become enormously popular. Goat cheese melts to a luscious creamy consistency and adds great flavor to pizza.

Blue cheese is another wonderfully robust cheese. It has a strong flavor, so use it sparingly over the top of the pizza. I prefer Italian Gorgonzola and English Stilton for the most distinctive flavor.

Equipment

1. **Pizza stone:** Baking a pizza on a pizza stone or tiles at high temperature is the best way to re-create the taste of pizza cooked in the brick ovens of Italy. The pizza stones are made of flat man-made tile or porous stone and must be preheated up to 30 minutes, in order to be hot enough to sear the crust and release the moisture in the crust as steam. Clean, unglazed, porous quarry tiles arranged on a flat cookie sheet in your oven are an economical substitute. The topped pizza dough is then slid directly onto the hot tiles. The stones should never be washed with soap, but should be scraped clean, rinsed, and allowed to dry completely before re-using them.

2. **Pizza or baker's peel:** This thin, wide wooden board with a bevel at one edge and a handle at the other makes sliding the pizza in and out of the oven easy. It is an indulgence to be sure, but a very useful one if you make lots of pizza. Sprinkle the board with cornmeal and the pizza will slide as if on ball bearings.

Basic Pizza Dough

✓ *MAKE-AHEAD*

Everyone knows the perfect pizza begins with the perfect crust. Ultimately, the pizza is a balance of a well-made crust and some tasty toppings. The crust can be thin and crisp or thick and chewy, depending on how the dough is handled (and your preference). This dough will make enough for two large relatively thin-crust pizzas, or four small ones. While making the dough by hand may seem more than you want to do after a busy day at work, the end result is very satisfying. You might want to reserve the fun for Friday nights and use frozen pizza dough or ready-made rounds such as Boboli when you are in a rush.

2½ teaspoons dry yeast

1 cup warm water

3 tablespoons extra-virgin olive oil

3 cups all-purpose flour (or more depending on the humidity) *

1 tablespoon sugar

1 tablespoon salt

1½ tablespoons olive oil

2 to 3 tablespoons cornmeal

1. In a small bowl, sprinkle yeast over the warm water and extra-virgin olive oil. Stir until foamy.

2. In a large bowl, stir together the flour, sugar, and salt. Stir in the yeast mixture, beating until a stiff dough forms, about 2 minutes. Add more flour if the dough is too sticky to handle. The secret to a great dough is the moisture content. A chewy crust comes from a "wet" dough, or one that slightly sticks to your hands.

3. Turn the finished dough onto a lightly floured surface and knead until smooth, shiny, and elastic, adding flour if it is still too sticky; this takes 8 to 10 minutes.

4. Lightly oil a large bowl and put the kneaded dough into it. Brush the surface with oil. Cover and let it rise in a warm place (about 80°F is perfect) until double in bulk (two fingers poked into the surface will leave deep holes), up to 1 hour.

5. Punch the dough down by literally pushing your fist into it two or three times, taking out much of the air. Divide the dough into 2 equal pieces and form into 2 flat rounds that are each 6 inches in diameter. Cover with plastic wrap and refrigerate if not using immediately.

6. Place the dough on a large piece of parchment paper dusted with cornmeal. Roll the dough from the center out. If the dough bounces back as you roll or press it out, allow it to rest 5 minutes and then continue rolling into a 12-inch round about ¼ inch thick.

7. To form the rim around the pizza crust, place the knuckles of one hand about ½ inch inside the edge of the round. Working in a clockwise direction, use the other hand to press the edge of the dough against your knuckles, forming a raised edge.

Serving Suggestion

To make a quick flatbread, roll the dough out into individual rounds about 12 to 14 inches in diameter and ¼ inch thick, brush with olive oil, and grill on a hot grill or grill pan.

★TIP: I call for all-purpose **flour** in my basic pizza dough, especially when you are just beginning to experiment. Once you know you are going to make your own dough on a regular basis, try an unbleached, stone-ground bread flour for superior flavor. Many specialty shops and even some supermarkets are now carrying this type of flour.

Fresh Salad Pizza

✓ *EASY PREPARATION*   ✓ *SOMETHING SPECIAL*

Who needs salad on the side when you can have it on top—of a delicious crispy pizza crust. Homemade dough is ideal, but on a busy night or if you're just starting out making pizza, packaged pizza rounds are a good substitute.

2 heads watercress, cleaned and chopped

1 cup thinly sliced red onion, soaked in ice water for 10 minutes, then well drained (from 1/2 medium onion)

1 cup seeded deveined and thinly sliced red bell pepper (from 1 small)

4 cups seeded and diced vine-ripened tomatoes (from 4 large tomatoes)

½ cup marinated artichokes, drained and cut into thin wedges

4 tablespoons good-quality balsamic vinegar

1 teaspoon grainy Dijon mustard

¾ teaspoon salt

¾ teaspoon freshly ground pepper

¼ cup (4 tablespoons) fruity extra-virgin olive oil

2 to 3 tablespoons cornmeal

Two 12-inch pre-made thin pizza crusts, such as Boboli

4 cups shredded smoked Gouda cheese (from 1 pound)

1. Preheat a pizza stone in the oven at 500°F for 30 minutes.

2. In a large bowl, combine the watercress, onion, bell pepper, tomatoes, and artichokes. *

3. In a small bowl, combine the balsamic vinegar, mustard, salt, and pepper. Add the olive oil in a slow stream, whisking constantly, until the dressing thickens. Taste and adjust seasoning. Toss this dressing with the vegetables. Allow the mixture to stand at room temperature for 30 minutes.

4. Sprinkle cornmeal on the pizza peel, if using, or on a flat rimless cookie sheet. Place 1 premade pizza crust on the peel or cookie sheet.

5. Drain the vegetables well and toss them with ¼ cup of the Gouda cheese. Spread ¼ cup of the remaining Gouda cheese on the crust. Spoon ½ of the vegetable mixture over the cheese. Top with ½ cup of the remaining cheese. Repeat with the second crust.

6. Transfer the pizza from the peel or cookie sheet to the pre-heated pizza stone and bake 8 to 10 minutes, until the cheese melts. Remove the pizza from the oven and let it stand for 5 minutes before cutting and serving. Bake the second pizza the same way.

7. Cut the pizza into wedges and arrange on a board or heated serving platter.

SERVING SUGGESTIONS

Fresh herbs add a fantastic accent to this pizza. Good choices include basil, oregano, thyme, and parsley. Do not go overboard, though. Add one or two varieties, chopped, to the salad mixture just before heating the pizza.

Try serving this pizza with grilled chicken—or with roasted chicken from the supermarket.

*TIP: This pizza can be made with any type of peppery **salad green**. Try using a combination of arugula and spinach for a different version of this salad pizza.

Mushroom and Cheese Pesto Pizza

✓ *SOMETHING SPECIAL*

This aromatic and tasty pizza features a variety of flavorful mushrooms and pesto as the base instead of tomato sauce. I like to combine the mild fresh mozzarella cheese with Italian fontina and Parmigiano-Reggiano to give the pizza great flavor and richness. For an elegant appetizer pizza, roll out the dough into twelve two-inch rounds, top with the pesto, mushrooms, and some blue cheese, and bake until crusty.

1 recipe Basic Pizza Dough (page 57), premade dough for 2 pizzas, or 2 premade pizza crusts, such as Boboli

1 cup Pesto (page 77), or good-quality store-bought pesto

2 to 3 tablespoons cornmeal

1/2 pound button mushrooms, brushed, stemmed, and sliced

1/2 cup freshly grated Parmigiano-Reggiano cheese (from 2 ounces)

1 pound fresh mozzarella cheese, sliced

1/4 pound shiitake mushrooms, brushed and sliced (about 1 cup)

1/4 pound cremini mushrooms, brushed and sliced (about 1 cup)

1/4 pound enoki mushrooms, brushed and broken into small clusters (or substitute another mushroom or more of the others) (about 1 cup) *

2 cups shredded fontina cheese (from 8 ounces)

1. Preheat a pizza stone in the oven at 500°F for 30 minutes.

2. Make the pizza dough. Make the pesto. Then, roll each dough round into two 12-inch circles about 1/4 inch thick and create a 1/2-inch rim, or unwrap prepared crusts. Sprinkle cornmeal on the pizza peel, if using, or on a flat rimless cookie sheet. Place one round on the prepared peel or cookie sheet.

3. Spread 1/2 cup of the pesto onto each round. Distribute the button mushrooms evenly over the pizzas. Sprinkle each pizza with half the Parmigiano-Reggiano cheese, and place half the mozzarella slices over the Parmigiano-Reggiano. Divide the other mushrooms evenly over the pizzas. Spread the fontina cheese over the top.

4. Transfer the pizza from the peel or cookie sheet to the preheated pizza stone and bake for 10 minutes, until the crust is browned and the cheese is melted. Remove the pizza from the oven. Bake the second pizza the same way.

5. Cut the pizza into wedges and arrange on a board or heated serving platter.

SERVING SUGGESTION

To make this pizza a little bit heartier, add small strips of prosciutto or thin rounds of pepperoni or other sausage to the pizza after topping it with the mushrooms.

*TIP: When choosing **mushrooms**, look for those that are firm and even in color, avoiding those that are shriveled and broken. Store them in a paper bag in the refrigerator until ready to use. Mushrooms should be brushed off to clean them instead of washing, as they have a tendency to absorb too much of the water.

Gorgonzola, Escarole, and Roast Pepper Pizza

✓ *SOMETHING SPECIAL*

This pizza has a very robust flavor. The slightly bitter taste of the escarole, the robust smokiness of roasted peppers, and the tangy, salty flavor of the Gorgonzola cheese are wonderful together.

½ **recipe Basic Pizza Dough (page 57)**

2 to 3 tablespoons cornmeal

¼ **cup olive oil**

1 tablespoon thinly sliced garlic (from 2 medium cloves) or more if you like

1 large head escarole, separated into leaves, washed, well dried, and cut up (about 6 cups)

½ **cup stemmed peeled seeded roasted peppers, cut into thick strip (from about 1 small pepper) ✱**

Salt and freshly ground pepper, to taste (optional)

½ **cup crumbled Gorgonzola cheese (2 ounces)**

Pinch dried Italian herbs, crumbled with your fingers

1. Preheat a pizza stone in the oven at 500°F for 30 minutes.

2. Make the pizza dough. Then, roll the dough into one 14-inch circle about ¼ inch thick. Create a ½-inch rim . Sprinkle cornmeal on the pizza peel, if using, or on a flat rimless cookie sheet. Lay the round on the prepared peel or cookie sheet.

3. Heat 2 tablespoons of the oil in a large skillet. Add the garlic and toss just until tender, but not brown, about 1 minute. Be careful not to let it burn. Add the escarole, and toss to coat with oil and wilt slightly, 1 minute. Remove and set aside.

4. Brush the crust with olive oil and arrange the peppers in a single layer. ✱

5. Spread the escarole and garlic mixture over the peppers. Season with salt and pepper. Distribute the cheese on top and drizzle with remaining olive oil. Sprinkle with the herbs.

6. Transfer the pizza from the peel or cookie sheet to the preheated pizza stone and bake 7 to 10 minutes, until the crust is golden brown.

7. Cut the pizza into wedges and arrange on a board or heated serving platter. ✱

✱**TIP:** Roast the peppers by grilling or broiling them whole, turning from time to time, until they are well blackened on all sides and pocked with blisters. Cover the peppers with a damp paper towel or seal them within a paper or plastic bag. Set aside for 5 minutes to allow the steam to help loosen the skin from the flesh. Peel and seed the peppers, then slice.

✱**TIP:** You can turn this into a **"soufflé" style pizza** by simply tossing the escarole, peppers, and garlic with two lightly beaten eggs. Stir in the cheese and season with salt and pepper. Spread the filling mixture to just cover the crust and bake until the crust is golden. Serve hot.

✱**TIP:** To make this **on the grill**, lay the raw dough on a hot grill. Cover the grill and bake the dough until the first side is golden brown. Once the first side is done, flip it over and top the cooked side with the toppings. Return it to the grill, grilled side down and bake on the grill at low heat with the hood down until the Gorgonzola melts.

Roasted Vegetable and Fontina Pizza

✓ *EASY PREPARATION*   ✓ *SOMETHING SPECIAL*

Wednesday night is my family's pizza-making night and I love to make this simple whatever's-in-the-fridge pizza, being creative with the vegetables I have on hand. Feel free to do the same. It's fun! Try brushing the dough with chili oil or other flavored oil before building the pizza to add deeper flavor.

1 recipe Basic Pizza Dough
(page 57)

2 to 3 tablespoons cornmeal

2 medium Italian eggplants,
well washed, sliced on the bias into
¼-inch slices

¼ cup oil-packed sun-dried
tomatoes, drained and julienned

2 small zucchini, washed and sliced
lengthwise into ¼-inch slices

4 cups stemmed seeded and sliced
green bell peppers (from 2 medium
peppers)

2 large portobello mushrooms,
stemmed, dark gills removed from
the underside, and thinly sliced

2 bunches green onions (about
10 thin), cut into 6-inch lengths

1 tablespoon finely chopped garlic
(from 2 medium cloves)

¼ cup olive oil

Salt and freshly ground pepper,
to taste

3 cups grated
fontina cheese (from 12 ounces)

2 teaspoons dried Italian herbs
or a mixture of oregano, marjoram,
and thyme

1. Preheat a pizza stone in the oven at 500°F for 30 minutes.

2. Make the pizza dough. Then, roll out the dough, 1 round at a time, into two 12-inch rounds, forming a rim (see page 57). Sprinkle cornmeal on the pizza peel, if using, or on a flat rimless cookie sheet. Place 1 round on the peel or cookie sheet.

3. Brush vegetables with oil and spread in a single layer on a heavy baking sheet. Roast in the oven 6 to 7 minutes, turn, and continue roasting for 5 to 6 minutes more. Remove from heat.

4. Brush dough with olive oil. Scatter vegetables evenly over the two pizza circles. Season with salt and pepper. Top the vegetables with cheese and sprinkle with herbs. Drizzle with a little more oil, if you like.

5. Transfer the pizza from the peel or cookie sheet to the preheated pizza stone and bake 15 minutes, until crust is crisp and browned and the cheese is melted. Bake the second pizza the same way.

6. Cut the pizza into wedges and arrange on a board or heated serving platter.

SERVING SUGGESTION

If you like, serve some Italian cold cuts alongside the pizza.

Smoked Salmon and Goat Cheese Pizza

✓ *SOMETHING SPECIAL*

This is not your everyday pizza, but it's nice to do something different every now and then. Make it with a premade crust or with the handmade dough. Serve the pizza with a fresh green salad to make a quick meal.

1 recipe Basic Pizza Dough (page 57), 1 pound frozen dough, or 2 premade thin pizza crusts, such as Boboli

2 to 3 tablespoons cornmeal

2 tablespoons chili oil or garlic-infused oil

1/3 cup chopped fresh dill

10 ounces fresh soft goat cheese, such as Montrachet, at room temperature

1/4 cup chopped red onion

8 ounces smoked salmon, diced

1. Preheat a pizza stone in the oven at 500°F for 30 minutes.

2. Make the pizza dough. Then, roll out the dough into two 12-inch rounds and form a rim, or unwrap prepared crusts. Sprinkle cornmeal on the pizza peel, if using, or on a flat rimless cookie sheet. Place 1 basic dough round or 1 pre-made pizza crust on the peel or cookie sheet. Brush the dough lightly with chili oil. Sprinkle the crusts with the dill, and then crumble the goat cheese over it. Top with the onion and then the smoked salmon.

3. Transfer the pizza from the peel or cookie sheet to the pre-heated pizza stone and bake until the crust is golden brown and the goat cheese is soft and creamy.

This will take about 15 minutes with raw dough and 10 minutes with the fully baked premade crust. Bake the second pizza the same way.

4. Cut the pizza into wedges and arrange on a board or heated serving platter.

SERVING SUGGESTION

For a great appetizer to go with drinks, use a 2-inch biscuit or cookie cutter to cut the pizza dough into rounds. Build miniature pizzas and bake on the hot stone, 4 at a time, 7 to 10 minutes. Allow the small pizzas to cool slightly before serving. Makes about 12 rounds.

Grilled Chicken Pizza

✓ *SOMETHING SPECIAL*

This recipe will remind you of a crowd pleaser, the barbecued chicken sandwich. Just pick your favorite barbecue sauce to put on it—you can try varying the sauce for different tastes, such as smoky, spicy, or sweet.

4 large boneless skinless chicken breasts

1 tablespoon olive oil

1 cup barbecue sauce

1 recipe Basic Pizza Dough (page 57)

2 to 3 tablespoons cornmeal

4 cups shredded smoked Gouda (from 16 ounces)

1 cup finely chopped red onion (from 1 small onion)

1. Preheat a pizza stone in the oven at 500°F for 30 minutes.

2. Preheat the grill or grill pan over medium-high heat. Grill the chicken breasts, brushing several times with olive oil and turning several times, until the chicken reaches a temperature of 160°F on an instant-read thermometer when inserted into the thickest part of the breast, 25 to 30 minutes. Cool slightly and then use two forks to pull the meat into shreds.

3. Combine the shredded chicken with ¼ cup of the barbecue sauce in a small bowl.

4. Make the pizza dough. Then, roll out the dough, 1 round at a time, into two 12-inch rounds, forming a rim (see page 57). Sprinkle cornmeal on the pizza peel, if using, or on a flat rimless cookie sheet. Place 1 round on the peel or cookie sheet.

5. Spread both crusts lightly with barbecue sauce, and then top each crust with about 1 cup of the cheese. Arrange the chicken over the crusts. Spoon a little of the barbecue sauce over the chicken. Distribute the red onion evenly over the chicken and then drizzle with more barbecue sauce. Spread the remaining cheese on top.

6. Transfer the pizza from the peel or cookie sheet to the preheated pizza stone and bake about 15 minutes, until the cheese melts and the crust is golden. Bake the second pizza the same way.

7. Cut the pizzas into wedges and arrange them on a board or heated serving platter.

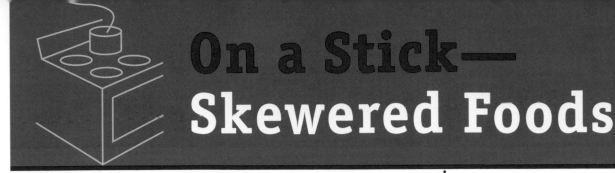

On a Stick—
Skewered Foods

There is something really rewarding about cooking food on a stick. A big plus is that skewers are quick to make and clean up. The food also gets that great rich, smoky taste all the way through it, with more surface area exposed to the grill or broiler. And it's fun for kids and adults alike—you get to eat with your hands or right off the stick, if you like.

The "stick" can be a toothpick, a bamboo skewer, or even a piece of sugar cane. What the skewered foods are depends on how creative you are. You can use almost any kind of meat, seafood, or vegetables, even pound cake. Look in the refrigerator, in the freezer, on the shelf, and see what you come up with.

Skewered foods may not be what you would consider a full meal, so also think about what you would serve with them. You may want to add a salad, or even some couscous or rice.

Kids will love the skewer concept. Make it even more appealing by getting them involved with the preparation. Bring them into the kitchen while you are preparing the skewers, so everyone can create his or her own to suit personal tastes. Even the most finicky eaters can find a combination they like!

Tips for Skewered Foods

- **Try different skewers.** The most common skewers are metal (the sturdiest) and wood, but I also like to use different types of skewers, depending on the flavor that I want to impart. A softer skewer may not easily thread through foods, so try making a small hole in the foods with a paring knife or ice pick and then thread it through the holes.

If you notice that the skewers are beginning to burn before the food is done, cover the ends of the skewers with foil. If you are cooking

on the grill, place a piece of the foil at one end of the grill, then line the skewers across the foil with the food directly on the grill and the bare ends of the skewers on the foil. The foods can be threaded on:

Wooden skewers (usually made from bamboo): Soak the skewers in water to cover for at least 30 minutes before you use them. This slows the heating of the skewers when you put them on the grill, in the broiler, or in the oven, and keeps them from burning. They can be used for any type of skewered food.

Metal skewers (usually made from stainless steel, chrome, or nonstick finishes): Foods hold more securely on metal skewers that are flat rather than round; the nonstick skewers clean easily. Metal skewers are also dishwasher safe. I particularly like to use metal skewers for meat and thick vegetables. Heat is transferred into the interior of the foods by the metal.

Rosemary stems: When you use rosemary for seasoning other dishes, save the stripped stems to use as skewers. Remove all of the leaves off the base of each stem. Dry them in a cool (175°F) oven, cool completely, and then store in a resealable plastic bag. When ready to use, soak in water for 20 to 30 minutes. Then thread with the food pieces.

Other skewers: Lemongrass stalks work very well with fish and vegetables if you want something that really infuses flavor. For desserts, I have used everything from raw sugarcane to candy canes.

- **Cut ingredients into equal pieces.** Everything should be cut to a uniform size so it all cooks evenly. With appetizer skewers, you should cut the ingredients into bite-sized pieces; with main-dish skewers, ingredients should be cut evenly and no larger than a 2-inch square so that they won't over-brown in the time they take to cook through.

- **Don't overfill the skewers.** Ingredients caramelize better and cook more evenly if the skewer isn't loaded from tip to tip. An appetizer, which should be served on a two- to three-inch skewer, should have only two or three pieces of food to make it easy to eat. On a main-dish skewer, eight to ten pieces is the maximum.

- **Watch cooking times.** Make sure foods that cook at the same rate are on the same skewer. Put the foods that take longer to cook, such as those containing chunks of meat, on the same skewer, then put those in the oven or on the grill first. The fast-cooking skewered foods such as fish and fruit can go on later. The overdone tomato or bell pepper that sat on the skewer waiting for the meat to get cooked will be a thing of the past.

Chicken Skewers with Quick Mole Sauce

MAKES 4 SERVINGS

I love the Latin America-inspired flavor of the mole sauce—a blend of tomatoes, cinnamon, cayenne, and unsweetened chocolate. Marinating the chicken in the sauce makes them deliciously succulent. For a light meal, slide the chicken off the skewers onto a piece of crisp lettuce such as butter leaf and roll up like a wrap. You can substitute pork or flank steak for the chicken in this recipe.

Quick Mole Sauce (below)

2 teaspoons light soy sauce

1/4 cup sugar

2 teaspoons finely chopped garlic (from 2 medium cloves)

1/3 cup vegetable oil, preferably peanut

2 large boneless skinless chicken breasts, halved horizontally into 2 thin cutlets, then sliced lengthwise into twelve 1-inch-wide strips *

Salt and freshly ground pepper, to taste

2 tablespoons toasted sesame seeds

Twelve 8-inch wooden skewers, soaked in water for 30 minutes

1. Make the mole sauce. Then, in a medium bowl, combine soy sauce, sugar, garlic, and oil. Marinate the chicken strips in the soy sauce mixture for 15 minutes, or longer if you like, refrigerated, up to 1 hour. *

2. Season the chicken with salt and pepper and sprinkle with sesame seeds. Thread each chicken strip on a skewer, weaving the skewer in and out of the chicken strip to secure it. Brush with the marinade.

3. Wrap foil around the exposed ends of the skewers to prevent burning, or place a strip of foil across one end of the grill and lay the exposed ends of the skewers on it. Grill skewers for 3 to 4 minutes, turning only once, after about 2 minutes.

4. Serve 3 skewers per person, with the mole sauce on the side.

SERVING SUGGESTION

Prepare vegetable skewers as well as the chicken skewers, and add freshly steamed rice. Spread the rice on a plate and lay the skewers on top. Drizzle with a little of the hot Quick Mole Sauce and serve. Pass the extra sauce in a bowl at the table.

✱ TIP: Before slicing **chicken** into strips, place the cutlets between two pieces of plastic wrap and pound them flatter, being careful not to tear the meat. This makes the chicken even more tender.

✱ TIP: Marinating can be a great way to add flavor to skewered foods. I marinate foods in a resealable plastic bag. Foods being marinated can sit as little as 15 minutes for added flavor, but there are maximum times too, depending on the food. If something marinates too long, the food proteins break down and the food can get mushy or, if there is acid in the marinade, it can become partly "cooked," which is further than you want if you plan to grill, roast, or fry following the marinating. You can marinate firm-fleshed fish for up to 4 hours in the refrigerator. Chicken and pork can marinate for up to 24 hours, beef and lamb for 48 hours.

Quick Mole Sauce

Traditional moles have been served in Mexico, Central America, and South America for hundreds of years. What distinguishes them is the normally extensive combination of ingredients and the slow cooking that reduces the sauce to give it a deep flavor and color. My sauce is a quick variation for weeknight cooking. The unsweetened chocolate is an authentic addition that provides richness, flavor, and color. This sauce can be made ahead, refrigerated, and reheated when ready to use.

1 small onion, quartered

1/2 cup chili-style canned diced tomatoes

2 teaspoons peeled and finely chopped garlic (2 medium cloves)

2 tablespoons dry bread crumbs

1/2 teaspoon ground cinnamon

1/4 cup roasted salted peanuts (1 ounce)

Salt and freshly ground pepper, to taste

1 tablespoon sesame seeds, toasted

1 teaspoon cayenne pepper

1 ounce unsweetened chocolate, broken up or chopped

2 tablespoons olive oil

1 cup low-sodium chicken broth

1. In the bowl of a food processor or in the container of a blender, combine all the ingredients except the olive oil and broth. Blend until coarsely smooth.

2. Heat the oil in a heavy skillet over medium-high heat. Pour in the pureed mixture. Let it cook for about a minute at this heat, then turn the heat to low and allow it to reduce slowly, stirring to prevent burning.

3. Cook 5 minutes, then beat in the chicken broth. Raise heat and cook on medium-high until heated through, about 3 minutes more.

4. Serve hot, drizzled over and alongside the chicken skewers.

Shrimp and Cucumber Sticks with Spicy Tomato Sauce

✓ *EASY PREPARATION*   ✓ *MAKE-AHEAD*   ✓ *SOMETHING SPECIAL*

These tantalizing skewers will remind you of a quick trip south of the border and are great for a warm night when you don't want to do a lot of cooking. To really save time, buy the shrimp already cooked; then all you have to do is make the sauce, thread the ingredients, and serve.

Spicy Tomato Sauce (below)

1 large ripe avocado, peeled, halved, stoned, and cut into 8 chunks

1 teaspoon fresh lemon juice

24 medium (31-35 per pound) shrimp, peeled, deveined, and rinsed

Eight 8-inch wooden or metal skewers (soak wooden ones in water for 30 minutes)

1 large cucumber, peeled, quartered, seeded, and cut into sixteen 1-inch sticks (see Tip on page 70)

8 cherry tomatoes

Salt and freshly ground pepper, to taste

1. Prepare the tomato sauce. Then, toss the avocado gently with the lemon juice in a small bowl.

2. Bring 4 quarts of water to a boil in a large saucepan. While you wait, fill a bowl that will hold the shrimp with ice water.

3. Cook the shrimp in two batches: toss half of the shrimp into the boiling water. Once the shrimp turn pink and are firm, after about 3 minutes, lift them out of the water with a slotted spoon and immediately place them in the ice water to stop the cooking. Allow the cooking water to return to a boil and cook the second batch of shrimp. Remove the shrimp from the ice water bath as soon as they are cool, and pat dry with paper towels.

4. To prepare the skewers, thread 1 shrimp, 1 piece cucumber, 1 cherry tomato, 1 shrimp, 1 piece avocado, and 1 shrimp on each skewer. Dust with salt and pepper. Serve chilled or at room temperature.

SERVING SUGGESTIONS

Place the skewers on a bed of crisp lettuce on a large platter. Garnish, if you like, with Fresh Picante Salsa (page 54), Fresh Guacamole (page 53), sour cream, tortilla chips, and cilantro. Pass the tomato sauce alongside.

Try tossing the ingredients together with the sauce to serve this dish like a salad instead of on skewers. Serve jarred salsa and guacamole on the side, if you like.

Spicy Tomato Sauce

✓ *EASY PREPARATION*

The trick to making this great sauce is to use a high-quality canned tomato. American canned tomatoes are often very high in acid, and sometimes have sodium and sugar added. Try Italian canned tomatoes, such as Pomi, or organic canned tomatoes for the best flavor.

2 tablespoons olive oil

2 cloves garlic

½ teaspoon crushed red pepper

1 cup drained canned diced tomatoes

Salt and freshly ground pepper, to taste

1 tablespoon chopped fresh cilantro ✳

1. Heat the oil in a medium heavy skillet. Add the garlic and pepper and cook, stirring, for 1 minute. Add the tomatoes and cook over high heat until thickened, 6 to 8 minutes.

2. Pour the tomato mixture into a blender or food processor and puree until smooth. Season well with salt and pepper; stir in freshly chopped cilantro. Taste and adjust seasoning, if necessary. Serve at room temperature.

✳ TIP: Cilantro is the name for the leaves of the coriander plant, which is why you may also see it referred to as fresh coriander. Some people just love it and others hate it. I find that cilantro can add sweetness and a refreshing quality to many dishes. Use the chopped leaves for a garnish, but if making something with cilantro in the blender or food processor, use both the leaves and stems for even more flavor.

Lamb Fingers on Skewers with Tzatziki

✓ SOMETHING SPECIAL

This recipe is a tribute to the Mediterranean—Greece, in particular. Loaded with incredible flavors, these delicious finger-shaped lamb kebabs are the centerpiece of a wonderful meal. Tzatziki is a refreshing minty yogurt-cucumber sauce that goes well with this dish or any well-seasoned meats and fish.

Tzatziki (below)

1 pound ground lamb

1 teaspoon onion juice (from 2 table-spoons grated onion or bottled) *

¼ cup finely chopped onion

3 teaspoons finely chopped garlic (3 medium cloves)

1½ teaspoons ground coriander

Salt and cayenne pepper, to taste

2 tablespoons chopped fresh cilantro

Twelve 8-inch wooden skewers, soaked for 30 minutes in cold water

1. Preheat the grill. Meanwhile, make the tzatziki.

2. In a large bowl, mix all the remaining ingredients with a wooden spoon until very well combined. Use your hands to mold the meat mixture into 12 small logs or fingers, about 4 inches long and 1 inch wide. Mold 1 log around each skewer. Place each finished skewer on a cookie sheet. *

3. Spray the grill with nonstick spray. Wrap foil around the exposed ends of the skewers to prevent burning, or place a strip of foil across one end of the grill and lay the exposed ends of the skewers on it.

4. Grill the skewers over medium-hot heat for 3 to 4 minutes per side, about 6 or 7 minutes total. Serve 3 skewers per person with tzatziki on the side for dipping.

SERVING SUGGESTION

Serve these lamb fingers on the skewer on a large platter of couscous along with Vegetable Skewers (page 71) and the Tzatziki in a bowl in the center of the platter.

*TIP: Fresh **onion juice** is a way to add the wonderful flavor of onion without injecting additional texture to the final dish. It is easy to grate onion on a box grater. Put the grated onion into a small fine-mesh strainer and press well to extract all the juice.

A quick substitute can be found in your supermarket in a small bottle like that for lemon juice.

*TIP: To secure the **lamb fingers** on the skewers: For each, hold a skewer in one hand, a lamb finger in the other. Gently press the wooden skewer through the log, then reshape the meat around the skewer to secure.

Tzatziki

✓ EASY PREPARATION   ✓ NO COOKING NEEDED

This simple Middle Eastern sauce is great for many different types of skewers. I use it with the lamb fingers or even with small cubes of salmon that are tossed in olive oil, skewered, and grilled.

2 cups fresh plain yogurt (1 pint)

3 tablespoons chopped fresh mint

¾ cup peeled halved seeded and thinly sliced cucumber (from 1 small cucumber) *

2 teaspoons finely chopped garlic (from 2 medium cloves)

1 teaspoon fresh lemon juice

Salt and freshly ground pepper, to taste

Combine all ingredients in a small bowl; taste and adjust seasoning, then chill. Keep in mind that chilling tends to reduce the flavor of the seasonings, so don't be stingy with the salt and pepper.

*TIP: To prepare the **cucumber**, peel it, then slice it in half lengthwise. Run the sharp tip of a teaspoon down the middle of the cucumber halves to remove the seeds. Slice, grate, or chop the cucumber.

Vegetable Skewers with Louis Dressing

✓ *SOMETHING SPECIAL*

Vegetable skewers make fantastic appetizers with a dipping sauce such as the Louis Dressing, and great side dishes alongside meat skewers. In this recipe you will need to precook the potatoes and the onions, as they would take too long to cook on the skewer with the other vegetables. Substitute different vegetables such as blanched broccoli and cauliflower, or squares of red or green pepper for even more variety.

16 tiny new potatoes

Louis Dressing (below)

16 cherry tomatoes

8 boiling onions, peeled and boiled until just tender, drained

2 small zucchini, cut into 8 chunks, blanched 2 minutes in boiling salted water, drained

16 small mushrooms

Olive oil

Eight 12-inch wooden skewers, soaked in water for 30 minutes

Salt and freshly ground pepper, to taste

1. Cook the potatoes in salted boiling water until just barely tender. Drain when done. Meanwhile, make the dressing.

2. Then, preheat the grill, grill pan, or broiler to medium-high. Brush the vegetables with olive oil.

3. To assemble the skewers, thread 1 potato, 1 tomato, 1 mushroom, 1 onion, 1 piece zucchini, 1 mushroom, 1 tomato, and 1 potato onto each skewer. Season lightly with salt and pepper. ✱

4. Wrap foil around the exposed ends of the skewers to prevent burning, or place a strip of foil across one end of the grill and lay the exposed ends of the skewers on it. Grill the skewers over medium-high heat, turning frequently, until browned, 8 to 10 minutes total cooking time. Serve warm, 2 skewers per person, with dressing for dipping.

✱TIP: The temperature of the **grill or grill pan** should be 450°F to 500°F when the skewers go on. You can tell how hot it is with an oven thermometer placed on the grill or by putting your hand three to four inches above the cooking surface and counting: one thousand one, one thousand two, one thousand three, one thousand four. If you pull your hand back between four and five (because it's HOT!) the grill is between 450°F and 500°F.

Louis Dressing

✓ *EASY PREPARATION*   ✓ *SOMETHING SPECIAL*

Crab or shrimp salad with Louis Dressing is a tradition on the West Coast. No one is quite sure who Louis was, but this tantalizing blend of mayonnaise and chili sauce is out of this world and works with many other dishes. In just a matter of seconds this sauce can turn a vegetable, fish, or meat skewer into something spectacular. Make a double batch to have some for another time.

½ cup mayonnaise

⅓ cup bottled chili sauce

3 tablespoons finely chopped onion

3 tablespoons sour cream

Cayenne pepper, to taste

1 tablespoon chopped fresh Italian flat-leaf parsley

Beat together all the ingredients in a small bowl. Store, covered, in the refrigerator.

Freshly Grilled Tuna Kebabs with Creamy Curry Sauce

✓ *EASY PREPARATION*　　✓ *SOMETHING SPECIAL*

Enhance the great flavor of this dish by adding a big mound of fragrant steamed basmati rice to the platter. Drop a little bit of saffron and butter into the water before cooking the rice to make a fantastic side dish.

Creamy Curry Sauce (below)

3 tablespoons olive oil

2 tablespoons fresh lime juice

1 teaspoon ground cumin

1 tablespoon soy sauce

1½ pounds high-quality tuna fillet or steak, in one 1½-inch-thick piece, cut into 1½-inch chunks, 24 in all *

Eight 8-inch wooden skewers, soaked in water for 30 minutes

16 cherry tomatoes

1. Preheat the grill for 10 minutes to medium-high. Meanwhile, prepare the curry sauce.

2. Combine the oil, lime juice, cumin, and soy sauce in a resealable plastic bag. Add the tuna chunks and marinate for 15 minutes. Remove the tuna to a plate and discard the marinade.

3. To assemble the skewers, thread 1 piece tuna, 1 tomato, 1 piece tuna, 1 tomato, and 1 piece tuna on each skewer.

4. Wrap foil around the exposed ends of the skewers to prevent burning, or place a strip of foil across one end of the grill and lay the exposed ends of the skewers on it. Grill at medium-high heat, turning to cook all 4 sides, until seared on the outside but still rare inside, 5 to 7 minutes total. Serve the skewers hot or warm, with curry sauce on the side.

✴ TIP: When shopping for **fish**, don't follow your shopping list; let the freshness at the market determine your choice. If fresh tuna's not available, try halibut, swordfish, or even thick-cut salmon or ask the fish seller for advice. Make sure that the fish smells fresh and is moist. When you bring it home, take it out of the paper, and put the bag with the fish in it on ice in a colander over a bowl. As the ice melts, it will drain and the water will stay away from the fish. Use it within 48 hours.

Creamy Curry Sauce

✓ *EASY PREPARATION*

I love this sauce! The yogurt gives it a slightly tart flavor; the addition of the lime zest gives it a really bright, refreshing flavor. It pairs well with tuna and salmon, and even with cold chicken or pork.

1 cup plain yogurt (½ pint)

¼ cup heavy cream

2 tablespoons hot or mild curry powder

⅓ cup white and light green, very thinly sliced green onions (1 bunch or about 5 thin onions)

Salt and freshly ground pepper, to taste

1 teaspoon fresh lime zest (from 1 medium lime) *

1 tablespoon chopped fresh cilantro

Beat together all the ingredients in a small bowl. Taste and adjust the seasonings. Chill.

✴ TIP: Zest comes from the outside rind or peel of a citrus fruit—lemon, lime, and orange are commonly used. When removing the zest, it is important to remove only the bright shiny colorful outer part of the rind, not the bitter white pith right underneath, for the best flavor.

Grilled Fresh Fruit Sticks with Honey-Ginger Yogurt Sauce

✓ EASY PREPARATION ✓ NO COOKING NEEDED

This fantastic home-style dessert will please everyone. The process of grilling the fruit caramelizes the fruit sugars, letting the flavor burst through. In summer, substitute other fruit if you like, such as peaches or mangoes. In early autumn, try skewers of cut-up apples and different kinds of pears.

Honey-Ginger Yogurt Sauce (below)

2 tablespoons sugar

3 tablespoons butter, melted

Eight 8-inch wooden skewers, soaked in water for 30 minutes

1/2 fresh pineapple, peeled, cored, and cut into 16 chunks

4 hard-ripe plums, quartered and stoned (8 pieces)

2 ripe nectarines, halved, stoned, and halved across (8 pieces)

1. Prepare the yogurt sauce. Then, dissolve the sugar in the melted butter in a small saucepan over medium-low heat. Remove from the heat as soon as the sugar is dissolved.

2. Preheat the grill to medium-high for 10 minutes. To assemble the skewers, thread 1 cube pineapple, then 1 quarter plum, then 1 quarter nectarine, and finally 1 cube pineapple on each skewer. Brush the fruit with butter and sugar mixture. ✱

3. Wrap foil around the exposed ends of the skewers to prevent burning, or place a strip of foil across one end of the grill and lay the exposed ends of the skewers on it. Cook over a medium-hot grill about 15 minutes, turning and basting every 5 minutes with the sweetened butter. Serve with the yogurt sauce.

SERVING SUGGESTION

For a more substantial variation, serve the fruit skewers with pound cake grilled on skewers, and the yogurt sauce on the side.

✱TIP: When **grilling fruit** with a peel, keep the skin on and turn the fruit so the skin faces up. The skin adds color and helps hold the fruit together as it cooks and gets soft. Most fruit without skin is too fragile to grill on skewers, though it can be grilled halved or in large pieces on a vegetable screen on top of the regular grill grid.

Honey-Ginger Yogurt Sauce

✓ EASY PREPARATION

Desserts can be quick, easy, and fun with sauces. This one can be used as a dipping sauce for fruit skewers, drizzled over berries, or poured into a cantaloupe half. Experiment with your own combination of fruit or cake, or both.

3 tablespoons honey

1 1/2 tablespoons boiling water

1 1/2 cups best-quality vanilla yogurt (3/4 pint)

3 tablespoons finely chopped candied ginger

1. Dissolve the honey in boiling water in a small saucepan, and cool slightly.

2. Beat the warmed honey into the yogurt with a fork in a small bowl, and stir in the ginger. Let stand 15 minutes or more to give the flavors time to blend.

Wok Works

In the 1970s, when I was a child, my mother loved making lots of different stir-fry dishes in the wok. It was a fun, exotic way to cook and eat, and at the time, everyone was "wokking." Like many fads, this one seemed to fade. But it never completely disappeared from my family's kitchens, and if you don't already make stir-fries, I'm here to get you started. The ease and healthfulness of stir-frying make it an inspired way to cook quickly Monday through Friday.

Although the technique is classically tied to Asian foods, many different dishes can be cooked as stir-fries—in other words, cooking foods over high heat while stirring constantly. It even works in a regular frying pan. Depending on the ingredients and seasonings you use, you can cook dishes from around the world this way.

The recipes I've included here begin with a traditional stir-fry, seasoned mainly with soy sauce and a little rice wine, and then move on to several recipes that have ingredients traditionally thought of as Mediterranean, Italian, Indian, and American. (It's fun to experiment.) You will also see that many quick side dishes can be made in the wok, even if the main dish comes off the grill, out of the oven, or from the frying pan.

Because stir-fry recipes tend to require a lot of ingredients, the ingredient preparation is what takes the most time. But most of the ingredients are available at supermarkets and once the prep is finished, the food cooks quickly.

The Basics of Stir-Frying

Although stir-frying is a classic Asian cooking technique, the methods of combining ingredients and then the actual "wokking" can and do vary—by cook, by country, by tradition. But basic stir-fry is intended to be economical and simple.

The wok, which is the principal stir-frying equipment needed, is a heavy slope-sided pot made of steel, shaped to fit tightly over a base centered over the fire or heat. It conducts heat evenly and efficiently. The stir-fry process was devised to be as efficient as the multi-purpose wok.

1. The first step is preparation. All the ingredients should be cut uniformly, in relatively small pieces that will cook quickly and evenly.

2. Strips or chunks of meat can be marinated to enhance flavor, and then brought to room temperature before stir-frying.

3. Before you begin, every element of the stir-fry recipe, down to the liquids, oils, and seasonings, should be arranged near the wok in the order they will be used so they are close at hand. Wok cooking is very quick—you won't have time to chop or measure once things have begun to go into the wok.

4. Preheat the wok over high heat. Add a drop of water to the wok—when it sizzles away the wok is ready. Then add oil to the wok, swirling the wok as you add it to coat the interior evenly.

5. Test the oil temperature by adding a small piece of food or cube of bread to the wok; if it sizzles, the wok is ready.

6. Add the ingredients, starting with the most fragrant of the flavorings (called aromatics) such as ginger, garlic, and green onions. These will season the oil and give them a more pronounced flavor.

7. Next, add the more dense ingredients, followed in order by those that need progressively less cooking time.

8. Toward the end of the cooking, add the liquids and seasonings.

9. Finally, cornstarch dissolved in a little cold liquid can be added to thicken the sauce and lightly glaze the ingredients.

Pork, Broccoli, and Glass Noodle Stir-Fry

✓ *SOMETHING SPECIAL*

This is a good family pleaser. It's tasty and filling, and children like the way the clear noodles look and taste, so they may overlook that there's a green vegetable that goes along with them.

2 ounces glass (mung bean) noodles, or rice sticks ∗

2 tablespoons teriyaki sauce

1/3 cup peanut oil

1 tablespoon cornstarch

1/2 pound pork tenderloin, cut into 3/4-inch cubes

1 teaspoon finely chopped garlic

1 teaspoon freshly grated ginger (optional)

2 cups broccoli florets, boiled or steamed until crisply tender, and drained (about 1 pound)

Salt and freshly ground pepper, to taste

1/4 cup chicken broth

1/4 cup dry white wine, such as Sauvignon Blanc

Light soy sauce, for serving (optional)

1. In a deep bowl, pour enough boiling water over the noodles to cover them. (Have the same amount of boiling water ready for a second soaking.) Let the noodles soak, swishing them around the bowl from time to time, until they are softened, about 5 minutes. Cut at both ends of the bundles, leaving 6- to 8-inch lengths. Drain. Cover noodles again with boiling water and soak 3 to 4 minutes more. Drain well in a strainer until just before adding to the wok.

2. In a shallow bowl, combine the teriyaki sauce, 1 tablespoon oil, and the cornstarch, beating with a fork or small whisk. Add the pork cubes and mix to coat well.

3. Preheat the wok or a large, heavy skillet with sloping sides. Add the remaining oil and heat.

4. Add the pork and stir-fry over high heat until browned, 3 to 4 minutes. Add the garlic, ginger, and broccoli. Stir-fry 1 minute more. Season with salt and pepper. Push the browned pork and broccoli to one side of the wok with a flat spatula. Add the drained noodles to the empty side of the wok and fry, stirring just a little to coat with the oil, 2 to 3 minutes. (Be careful, they may sizzle and splatter, especially if not well drained.) The noodles will puff up when done.

5. Toss the pork and noodles together, add the broth and wine, and cook, tossing, 2 minutes more.

6. Divide the contents of the wok among 4 heated bowls and serve at once. Pass light soy sauce on the side if you like.

∗**TIP:** Glass or cellophane noodles often come in looped bundles or hanks, about 6 or 7 inches long. Soften them intact in boiling water, as they tend to shatter if you cut them when dry. Once they are soft, cut the bundles at both ends with a pair of kitchen shears. Cut into smaller pieces if you like.

Pesto Chicken and Vegetables

✓ *EASY PREPARATION*

Sometimes, just the sound of dinner sizzling can perk you up and get the family curious about what you're up to in the kitchen. Stir-fry doesn't have to be an Asian dish. Try this Italian-style chicken stir-fry with pesto and find out. Serve over a bed of Polenta (page 77).

½ cup Pesto (below) or store-bought pesto

3 tablespoons peanut oil

1 pound boneless skinless chicken breasts, cut into chunks

2 cups sliced yellow onion (from 1 large onion)

2 cups stemmed seeded and sliced red bell pepper (1 medium pepper)

2 small zucchini, cut into 2-inch-long strips

2 cups seeded and chopped vine-ripened tomato (2 large tomatoes)

4 ounces fresh shiitake mushrooms, sliced (about 1 cup)

¼ cup low-sodium chicken broth *

Salt and freshly ground pepper, to taste

1. Prepare the pesto. Then, heat a wok or large, heavy skillet over high heat; add 2 tablespoons of oil and swirl it in the wok to coat. When the oil is very hot, add the chicken pieces and stir-fry until lightly browned and just cooked through, about 3 minutes. Transfer the chicken to a dish and set aside.

2. Add 1 tablespoon of oil to the pan and swirl it in the wok to coat. When the oil is very hot, add the onion. Toss until the onion is softened, about 2 minutes. Add the bell pepper, zucchini, tomato, and mushrooms. Stir to coat with the oil and then return the chicken to the pan. Add the broth and heat through, about 3 minutes.

3. Remove the wok from the heat, add the pesto, and season with salt and pepper. Toss until the chicken and vegetables are coated with the sauce. Serve immediately.

SERVING SUGGESTION

Make the polenta very creamy and serve the chicken spooned over the polenta in a bowl.

★TIP: Because it is rare or unlikely that you will have home-made chicken stock on hand, seek out a good store-bought **chicken broth**. Look for a low-sodium variety that has good flavor. (Experiment to find the brand with flavor you like.) With regular broth, your food could be overly salty. The broth is absorbed or evaporates during cooking, leaving an intense saltiness in your food.

Pesto

✓ *MAKE-AHEAD*   ✓ *SOMETHING SPECIAL*   ✓ *TAKE-ALONG*

Pesto is wonderful on pizza, with beef, chicken, fish, vegetables, grilled polenta, even stir-fries. Make it ahead and it will keep in the refrigerator for up to one month, or in the freezer for up to three.

2 cups fresh basil leaves, firmly packed ✻

½ cup pine nuts (2 ounces)

½ cup olive oil

3 garlic cloves

Pinch of salt

½ cup freshly grated Parmigiano-Reggiano cheese (2 ounces)

1. Put the basil and pine nuts in the jar of a blender, and blend until coarsely chopped. Do not overblend. Spoon the mixture into a small bowl and beat in the olive oil with a wooden spoon. Mince the garlic and a pinch of salt together, crushing with the side of a heavy knife to form a paste. Add the garlic and cheese to the basil mixture and stir until combined.

2. Store in the refrigerator with some olive oil poured over the top. This pesto will keep for up to 1 month in the refrigerator.

✻TIP: Substitute **parsley or cilantro** for the basil and enjoy a different kind of pesto.

Polenta

✓ *EASY PREPARATION*

Polenta is a wonderful side dish. It can be made ahead and reheated when the stir-fry is ready.

4 cups water or whole milk

1 teaspoon sea salt

2 tablespoons unsalted butter

¼ teaspoon cayenne pepper

¾ cup instant polenta

½ cup freshly grated Parmigiano-Reggiano cheese (2 ounces)

1. In a medium saucepan, combine the water, salt, butter, and cayenne and bring to a boil over medium-high heat. Gradually add the polenta in a thin steady stream, whisking constantly so it doesn't lump. Lower the heat and continue to cook, stirring frequently with a wooden spoon, until the mixture is very thick and pulls away cleanly from the side of the pan, about 5 minutes.

2. Stir in the Parmigiano-Reggiano cheese. Remove from the heat and serve.

SERVING SUGGESTION

Leftover polenta can be spread in a flat pan and chilled. Once set, it can be cut with a knife or biscuit cutter into squares or rounds. Fry in butter and serve with grated cheese.

Shrimp Stir-Fry with Leeks and Yukon Mashed Potatoes

✓ *SOMETHING SPECIAL*

The sweetness of leeks goes very well with the shrimp. It may seem strange to match a stir-fry with mashed potatoes, but it's really just another kind of starchy food, like rice; try it and you'll see why it works. Of course, you can serve it over rice, if your family likes it better that way.

Yukon Mashed Potatoes (below)

3 tablespoons peanut oil

4 leeks, white part with 1 inch of the green, slivered (about 2 cups) *

2 teaspoons grated fresh ginger

2 large cloves garlic, chopped, then mashed with the back of a knife until creamy

2 pounds medium (31-35 per pound) shrimp, peeled, deveined, and rinsed

1/4 cup dry sherry

1/4 cup light soy sauce (low sodium is fine)

1/4 cup pine nuts, toasted in a hot, dry wok until brown, set aside (4 tablespoons or 1 ounce)

1 teaspoon sesame oil

1 teaspoon chili oil

1/2 teaspoon salt (optional)

1 teaspoon orange zest

1. Prepare the potatoes. Then, heat the wok or large, heavy skillet over high heat, add 2 tablespoons of the peanut oil, and swirl it in the wok to coat. When the wok is very hot, add the leeks and stir or toss them slightly, until softened and nearly transparent. This will take about 5 minutes. Add the ginger and the garlic to the wok and toss for 1 minute. Transfer the entire mixture to a dish and set aside.

2. Add the remaining oil to the wok, swirling to coat the pan. Add the shrimp and stir-fry until pink and firm, 2 to 3 minutes. Add the sherry, soy sauce, and the reserved leek mixture and bring to a boil. Add the pine nuts, sesame oil, chili oil, salt, and zest. Toss and cook 1 minute more. Adjust the seasonings and serve immediately.

3. To serve, make a shallow bed of potatoes on each serving plate and spoon the shrimp mixture over the top.

*TIP: When choosing **leeks**, pick the smaller ones. Cut off all of the green from the leek except for 1 inch and use all of the white. Leeks can be very dirty. To clean them properly, cut them in half lengthwise, then fan open the layers and rinse out all of the dirt with cold water. Cut the leeks lengthwise into slivers after they are clean.

Yukon Mashed Potatoes

✓ *EASY PREPARATION*   ✓ *MAKE-AHEAD*   ✓ *SOMETHING SPECIAL*

The best tool for mashed potatoes is a ricer or a masher. Using an electric mixer for mashed potatoes can result in a gluey final dish rather than one that is light, fluffy, and lump-free. You can make these ahead and reheat them in the oven in a casserole dish to warm them through. The secret to reheating them is to make them very wet, so add about 1 cup of extra milk. Reheat them at 375°F for 20 to 30 minutes.

3 pounds Yukon gold potatoes, cut into quarters *

2 cups whole milk, warmed

4 tablespoons unsalted butter, at room temperature (¼ cup)

Salt and freshly ground pepper, to taste

2 tablespoons finely chopped fresh Italian flat-leaf parsley, for garnish

1. Place the potatoes in a stockpot, and cover with salted water, and bring to a boil. Boil until the potatoes are tender, about 15 minutes.

2. Let the potatoes cool for 10 minutes, then peel them. Press them through a ricer or use a masher to pulverize them. Stir in the milk, then the butter. Season generously with salt and pepper. Taste and adjust seasoning. Sprinkle with parsley and serve.

✱TIP: To make great mashed potatoes or potato salad, start with a good **boiling potato**. A Yukon gold potato or a red potato is perfect for boiling, steaming, or roasting. The lower starch content gives them great texture and they won't get gluey or heavy when mashed.

Orange Beef with Snow Peas

✓ *SOMETHING SPECIAL*

The sweet and sour marinade can be used with just about any meat. Try making this with shrimp or chicken for a great variation. Serve this with Steamed White Rice (page 128) and you will have a complete meal.

Sweet and Sour Marinade (at right)

1½ pounds trimmed flank steak

AROMATICS

1 tablespoon finely chopped fresh ginger

2 tablespoons finely chopped garlic

3 tablespoons thinly sliced green onion, white and up to 1 inch of green

SAUCE

1½ cups low-sodium chicken broth

2 tablespoons soy sauce

2 tablespoons balsamic vinegar

1 tablespoon dry sherry or rice wine

1 tablespoon sugar

3 tablespoons olive oil, for stir-frying

½ cup fresh snow peas, stringed if necessary, and cut in half

1 teaspoon orange zest

1. Prepare the marinade.

2. Cut the beef with the grain into several long strips about 2 inches wide. Holding your knife at a sharp angle to the cutting board, cut each strip across the grain into ribbons about ⅛ inch thick.

3. Pour the marinade into a bowl large enough to hold all the beef; add the beef to the bowl and toss to coat each slice.

4. In a small bowl, combine the aromatics, the ginger, garlic, and green onion, and cover until ready to use. In another small bowl, combine the sauce ingredients, the chicken stock, soy sauce, vinegar, sherry, and sugar, and set aside.

5. Place a wok or large, straight-sided skillet over medium-high heat. Add 2 tablespoons of the olive oil. When a piece of green onion sizzles when tossed into the oil, add half the aromatic mixture, reduce the heat to medium, and add half the beef to the pan with a slotted spoon. Toss the beef until it is fully cooked and golden brown, 3 to 4 minutes. Remove the beef from the wok, set aside, and add the remaining olive oil, ginger, garlic, and green onion, to the wok. Stir until fully fragrant, 20 to 30 seconds, adjusting the heat so the mixture foams without browning, then add the remaining beef and stir-fry until fully cooked.

6. Remove the beef from the wok and set aside. Stir the sauce and add it to the pan. Raise the heat to high and bring the sauce to a boil, scraping the pan while it reduces. Lower the heat, add the reserved beef, and the snow peas. Warm over medium heat about 3 minutes. Add the orange zest. Serve immediately.

Sweet and Sour Marinade

✓ *MAKE-AHEAD*

I like to keep a jar of this marinade on hand in the refrigerator so it will be instantly available to brush on fish fillets, chicken breasts, or even pork chops. Fun food with little or no trouble.

½ cup soy sauce

2 tablespoons dry sherry or rice wine

¼ cup packed brown sugar

2 tablespoons cornstarch

Combine all the marinade ingredients in a small bowl.

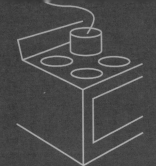

Mix-and-Match Pastas and Sauces

In Italy, pasta has long been the first course of a meal, though these days Italians often eat their daily pasta for lunch, choosing to eat lighter dishes for dinner.

You can follow the Italian tradition and serve smaller portions of pasta before another course. But, because pasta may be all you need to be satisfied, you can, of course, serve it as a main course. You can create beautiful and delicious pasta dishes that come together quickly, but seem to have taken a tremendous amount of time. The key is a good dry or fresh pasta and a simple, but wonderfully flavored, sauce.

A Guide to Perfectly Cooked Pasta

- Always use a large pot of water. For 1 pound of pasta you will need 5 to 6 quarts of water.

- When the water starts to boil vigorously, add salt and then pasta. The water should be pretty salty, so you can add a good 2 tablespoons of salt. I especially like sea salt, as it has a more concentrated flavor than iodized salt or kosher salt, or whatever is in your pantry. Cover the pot partway (or the pasta starch will build quickly into a rising foam and boil over) and bring the water back to a boil.

- Lift the lid and stir the pasta occasionally. If you have enough water, the pasta will not stick together. (Oil in the water is not necessary—and some experts say it makes the sauce slide off later.) Replace the lid.

- Taste the pasta for doneness. The pasta should be tender but still firm—al dente. Also keep in mind that the residual heat of the pasta continues to cook it even after it is drained.

- Dried factory-made pasta can be wonderful. In Italy, especially in the south, this product is not inferior to fresh pasta, only different. Most Italians use both fresh and dried, choosing the one that is best for each dish. I urge you to find the finest Italian-made dried pasta that you can. Brands such as Del Verde and DeCecco, which are made from 100% semolina flour, are very good and can be found in many supermarkets. If you make pasta a lot, look for more uniquely shaped artisanal dried pastas for variety or a special meal. They are expensive but worth a splurge, especially if you are keeping the rest of the meal fairly simple, such as by topping the pasta with a simple tomato sauce and serving it with a salad.

- Mixing and matching is easy. The one rule of thumb is that the thicker the sauce, the more nooks and crannies the pasta should have in order to hold on to it. Cream sauces are an exception—they really should be served over larger flat noodles such as fettuccine or pappardelle. Here are our sauces and some of the pasta shapes you might choose.

Sauces	Pasta
10-Minute Tomato-Basil Sauce	Angel Hair, Spaghetti, Linguine
White Clam Sauce	Linguine, Angel Hair
Puttanesca Sauce	Penne, Spaghetti, Linguine, Angel Hair
Primavera Sauce	Rigatoni, Rotelli, Radiatore, Fettuccine, Pappardelle
Mushroom Cream Sauce	Fettuccine, Penne, Orrecchiete

Angel Hair with 10-Minute Tomato-Basil Sauce

✓ *MAKE-AHEAD*   ✓ *SOMETHING SPECIAL*

Everyone needs a "straight-from-the-pantry" tomato sauce. Use this one for pasta, for pizza, or for whatever else you can think of. It freezes well, so make extra and keep some in the freezer.

3 tablespoons olive oil

¾ cup finely chopped onion

¾ cup finely chopped green bell pepper (¾ medium pepper)

3 teaspoons finely chopped garlic (3 medium cloves)

6 cups halved seeded and chopped tomatoes (6 large tomatoes) or, in a pinch, one 35-ounce can plum tomatoes, drained and chopped

1 teaspoon sugar

Salt and freshly ground pepper, to taste

2 to 3 tablespoons freshly chopped basil

½ pound fine-quality angel hair or linguine

1. Heat the oil in a heavy skillet over medium heat. Add the onion and green pepper. Cook, stirring, until the onion is transparent, 5 minutes. Add the garlic and cook, stirring, 1 minute more.

2. Stir in the tomatoes, sugar, salt, and pepper. Reduce heat; add the basil and simmer 3 to 4 minutes more. ✱

3. Cook the angel hair in 6 quarts of boiling salted water until al dente, 6 to 9 minutes. Drain and turn into a heated serving bowl.

4. Ladle the sauce over the angel hair. You can also use any of your favorite hot pastas, but this thin, chunky sauce is especially good with thin pasta. It can be served with your favorite grilled fish as well.

✱TIP: Adding a little **sugar** to a fresh tomato sauce will cut the slight acidity in tomatoes, especially for a quickly cooked sauce. The sugar can balance the flavor of even the best canned tomatoes.

Linguine with White Clam Sauce

✓ EASY PREPARATION   ✓ SOMETHING SPECIAL

For the most traditional version of this pasta, use good linguine. I like to keep canned clams and packages of linguine in the pantry for a dinner that can be on the table in minutes. If you don't have any linguine on hand, basic spaghetti is equally delicious. I like to add a lot of parsley for flavor and color; use as much as you like.

★TIP: To get rid of the grit and sand in the fresh **clams**, soak them for three hours in 1 gallon of water before cooking.

½ pound best-quality dried
or fresh linguine, or spaghetti

2 tablespoons olive oil

2 tablespoons unsalted butter

3 teaspoons finely chopped garlic
(3 medium cloves)

½ teaspoon dried thyme, or more,
to taste

2 dozen small hard-shell clams,
scrubbed and drained, or one
14-ounce can whole clams, or two
6½-ounce cans chopped clams ★

1 cup bottled clam juice

½ cup dry white wine, such as
Sauvignon or Pinot Blanc

Salt and freshly ground pepper,
to taste

¼ to ½ cup finely chopped fresh
Italian flat-leaf parsley, plus more
for garnish

1. Cook the pasta in 6 quarts of boiling salted water for 6 to 9 minutes for dried pasta, 3 minutes or less for fresh. Drain.

2. Heat the oil and butter in a heavy skillet. Add the garlic and thyme and cook, stirring, 1 minute. Add the clams and shake to cover with oil. Stir in the clam juice and wine. Cover and cook 2 to 3 minutes. Season with salt and pepper.

3. Stir in parsley and boil 1 minute. If using clams in the shell, all the shells should be open by this time. Discard any that are not.

4. Toss the drained linguine with a small amount of the sauce. Place the pasta on a warm platter and then pour the remaining sauce and clams over it. Drizzle with a little more olive oil, if you like, and garnish with more parsley.

Penne with Puttanesca Sauce

MAKES 4 SERVINGS

✓ *MAKE-AHEAD*   ✓ *SOMETHING SPECIAL*

This fantastic quick sauce combines anchovies and tomatoes. It can be seasoned with chili powder if you like, for a spicier version. One of my favorite ways to eat it is as leftovers—right out of the refrigerator or at room temperature. If anchovies are not your favorite flavor, you can leave them out, but the resulting sauce is somewhat plain and it might be better to choose one of our other sauces.

2 tablespoons olive oil

2 tablespoons very thinly sliced garlic (2 medium cloves)

1/2 cup finely chopped onion (1/2 small onion)

1/2 teaspoon dried oregano

6 to 8 anchovy fillets, chopped

1 tablespoon capers, drained and chopped (optional but highly recommended)

Pinch crushed red pepper, or more to taste

Two 14½-ounce cans Italian-style diced tomatoes, drained

Salt and freshly ground pepper, to taste

2 tablespoons finely chopped fresh Italian flat-leaf parsley

1/3 cup Kalamata olives, pitted and halved

1/2 pound penne

1/2 cup freshly grated Parmigiano-Reggiano cheese (2 ounces)

1. Heat the oil in a large, heavy skillet over low heat. Add the garlic, onion, oregano, and anchovies. Cook, stirring, until the onions are transparent and the anchovies have nearly melted, about 5 minutes. Stir in the capers and crushed pepper. Cook 30 seconds. Stir in the tomatoes. Simmer gently 10 minutes. Season with salt and pepper and stir in the parsley and olives. Simmer until thickened, 10 minutes more.

2. Cook the penne in 6 quarts of boiling salted water until al dente, 6 to 9 minutes. *

3. Serve the sauce tossed with penne—or one of your favorite shapes with nooks and crannies to capture the sauce (rotelli or radiatore are great choices)—and garnished with freshly grated Parmigiano-Reggiano cheese.

*TIP: The term "al dente" actually means "to the tooth," or firm to the tooth. To test the pasta for doneness, remove a piece of pasta from the water and allow it to cool slightly. Then bite it. Perfectly cooked pasta will feel tender enough to bite through easily, but will still have a little firmness at the center.

Rigatoni and Fast and Crunchy Pasta Primavera

Dotted with peas and freshly steamed vegetables, this cream-thickened sauce binds these beautiful ingredients. Add strips of ham or even prosciutto for a more filling meal. Rigatoni or penne is ideal for this type of recipe.

1 cup asparagus tips, about 1½ inches long (cut from about 1 pound asparagus spears)

2 carrots, cut into 1-inch lengths and then thinly sliced lengthwise (about 1½ cups)

½ cup fresh green beans, cut diagonally into 1½-inch pieces (about 4 ounces)

½ cup garden peas, or frozen peas, defrosted (about ½ pound in the pod)

1 cup fresh broccoli florets, or frozen broccoli florets, defrosted

1 small zucchini, cut into thin 1-inch sticks

5 to 6 green onions, cut into 1½-inch lengths up to the dark green

½ pound rigatoni

½ cup heavy cream

1 large egg

½ cup freshly grated Parmigiano-Reggiano cheese, plus more for garnish (2 ounces)

2 tablespoons chopped fresh Italian flat-leaf parsley

Salt and freshly ground pepper, to taste

1. Steam the vegetables, each type separately, in a basket or strainer over boiling water until crisply tender, for 4 to 6 minutes. Rinse under cold water to stop cooking, then keep warm over simmering water.

2. Cook the rigatoni in 6 quarts of boiling salted water until al dente, 6 to 9 minutes.

3. While the rigatoni is cooking, beat together the cream, egg, and cheese in a large bowl. Drain the pasta and toss, while still very hot, with the egg and cream mixture. Toss in the vegetables and parsley. Season with salt and pepper. Serve very hot with more grated Parmigiano-Reggiano cheese on the side.

SERVING SUGGESTION

To make this dish a little more elaborate, cook the pasta, then toss it with the sauce and vegetables. Spoon the mixture into a casserole dish, top with a good sprinkling of grated Parmigiano-Reggiano, and bake at 375°F for 20 minutes.

86 KITCHEN COACH: WEEKNIGHT COOKING

Parsley and Herb Garlic Bread

✓ *MAKE-AHEAD*   ✓ *TAKE-ALONG*

My mother has long rounded out her pasta meals with this fantastic garlic bread. You can make the seasoned butter up to three days ahead. Then all you will need to do is spread it on the bread, top it with cheese, and bake.

1 cup (2 sticks) unsalted butter, at room temperature (1/2 pound)

1 tablespoon freshly chopped basil

1/3 cup finely chopped fresh Italian flat-leaf parsley

1 teaspoon salt

1/2 cup freshly grated Parmigiano-Reggiano cheese, plus 1 cup for sprinkling (6 ounces total)

1 tablespoon creamed garlic (1 to 2 cloves garlic, smashed with the back of a heavy knife)

1/2 teaspoon freshly ground pepper

One large round French or sourdough bread loaf or two baguettes *

1. Preheat the oven to 375°F. Place all of the ingredients except 1 cup of the cheese and the bread in a bowl or in a food processor and mix them together to form a smooth butter. It will be green and full of flavor.

2. Slice the round loaf into 1/2-inch slices or the baguette into 2 long slices lengthwise. Spread the butter on each slice of the round loaf or on the 2 long pieces of the baguette. Sprinkle with the remaining cheese. Put the slices together to form a loaf again and wrap in foil.

3. Bake for 30 minutes. Serve hot.

SERVING SUGGESTION

In a hurry? Brush the individual slices with the parsley herb butter, sprinkle with cheese, and broil until the cheese is melted. Try adding some mozzarella on top to make a delicious cheese bread.

✽TIP: While my mother preferred to cut the **bread** into thick slices and cook them individually on a baking sheet, I find the loaf will be more moist and flavorful when it is baked as an entire loaf. If you want the crust to be crunchier, just take the loaf out of the foil about two-thirds of the way through the cooking. Put the slices on a cookie sheet at that time and bake until bubbling. This will allow the crust to get crispy without getting dried out.

Fettuccine with Mushroom Cream Sauce

✓ SOMETHING SPECIAL

This mushroom sauce is perfect on pasta, but can also be used with chicken or meat. Choose high-quality Italian canned tomatoes to keep in your pantry, ready anytime.

3 tablespoons olive oil

1 pound white mushrooms, or any mixture of available mushrooms, wiped clean and sliced (4 to 5 cups) ✱

1 teaspoon finely chopped garlic, or more, to taste (1 medium clove)

1 tablespoon dried Italian herbs

½ cup dry white wine, such as Sauvignon Blanc or Chardonnay

One 14-ounce can petite-diced tomatoes, undrained

2 teaspoons tomato paste ✱

¾ cup heavy cream, or fat-free half and half

Salt and freshly ground pepper, to taste

1 pound dried or fresh fettuccine

2 tablespoons finely chopped fresh Italian flat-leaf parsley, plus more for garnish

Extra-virgin olive oil, for garnish

1. Heat the olive oil in a large, heavy skillet over medium-high heat. Stir in the mushrooms and cook, stirring and shaking from time to time, until browned, about 5 minutes. Stir in the garlic and herbs. Cook 1 minute. Add the wine and boil the sauce for 1 minute. Stir in the tomatoes, tomato paste, and cream. Season with salt and pepper. Reduce the heat and simmer, stirring from time to time, until the sauce thickens slightly, 10 to 15 minutes.

2. While the sauce is thickening, cook the fettuccine in 6 quarts of boiling salted water until al dente, 3 minutes for fresh pasta, 6 to 9 minutes for dried. Drain.

3. Stir the parsley into the sauce and serve hot over the fettuccine. Fettucine has enough width to hold onto the sauce. Rigatoni, penne, and other nook-and-cranny pastas are also quite good. Finish with a drizzle of extra-virgin olive oil and some chopped Italian flat-leaf parsley.

✱ **TIP:** Look for **mushrooms** that are firm and even in color, avoiding those that are shriveled, slimy, or broken. Place them in a paper bag and store them in the refrigerator until ready to use. To clean mushrooms, brush them off or wipe them with a moist towel instead of washing them; if they get soaked, they absorb too much of the water and become soggy.

✱ **TIP:** Look for Italian **tomato paste** in a tube for the best flavor and ease of use—any left over remains safely in the tube for future cooking.

Hearty Pasta and Noodle Dishes

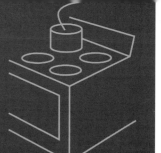

What's not to love about pasta? Pasta or noodles with a simple sauce can make a quick meal as in the previous chapter, but there are also more complex and more substantial dishes to explore—from pasta with vegetables or meat to baked pastas to excellent Asian dishes.

Pasta dishes come together so easily that they are perfect for the day when I want to put something on the table fast, yet still not sacrifice flavor. I find the best thing to do when I step in the door after a busy day is to go directly to the stove and start boiling a pot of water. This sets my gears in motion, lets me begin to disconnect from the day's business, and gets me into the rhythm of my kitchen.

If you are used to making only Italian pasta dishes, Asian noodles may seem exotic, but they are not complicated to work with and they offer delicious variety to a meal. Once you know how to work with them, you may find them almost easier to use than spaghetti or other pastas. You may find a selection of noodles in the supermarket but visit an Asian market for more variety. Here is a quick guide to the four basic types of Asian noodles.

Mung bean or bean thread noodles are also called glass (or cellophane) noodles. When soaked and flexible, they are transparent. One of the nicest aspects of these noodles is that they will not become mushy, even if left in the sauce for some time. Preparation is easy. They can be soaked in either warm or boiling water for a few minutes and then drained. They can be simmered in water or broth for 2 to 3 minutes and then drained. Or they can be fried in hot oil when dry—they will puff up and become crispy—to make a delightful base for some stir-fries.

Rice noodles are similar in texture to glass noodles. They are pre-cooked during the manufacturing process and only need to be softened by soaking in hot or warm water. They should be well drained.

Wheat noodles, including buckwheat or soba noodles, can be simmered in water or broth for 2 or 3 minutes, or can be cooked by covering with boiling water several times, draining well between soakings. These noodles are best when tossed with a tablespoon or two of oil after they are drained and before they are added to the final dish.

Fresh Asian noodles should be treated just like the more familiar fresh Italian pasta. They can be simmered for 3 to 4 minutes, or steamed over hot broth or sauce until just cooked.

Rotelli with Roasted Asparagus, Mushrooms, and Shaved Parmigiano

✓ *SOMETHING SPECIAL*

Serve this quick and satisfying pasta dinner with a tomato salad and a loaf of hot crusty bread. Dinner will be ready even before you can get the table set. Shaving the Parmigiano into slices rather than grating it is a simple way to add an elegant garnish and more substance and flavor to every bite.

½ pound portobello mushrooms

½ pound fresh asparagus, cut into 8-inch spears

1 large sweet onion, cut into ¼-inch slices

¼ cup olive oil

Salt and freshly ground pepper, to taste

½ pound rotelli

1 tablespoon chopped fresh Italian flat-leaf parsley, for garnish

2 ounces Parmigiano-Reggiano, freshly shaved, for garnish

1. Preheat the oven to 450°F.

2. Brush the mushrooms, asparagus, and onion with about 2 tablespoons olive oil. Sprinkle with salt and pepper. In a roasting pan, arrange the vegetables in a single layer. Roast, turning twice, 10 to 12 minutes, until just tender when tested with a knife. Remove from the oven and let cool slightly.

3. Cook the rotelli in 6 quarts of boiling salted water until al dente, 6 to 9 minutes. Drain.

4. Slice the mushrooms, cut the asparagus into 2-inch lengths, and cut the onion slices into thirds.

5. In a heated serving bowl, toss the drained pasta with the remaining olive oil. Add the roasted vegetables and toss with the pasta. Garnish with the parsley and top with the Parmigiano-Reggiano. ✳

✳ TIP: Use a **vegetable peeler** to make very thin, wide strips of Parmigiano-Reggiano to garnish this dish.

Fettuccine with Smoked Chicken, Goat Cheese, and Vegetables

✓ *SOMETHING SPECIAL*

This dish adds a delicious sauce and vegetables to precooked chicken and pasta. It's creamy, flavorful, and satisfying—and quick to make. The sauce begins like a classic French sauce called beurre blanc, but don't let the name scare you. All you do is reduce the wine, vinegar, and shallots by half and then whisk in the softened goat cheese.

1 cup dry white wine, such as a California Chardonnay

1 teaspoon white wine vinegar

2 tablespoons finely chopped shallots (about 2 medium bulbs)

5 ounces soft goat cheese, such as Montrachet, at room temperature

1 teaspoon salt, and more for cooking the pasta

1/2 teaspoon freshly ground pepper

2 tablespoons olive oil

1 cup finely chopped yellow onion (from 1 medium onion)

1 cup stemmed seeded deveined and finely diced red bell pepper (from 1 medium pepper)

1 cup stemmed seeded deveined and finely diced yellow bell pepper (from 1 medium pepper)

2 cups seeded and chopped vine-ripened tomatoes (from 2 large or 3 small tomatoes)

1 teaspoon crushed red pepper

8 ounces precooked smoked chicken, cut into strips *

1 pound fresh fettuccine

2 tablespoons fresh basil, cut into chiffonade, for garnish *

1. In a medium saucepan, combine the white wine, vinegar, and shallots. Over high heat, boil the liquid to reduce by half. Whisk in the goat cheese until melted, season with the salt and pepper, and set aside.

2. Heat a large, heavy skillet over medium-high heat. Add the olive oil and the onion. Cook, stirring, until soft, about 5 minutes, and stir in the peppers. Cover and steam over medium heat until tender, about 5 minutes. Add the tomatoes, red pepper flakes, and chicken. Cook until heated through, 2 minutes more.

3. Cook the fresh fettuccine in 6 quarts of boiling salted water until al dente, about 3 minutes. Be careful not to overcook it. Drain.

4. Combine the pasta with the goat cheese sauce and add the chicken and vegetable mixture. Toss to combine. Serve in warm bowls, garnished with the chiffonade of basil.

SERVING SUGGESTION

Add a rustic loaf of crusty bread and a bottle of Chardonnay—to me, this meal is heaven!

✱TIP: To cut down on prep time, I sometimes use good-quality **smoked chicken** from the supermarket, deli, or rotisserie chicken restaurant. Before cooking with it, taste it so you know if its seasonings may affect the flavor of the finished dish.

✱TIP: To cut basil into a **chiffonade** (ribbonlike strips), stack washed and dried leaves, then roll them into a tight cylinder from tip to stem. Slice very thinly across the roll to make strips. Toss the chiffonade to separate the pieces before sprinkling as a garnish. Lettuce can be prepared the same way and used as the base for salads.

Baked Penne with Basil, Tomatoes, and Sausage

✓ *EASY PREPARATION*   ✓ *MAKE-AHEAD*   ✓ *TAKE-ALONG*

I really love this all-in-one meal. Add a salad and maybe some Parsley and Herb Garlic Bread (page 87), and you're done.

You can find so many different types of delicious sausage these days. Use chicken sausage one night and turkey sausage on another night. I also like to use a pork sausage with fennel. The fennel in the mixture really complements the flavor of the overall dish. This makes a great take-along meal if you are gathering with friends for a potluck dinner.

2 tablespoons olive oil

1 cup finely chopped white onion (from 1 medium onion)

1 tablespoon creamed, fresh garlic (3 cloves smashed with the back of a heavy knife)

1 pound Italian sausage with fennel or with hot spices, casing removed, meat crumbled

1 pound penne

1 (35-ounce) can whole Italian plum tomatoes, chopped, with the juice (3 cups)

1/4 cup freshly chopped basil

Salt and freshly ground pepper, to taste

1 cup ricotta cheese

1 cup grated Parmigiano-Reggiano cheese (4 ounces)

1/2 cup finely chopped fresh Italian flat-leaf parsley

1/2 pound fresh mozzarella, cut into cubes

1. Preheat the oven to 400°F. Lightly oil a large baking dish.

2. Heat the olive oil in a large, heavy skillet over medium-high heat. Add the onion and cook, stirring, until soft, about 7 minutes. Add the garlic and the sausage and cook, stirring, until the sausage is browned, 5 to 7 minutes more. If the sausage has given off a lot of fat, pour it off before you continue. ✱

3. While the sausage is browning, cook the penne in 6 quarts of boiling salted water until al dente, 6 to 9 minutes. Drain the pasta well.

4. Add the tomatoes with all of the juice to the sausage, and let it simmer, uncovered, until it thickens, about 20 minutes. Add the basil and season with salt and pepper.

5. In a large bowl, mix the ricotta, half of the Parmigiano-Reggiano cheese, and the parsley. Season with salt and pepper. Toss the pasta into the cheese mixture. Add the sausage mixture and toss again. Add the mozzarella and pour everything into the prepared dish. Sprinkle with the remaining Parmigiano-Reggiano and bake, uncovered, about 20 minutes until lightly browned. Serve immediately.

✱ TIP: In many recipes the **onion and garlic** are added to the pan at the same time. But often, by the time the onion is cooked until translucent, the garlic is overcooked or burned—which adds an unpleasant taste to the final dish. Instead, add garlic a few minutes after the onion. In many cases, garlic can even be added at the last minute and cooked only slightly, which cooks out the bitterness of the garlic and highlights its wonderful aroma without burning it. Try this in all of your recipes for a softer garlic flavor.

Rice Noodles with Coconut Curry Shrimp

✓ *SOMETHING SPECIAL*

This Thai-style dish gives you an exotic but tasty way to indulge in the comfort and convenience of pasta or noodles—here with clear Asian noodles. Stir-frying is one of the quickest, nearly one-pot methods of creating dinner in a hurry after an exhausting workday. If you have an extra few minutes in the morning, or the night before, do all the cutting and chopping ahead of time, then cover the ingredients (separately) with plastic wrap and refrigerate. Dinner will be a snap.

6 ounces dried rice noodles

3 tablespoons peanut or other vegetable oil

3/4 cup peeled and chopped onion (from 1 small onion)

2 teaspoons finely chopped garlic (from 2 cloves)

2 to 3 tablespoons mild curry paste or powder, or use hotter curry, to taste

1/2 cup low-sodium chicken broth

1 cup unsweetened coconut milk (not the coconut cream used in drinks and desserts)

1 1/2 pounds medium (31 to 35 per pound) shrimp, peeled, tailed, and deveined

2 tablespoons chopped fresh Italian flat-leaf parsley

Salt and freshly ground pepper, to taste

2 tablespoons green onions (the white and up to 3 inches of dark green parts), thinly sliced, for garnish (from two onions)

1/4 cup shredded unsweetened coconut, for garnish (optional) *

1. Soak the rice noodles in boiling water in a large bowl for 3 minutes. Drain and toss with a fork to separate the strands.

2. Preheat a wok or a large, heavy skillet with sloped sides over medium heat. Add 2 tablespoons of the oil to the heated wok. Add the onion and garlic and cook, stirring quickly, until soft and transparent, about 5 minutes. Add the curry and stir-fry to release the spices, 30 seconds. *

3. Stir in broth and coconut milk. Boil until slightly reduced and thickened, 6 to 7 minutes. Stir in shrimp, reduce heat, and simmer until the shrimp are pink and just cooked through, 2 to 3 minutes. Stir in the parsley and season with salt and pepper.

4. Serve the noodles on the side, or toss the shrimp with the noodles. Garnish with the green onions and coconut. Serve very hot.

SERVING SUGGESTION

If you like, serve this dish as they do in Asia: divide the noodles among four to six large soup bowls. Ladle shrimp and sauce over the noodles and then garnish with green onions and coconut.

＊TIP: Unsweetened coconut is usually found in the freezer compartment of the supermarket.

＊TIP: Stir-frying is simple with these easy steps: 1. Preheat the wok or heavy slope-sided skillet. 2. Add oil and heat. 3. Reduce heat slightly and add first ingredients—usually the aromatics. Sometimes these ingredients are removed and set aside to keep them from over-cooking. 4. Raise heat slightly and add remaining ingredients. 5. Turn ingredients with a spatula or large flat spoon. 6. If adding liquid, raise heat again slightly and stir until sauce begins to thicken.

Cold Sesame Noodles with Pulled Chicken

✓ *MAKE-AHEAD*   ✓ *SOMETHING SPECIAL*   ✓ *TAKE-ALONG*

This is one of my very favorite ways to serve chicken and pasta. It can be served warm or cold like a salad, and it is an excellent dish for when your family's varied schedules prevent you from eating at the same time. Add a cold vegetable salad and whole-grain bread to complete the meal.

4 large chicken thighs

4 cups low-sodium chicken broth

1 teaspoon ground sage

1 teaspoon ground cumin

1 teaspoon ground thyme

Salt and freshly ground pepper, to taste

½ pound thin egg noodles

2 tablespoons light soy sauce (low sodium is fine)

2 tablespoons rice wine or dry sherry

2 tablespoons Asian sesame oil, or substitute hot sesame oil for 1 teaspoon if you like things spicy

2 tablespoons sesame seeds, toasted

3 tablespoons green onions (the white and up to 1 inch dark green parts), sliced (from 3 whole onions)

2 tablespoons finely chopped fresh Italian flat-leaf parsley

1. In a medium saucepan, simmer chicken thighs in enough broth to cover them, until the meat is very tender and falling off the bone, about 20 minutes. Remove the chicken from the broth and reserve ½ cup of the liquid. Remove the skin and bones from the chicken and put the meat into a medium bowl. Using two forks, shred the chicken meat. ✱

2. In a small bowl, combine the sage, cumin, thyme, salt, and pepper. Toss with the shredded chicken, moistening with a tablespoon or two of the reserved chicken broth if it appears too dry.

3. Cook the noodles in 6 quarts of boiling salted water (add very little salt if the noodles are made with salt) until just tender, 5 to 8 minutes, depending on their thickness. Drain well.

4. In a small bowl, combine the soy sauce, wine, sesame oil, sesame seeds, and green onions. Toss with the noodles.

5. Arrange the noodles in a deep serving plate. Pile the shredded, or "pulled," chicken on top and garnish with chopped parsley.

✱**TIP:** Shredding, or "pulling," meat or poultry produces a finer texture than chopping. With a fork in each hand, tear the chicken apart until it falls into thin strands.

It's Chicken, Tonight!

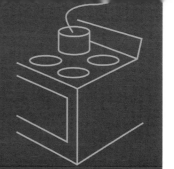

Easily prepared, reasonably priced, and infinitely versatile, chicken is one of the best foods to rely on for weeknight meals. From a chicken salad in the summer to a whole roasted chicken in cold months, a simple light sauté to crispy, soul-satisfying fried chicken, the choices are almost endless. By trying different herbs and spices you can make even more exotic dishes from around the world.

To enjoy a chicken dinner, you have to start with a really good bird. Below are some essentials for picking and preparing quality chicken—whether you are going to cook a whole chicken and make use of every part, or if you make dinner frequently with chicken breasts, as I often do. With good-quality chicken, the right techniques, solid recipes and flavoring ideas, and a little creativity, you can enjoy making chicken any or every night of the week.

Chicken Facts

The rising popularity of chicken has unfortunately led to the mass production of poultry. This has caused the bulk of chicken available to be commercially raised birds that lack flavor. Good chickens do exist and their availability is growing. You may need to spend a little time tracking them down, though.

What to Look For

If possible, buy chickens or chicken parts from a poultry store or a reputable food merchant whose staff knows about its products. Ask for the source of the chicken and what it has been fed. Free-range chickens, those allowed to hunt and peck for their food, are going to be more flavorful. This doesn't mean that all large-scale production chickens will be tasteless. Try to find out the source of the chicken and if they were fed a diet rich in grains.

Choose a chicken with the skin on and the bone in, unless the recipe specifies otherwise. The skin should be creamy yellow or white (usually the skin color is determined in part by what the bird eats) and should look moist. The fat should be well distributed. You should look for chickens that are packed on ice or are well chilled in a refrigerated case and that smell fresh.

Varieties of Chicken

Broiler-fryers: Young tender birds that are well suited for quick high-heat cooking. They range from 2½ to 4 pounds.

Roasters: Birds that are slightly older and heavier and are raised for roasting in the oven. They weigh 3½ to 8 pounds or more.

Stewing chickens: Older birds that are generally tougher and are best stewed or braised. They weigh from 3 to 5 pounds or more.

Capons: Male chickens that have been neutered as chicks, resulting in tender, flavorful large-breasted roasting birds. They weigh from 6 to 10 pounds.

Cornish game hens: Miniature hybrids of chicken and Cornish game-cock, each hen usually weighs about 1 to 1½ pounds and provides one large serving or two small.

Cleaning and Storing Chicken

As soon as you get it home, loosen the chicken from the wrapping and place it in the coldest part of the refrigerator. (Make sure that the package isn't leaking. If any liquid is seeping out, put the chicken in a plastic bag or in a bowl before placing it in the refrigerator.)

Cook the chicken within two days. Before cooking, rinse it with cold water and pat it dry with paper towels.

To freeze the chicken for up to 2 months, wrap it in a large airtight freezer bag. Thaw in the refrigerator for 24 hours.

Cutting Up a Chicken

Although for most nights you may find it easier to buy chicken already cut up, doing it yourself will save you money and provide more flavorful meals. The whole chicken will also yield extra pieces that can be used for stock. Try cutting it up during the weekend or on a weeknight when you aren't in a rush.

The techniques involved in cutting up or disjointing the chicken are fairly simple. A sharp boning knife or a good pair of poultry shears is all you will need. Some recipes call for quartered or halved chickens. You can do this or have the butcher do it for you. If you don't want to touch the chicken directly, you can wear close-fitting kitchen or surgical gloves (found in kitchen stores and drugstores), then discard them when you are done.

1. **Remove the legs:** Place the chicken on the cutting board, breast side up, with the legs facing toward you. Locate the joint by moving the leg, then cut through the skin between the thigh and body to remove the leg. Repeat on the other side.

2. **Separate the thigh and leg:** Bend the leg sharply to locate the joint between the leg and thigh. Cut through the joint to separate the two pieces. Repeat on the other side.

3. **Remove the wings:** Move the wing to locate the joint next to the body. Cut through this joint to remove the wing. Repeat on the other side.

4. **Cut off the back:** Starting at the neck opening, cut through both sides of the rib cage, separating both breasts from the remaining carcass.

5. **Remove the breastbone:** Holding the breast skin side down, slit the thin membrane covering the breastbone in the center. Grasp the breast and flex it upward to pop out the bone. Pull the bone free, using the knife if necessary.

6. **Cut the breast in half:** Place the breast skin side down on the cutting board. Cut along the center of the breast, through the cartilage, to split it in half.

Oven-Barbecued Chicken

✓ *EASY PREPARATION*

This is by far my favorite recipe for roasted chicken. For best flavor, the chicken is pan-browned, then roasted. Serve it with your favorite potatoes, carrots, or green beans, and a green salad. You will have a perfect meal every time. It's so easy, you will serve it often.

1 whole chicken (about 4 pounds), cut into pieces with skin intact, back discarded, or 3 to 4 pounds of whatever chicken parts you prefer

1 tablespoon olive oil

1 cup barbecue sauce (the spicier the better)

4 or 5 fresh rosemary sprigs or other herbs, for garnish (optional)

1. Preheat the oven to 400°F.

2. Rinse the chicken pieces and pat them dry. Allow the chicken to rest on a cookie sheet for 20 minutes.

3. Heat 1 tablespoon oil in a large, heavy ovenproof skillet or gratin dish. Brown the chicken on both sides, turning only once, cooking each side 5 to 6 minutes. Arrange chicken skin side up in the skillet. ∗

4. Brush with the barbecue sauce and roast in the oven for 25 minutes—longer if the breasts are very large—until the chicken reaches a temperature of 160°F on an instant-read thermometer inserted into the thickest part of the breast, basting several times with sauce. If the breasts and thighs are done but the legs—which have more fat—are not, remove the breasts to a platter and let the legs cook for a few more minutes.

5. Transfer the cooked chicken to a warmed platter. ∗

6. Garnish with rosemary sprigs, if you like. Serve the chicken very hot with the pan juices in a bowl on the side.

∗**TIP:** To brown chicken properly, follow these tips:

Bring chicken to about room temperature so it will cook more evenly.

Use a large pan to avoid crowding. (Overcrowding will cause the chicken to steam in its juices rather than brown.)

When the oil begins to bead and smoke slightly, add the chicken with the presentation side down first—this would be either the skin-on side, or the side that had the skin.

Brown the pieces until they are a light caramel color and then move them to a clean baking sheet.

∗**TIP:** Warmed plates and platters keep hot foods hot longer. You can warm them in a plate warmer if you have one, in a 200°F oven for 20 minutes, or in a clean sink full of hot tap water. Dry the plates or platters well before using.

Chicken with Grapes

✓ SOMETHING SPECIAL

When I was in college, I used to make a chicken dish with a mustard cream sauce that impressed all my friends. This enhanced version has the addition of sweet grapes to balance the tangy richness of the sauce.

4 medium boneless skinless chicken breasts, or if the breasts are more than 10 ounces each, use only 2 and slice them in half horizontally

Salt and freshly ground pepper, to taste

2 tablespoons unsalted butter

1 teaspoon finely chopped or creamed garlic *

1/2 cup dry white wine, such as Sauvignon Blanc

1/2 cup chicken broth

1 tablespoon Dijon mustard

1/2 cup heavy cream

1 cup seedless green grapes, halved

1 tablespoon chopped fresh Italian flat-leaf parsley, for garnish

1. Season the chicken well with salt and pepper.

2. Heat the butter in a heavy skillet over medium-high heat. Cook the breasts, turning once, until the chicken reaches a temperature of 160°F on an instant-read thermometer inserted into the thickest part of the breast, 12 to 15 minutes. Remove the chicken from the skillet and tent with aluminum foil to keep warm.

3. Add the chopped garlic to the same skillet and cook, stirring, for 30 seconds. Stir in the wine, chicken broth, and mustard. Raise the heat and boil the liquid until reduced by half. Beat the cream into the sauce. Boil until the sauce thickens a little, 3 to 4 minutes. *

4. Taste and season the sauce with salt and pepper if necessary.

5. Return the chicken breasts to the skillet with the sauce and add the grapes. Simmer gently until the chicken is heated through, 3 to 4 minutes. Do not overcook. Serve hot, garnished with a little parsley.

SERVING SUGGESTION

This would be great with some steamed carrots tossed with lemon juice and a 5-minute packaged couscous.

＊TIP: To **prepare garlic**, first separate the cloves from the head. Then, lay the clove on the work surface and quickly press the side of the knife down on the clove with the palm of your hand. The skin will come right off. Chop the garlic lightly. For a creamy texture, add a little salt, which will make it easier to work into a puree. Press the garlic repeatedly with the blade of the knife, rubbing it against the chopping board until it forms a creamy paste.

＊TIP: To see if a **sauce is the right thickness**, dip a spoon in the sauce and run a finger lengthwise down the back of the spoon. The sauce is thick enough when your finger draws a clean stripe, without the sauce seeping over the edges.

Tarragon Chicken Breasts

✓ *SOMETHING SPECIAL*

Tarragon, in discreet amounts, can be used to season tomatoes and salad dressings, and it goes especially well with chicken. Serve this dish with seasoned rice and fresh spinach, or Italian Green Beans with Tomatoes (page 165).

4 medium boneless skinless chicken breasts, tenderloins removed, ∗ or if the breasts are more than 10 ounces each, use only 2 and slice them in half horizontally, pounded to an even thickness ∗

Salt and freshly ground pepper, to taste

2 tablespoons unsalted butter

2 teaspoons finely chopped garlic (2 medium cloves)

3/4 cup fresh or thawed frozen tiny pearl onions

1/2 cup dry white wine, such as Sauvignon Blanc

1 1/2 teaspoons dried tarragon, or 2 tablespoons freshly chopped tarragon, or more, to taste

3/4 cup heavy cream

3 to 4 sprigs fresh tarragon, for garnish

1. Season the chicken well with salt and pepper.

2. Melt the butter in a heavy skillet over medium-high heat. Cook the chicken in the butter, turning once, until the chicken reaches a temperature of 160°F on an instant-read thermometer inserted into the thickest part of the breast, 8 to 10 minutes. Remove the chicken from the skillet and tent with aluminum foil to keep warm.

3. Stir the garlic and onions into the same skillet. Cook, tossing, until tender and golden brown, about 5 minutes. Stir in the wine and tarragon. Raise the heat and boil until the liquid is reduced by half, about 3 minutes. Stir in the cream.

4. Boil until the sauce thickens again slightly. Taste and season with salt and pepper if necessary.

5. Return the chicken to the sauce and simmer gently until heated through, 3 to 4 minutes. Serve the chicken on individual plates, sliced diagonally across the breast, with some of the sauce spooned over each serving. Garnish with fresh tarragon.

SERVING SUGGESTION

Arrange the sliced chicken on a bed of rice and vegetables. Then drizzle or spoon the sauce over and garnish with fresh tarragon.

∗**TIP:** To remove the tenderloin from each boneless breast: slide a paring knife under the tendon (the tough white strip that holds the tenderloin to the breast). Place the tenderloin, tendon down, on the cutting board. With the knife against the tendon, pull on the tendon, moving it gently from side to side with your other hand, until it pulls away.

∗**TIP:** To make the chicken breasts even, place each chicken breast in a plastic bag or between two sheets of plastic wrap. Gently flatten with the side of a meat mallet so that the breast is the same thickness all over. Make sure you don't pound the breasts too thin. These are not cutlets; you are only assuring that the meat will cook evenly. If it gets too thin, it may tear and dry out very quickly during cooking.

Chicken Niçoise Salad with Walnuts and Blue Cheese Vinaigrette

✓ *SOMETHING SPECIAL*   ✓ *TAKE-ALONG*

A traditional composed niçoise salad features many small but delectable and separate components such as tomatoes, olives, and green beans, with the main focus being tuna. This is a simpler but lovely composed salad using chicken. (Of course, you can substitute tuna or salmon for the chicken, if you like.) In winter, use vine-ripened tomatoes, or leave them out if the tomatoes aren't tempting. Though it isn't at all classic, I like to add some boiled potatoes for a heartier salad.

2 boneless skinless chicken breasts

2 cups low-sodium chicken broth

Salt and freshly ground pepper, to taste

½ pound smallest green beans, tipped and tailed, or frozen baby green beans

Blue Cheese Vinaigrette (below)

4 cups mixed greens of your choice (bagged greens are fine)

½ English-style cucumber, washed but unpeeled, very thinly sliced

3 small ripe tomatoes, cut into wedges, seeds removed

3 hard-boiled eggs, peeled and quartered ✱

½ cup oil-cured black olives

⅓ cup walnut halves, toasted

1. In a medium saucepan, poach the chicken breasts in simmering chicken broth until the chicken reaches a temperature of 160°F on an instant-read thermometer inserted into the thickest part of the breast, 8 to 10 minutes. Remove the chicken from the broth, cool, and slice the breasts across the grain on the diagonal. Season with salt and pepper.

2. Bring 4 quarts of water to a boil in a large saucepan. Add the green beans and cook until just crisply tender, 3 to 4 minutes. Drain well and refresh quickly by dunking them in a bowl full of ice water. Dry the green beans with a clean cloth towel. If using frozen green beans, steam over boiling water for 5 minutes and then dry with a clean cloth towel.

3. Make the vinaigrette.

4. To serve, arrange a bed of greens on a large serving platter. Layer the vegetables on top of the greens in an attractive pattern. Top with egg wedges, and scatter with olives and walnuts. Drizzle with a little of the vinaigrette and pass the remaining vinaigrette in a separate bowl.

✱**TIP:** To make perfect **hard-boiled eggs**, place 6 eggs at room temperature in the bottom of a medium saucepan. Add water to 1 inch above the eggs. Bring the water to a boil over high heat. After it comes to a boil, remove the pan from the heat and cover. Allow the eggs to sit 12 minutes, then soak the eggs in ice water for 6 minutes. Peel each egg by tapping it all over on the counter, rolling the egg to loosen the shell, then peel.

Blue Cheese Vinaigrette

This richly flavored vinaigrette is a great option for salads. Also try it as a dipping sauce for vegetables or barbecued chicken.

2 tablespoons white wine vinegar

2 teaspoons Dijon mustard *

Salt and freshly ground pepper, to taste

1 teaspoon finely chopped garlic

½ cup extra-virgin olive oil

⅓ cup crumbled blue cheese (1½ ounces)

In a small bowl, beat together the vinegar, mustard, salt, pepper, and garlic. Beat in the olive oil. Stir in the blue cheese. Let the dressing stand 15 minutes or longer to develop the flavor. Serve or store in a covered container in the refrigerator up to 2 hours.

∗ TIP: Dijon mustard is made from the finest mustard seeds perfectly blended with herbs, spices, and white wine. I have at least four different types of mustard in the pantry at all times to use in marinades, glazes, and sauces.

Chicken Scaloppine with Sesame Noodles

✓ *SOMETHING SPECIAL*

This dish combines the naturally great flavor of chicken with a wonderful lemon-parsley sauce. What makes it even more interesting is that it's served over tasty sesame noodles. Pound the chicken as in the Tarragon Chicken Breasts recipe (see the Tip on page 99), though these should be pounded into very thin cutlets.

Sesame Noodles (below)

¼ cup all-purpose flour

Salt and freshly ground pepper, to taste

4 boneless skinless chicken breasts, each breast halved horizontally into 2 thin fillets and pounded to an even ¼-inch thickness

2 tablespoons butter

1 tablespoon olive oil

2 tablespoons fresh lemon juice

2 tablespoons finely chopped fresh Italian flat-leaf parsley *

1. Preheat the oven to 200°F. Prepare the sesame noodles.

2. In a shallow bowl, combine the flour, salt, and pepper. Dredge the chicken breasts in the flour mixture, shaking off any excess.

3. Melt the butter with the olive oil in a large, heavy skillet over medium-high heat. Add the chicken and cook it, turning once, until it is golden brown and reaches 160°F on an instant-read thermometer inserted into the thickest part of the breast, 7 to 8 minutes (or less if the cutlets are very thin).

4. Mound the sesame noodles in the bottom of a heated serving platter.

5. Remove the chicken from the skillet and arrange over the noodles; keep warm in the oven.

6. Stir the lemon juice and parsley into the juices remaining in the skillet; cook 1 minute. Spoon over the chicken and serve at once.

✱ TIP: Parsley comes in different varieties but I think the best for seasoning dishes is the flat-leaf variety, sometimes called Italian parsley. When buying it, look for firm stems and leaves. At home, trim the stems at the base. Place the parsley in a small glass of water; loosely cover it with plastic wrap or a thin plastic bag and store in the refrigerator. It will stay fresh for about 2 weeks.

Sesame Noodles

✓ *EASY PREPARATION*

Asian noodles are becoming much more available in stores around the country. One of the most popular noodles in Japan is soba, made from buckwheat flour. You may find them sold fresh in the produce department, or dried in the Asian section of your supermarket. Once they're cooked, just toss them with chicken, vegetables, and dressing for a fantastic quick meal with a different flavor.

8 ounces fresh or dried soba noodles

1 tablespoon plus 1 teaspoon light sesame oil

¼ cup low-sodium chicken broth, hot

2 tablespoons light soy sauce

2 tablespoons Asian sesame paste

2 tablespoons very thinly sliced green onions (from 2 to 3 whole onions) *

2 tablespoons finely chopped fresh Italian flat leaf parsley

1. Cook the noodles in 6 quarts of boiling salted water, 3 to 4 minutes for fresh noodles, 6 to 9 minutes for dried noodles. Drain well, and turn into a warm serving bowl.

2. Toss the drained noodles with 1 tablespoon sesame oil.

3. In a small bowl, beat together the chicken broth, soy sauce, sesame paste, and 1 teaspoon sesame oil. Toss with the hot noodles and keep warm.

4. Just before serving, toss the noodles gently with the green onions and parsley.

★TIP: Green onions (often called scallions), are thin, quick-growing, and mature onions. While most have a white undeveloped root end, some have a small but rounded bulb. Store in a plastic bag in the refrigerator. When a recipe calls for them, use the trimmed white part and about 2 inches of the tender green.

Coconut Chicken Curry with Basmati Rice

✓ SOMETHING SPECIAL

For many people, curry has come to mean a generic but fragrant spice mix sold in the supermarket, usually containing turmeric, cumin, and cayenne among other seasonings. However, in India and other countries in the East, there are numerous curry flavoring combinations. "Curry powder" can represent almost any blend of spices used to create a savory dish. So if you don't like a traditional curry powder, blend your favorite spices to create your own.

1 cup basmati rice ∗

2 cups water

Salt, to taste

1 tablespoon fresh lime juice

1 cup unsweetened coconut milk

2 tablespoons mild curry paste or powder, or more, or hotter, to taste

1 teaspoon sugar

1 bunch (about 5 thin) green onions, cut into ¼-inch slices

3 tablespoons chopped fresh cilantro

1 tablespoon vegetable oil (peanut is preferred)

3 boneless skinless chicken breasts, halved across and cut into ½-inch-wide strips

1 teaspoon finely chopped garlic (1 medium clove)

1. In a medium saucepan, stir together the rice, water, and salt. Bring to a boil, stir once, and reduce heat to a simmer. Simmer until all the water is absorbed, about 15 minutes. Cover the pot with a kitchen towel and then the pot cover. Remove from heat and set aside for 10 minutes.

2. While the rice is cooking, in a small bowl, combine the lime juice, coconut milk, curry paste or powder, sugar, green onions, and cilantro.

3. Heat the oil in a wok or heavy skillet over high heat. Toss the chicken breast slices in the wok and stir-fry for 2 to 3 minutes.

Add the garlic and cook, stirring, 1 minute more. Pour in the coconut milk mixture, lower the heat, and simmer 4 minutes more.

4. Use a fork to stir the rice in the pot and then turn into a serving bowl. Spoon the chicken and sauce on top and serve immediately.

SERVING SUGGESTION

You can add steamed vegetables such as green beans or asparagus. Spread the rice in the bottom of a heated serving platter. Layer with vegetables and then the chicken and sauce.

∗ **TIP:** Basmati rice is special long-grain rice often used in Indian cooking. It has a light texture and is very fragrant. There is no need to rinse the basmati rice before cooking. Just make sure to use about 1 part rice to 2 parts liquid to cook it.

Chicken Saltimbocca

✓ *EASY PREPARATION*

Chicken breasts are easy to cook, and dishes based on them come together quickly. This classic but always exciting combination of sage, ham, and chicken will really spice up a weeknight dinner.

8 thin slices prosciutto or smoked ham, cut to the size of each piece of chicken

4 boneless skinless chicken breasts, sliced in half horizontally to make 8 thin cutlets (or, if the breasts are more than 10 ounces each, use only 2 and slice them in half horizontally to make 4 thick cutlets, then slice them in half horizontally again to yield 8 thin cutlets)

8 large fresh sage leaves or 1/2 teaspoon dried sage *

Salt and freshly ground pepper, to taste

2 tablespoons butter

1 tablespoon olive oil

1/4 cup dry white wine, such as Sauvignon Blanc

1/4 cup chicken broth

1. Lay 1 slice prosciutto on each chicken cutlet. Top each package with a sage leaf and skewer it to the ham and chicken with a round-edged (not flat) toothpick. (If using dried sage, sprinkle a little on the chicken before topping with the ham and skewering with the toothpick.) Dust with salt and pepper.

2. In a heavy skillet large enough to hold all the cutlets in one layer, heat the butter and oil over medium-high heat. Quickly brown the chicken cutlets on both sides, 1 to 2 minutes per side. Turn cutlets ham side up. Stir in the wine and chicken broth. Lower the heat and simmer gently until the chicken reaches a temperature of 160°F on an instant-read thermometer inserted into the thickest part of the breast, about 5 minutes.

3. Serve hot, sage leaf up, with the sauce spooned over the cutlets.

SERVING SUGGESTION

Serve with rice pilaf and steamed green beans.

*TIP: Dried herbs and **spices** can be a cook's saviors in the kitchen. Remember that dried spices last 1 1/2 months and dried herbs last only one year. Once you bring them home from the store, immediately mark them with the date. To store them, keep in a cool dark place where they won't dry out. When they lose their color, they have lost a lot of their natural oils, which give them their flavor. To use dried herbs, either toast them in a skillet or crumble them between your fingers to activate the oils.

Chicken Sausages with White Beans and Fresh Greens

✓ *MAKE-AHEAD*   ✓ *SOMETHING SPECIAL*

This hearty, delicious recipe is a quick and easy all-in-one meal even the kids will love.

12 chicken or turkey sausages *

2 cups dry white wine, such as Sauvignon Blanc

3 tablespoons olive oil

1 tablespoon finely chopped garlic (from 3 large cloves)

2 cups chopped white onions (from 2 small onions)

3 cups seeded deveined and chopped red bell pepper (from 3 medium peppers)

1 serrano chile, stemmed, seeded, deveined, and finely chopped

¼ cup fresh thyme, stemmed, leaves chopped

Three 14-ounce cans cannellini beans, drained and rinsed

Salt and freshly ground pepper, to taste

3 bunches fresh greens, such as arugula, spinach, or watercress

1. Place the sausages in a large, heavy skillet, and pierce each one with a fork. Add ¼ cup of the wine. Cover the pan and simmer the sausages over medium heat for 5 minutes. Uncover and increase the heat to high. Cook, turning the sausages occasionally, until the wine evaporates and the sausages are browned, about 10 minutes. Transfer the sausages to a plate. After they have cooled, slice them on the diagonal into 1-inch pieces.

2. Pour off all but ¼ cup of the drippings from the pan. Add the olive oil and heat the skillet over medium heat. Add the garlic, onion, red pepper, chile, and thyme, and cook, stirring, until the vegetables are tender, about 10 minutes. Increase the heat to high and add the remaining wine. Boil until the liquid is reduced by half, about 3 minutes, scraping the pan with a wooden spoon so all the nice brown bits in the pan are incorporated into the sauce. Add the beans and sausage, and season with salt and pepper. Stir until heated through, about 10 minutes.

3. Divide the fresh greens among the plates and top with the sausage mixture.

SERVING SUGGESTION

This is a good dish for evenings when latecomers will have to eat after the main meal. Refrigerate their portions, which can later be microwaved on high for about 2 minutes, until good and hot.

*TIP: Sausages come in many great flavors. I have made this dish with chicken-apple sausage, fennel-pork sausage, and many others. Find your favorites and then enhance the dish by seasoning it with more of the herbs and spices found in the sausages. Sausages will keep in the freezer for several months, so always keep them on hand.

Catch of the Day

Fish and shellfish are an important part of today's diet. Due in part to the demands of a more health-conscious public and to improved preservation and transportation techniques, good seafood is now widely available. Cooking time is short, and the flavors are so adaptable that fish and shellfish can make the perfect after-work dinner. Fish fillets and steaks, such as tuna or salmon, are versatile cuts that can be prepared by many different cooking methods.

You should aim to cook "the catch of the day"—meaning the freshest fish available the day you want to cook it. Try to buy fish at seafood stores and supermarkets with a dedicated fish counter. Choose from the fish that is not prepackaged so you can look at, feel, and smell the fish—all of which are prime ways to determine freshness.

Of course, certain fish aren't available everywhere all the time, so talk to the fish seller at your market. Some fish and shellfish can be substituted for one another, so be flexible—maybe the halibut looks great one week, and the sole another week.

Fresh fish should look shiny, not dull. If the fish is whole, the eyes should be luminescent and clear, not opaque and sunken in. The surface of the skin should be wet but not slimy, and the flesh should feel resilient when you touch it, not in the least spongy or mushy. And the fish should smell faintly of the ocean and water. If the smell is very strong, similar to ammonia, or even slightly unpleasant—leave it alone.

Try to have on hand a list of substitutions you can use for various types of fish. Here are a few of the most common and some comparable exchanges:

- Red snapper fillets: striped bass, catfish, tilapia, or tilefish

- Haddock and cod can be used interchangeably.

- Mackerel: bluefish, mahi-mahi, tilapia, and swordfish

- Tuna steaks: Mahi-mahi and swordfish

- Salmon: Salmon has a unique taste, so there really isn't a substitute. Tuna can be used in a salmon steak recipe, but will have a different taste.

There will likely be times when you need to plan ahead and buy fish in advance. Flash-frozen fish can still yield flavorful dishes, but check the date to make sure it hasn't been sitting in the store too long. If wrapped and stored carefully, fish steaks and fillets can keep in your freezer for up to two months.

Whatever fish you choose, be sure to treat it with care; refrigerate it at all times, even going so far as to take a chilled cooler to the supermarket when you are buying fish in the summer.

Keep in mind Rule Number One when preparing fish: do not overcook!

Roasted Salmon with Pesto

✓ *EASY PREPARATION*   ✓ *SOMETHING SPECIAL*

You cannot beat a quick salmon dish for a midweek supper. This very simple recipe requires really fresh fish. With so few ingredients, the flavor of the salmon will be the star. If salmon is not your favorite, try tuna.

I find that having a container of pesto in the refrigerator is a wonderful way to be ready for nearly any culinary occasion and makes this a super-quick meal.

¼ cup prepared Pesto (page 77)

Four 4- or 5-ounce salmon fillets

Salt and freshly ground pepper, to taste

1 tablespoon olive oil

1. Prepare the pesto.

2. Preheat the oven to 475°F.

3. Season the salmon with salt and pepper, and then brush on all sides with olive oil.

4. Preheat a heavy ovenproof skillet or grill pan large enough to hold the fillets in one layer. Brush lightly with olive oil. Sear the salmon on both sides, 1½ to 2 minutes per side, then spread 1 tablespoon pesto over each fillet.

5. Place the skillet or grill pan in the oven and roast 5 to 7 minutes, until salmon just begins to flake easily, but remains pink at the very center. ✱

6. Remove the skillet from the oven. Let stand 2 to 3 minutes. Serve very hot.

SERVING SUGGESTION

Serve on a bed of Cannellini Beans with Basil and Fresh Tomatoes (page 171).

> ✱ **TIP:** If your pan does not have an **ovenproof handle**, cover the handle with two layers of aluminum foil to keep it from burning.

Roasted Herb-Crusted Salmon with Extra-Virgin Olive Oil

✓ *EASY PREPARATION*   ✓ *SOMETHING SPECIAL*

Here, the salmon is coated with coarse bread crumbs and herbs to create a wonderfully crunchy and flavorful meal. Herbes de Provence is a commercial blend of herbs, combining lavender, rosemary, fennel, thyme, tarragon, and oregano, among others.

Lemon Vinaigrette (page 16)

2 teaspoons ground cumin

6 tablespoons herbes de Provence

Salt and freshly ground pepper, to taste

1 cup panko bread crumbs or unseasoned dried bread crumbs *

Eight 4- to 6-ounce center-cut salmon fillets, with the skin removed

1/4 cup olive oil

3 cups fresh salad greens of your choice

Extra-virgin olive oil, for garnish

1. Prepare lemon vinaigrette. Preheat the oven to 450°F.

2. On a sheet of wax paper, combine the ground cumin, herbes de Provence, salt, pepper, and panko bread crumbs. Roll the salmon fillets in the herb and crumb mixture, patting gently so the coating will adhere to the fish.

3. Heat the 1/4 cup olive oil in an ovenproof skillet large enough to hold all the fillets in one layer, over medium-high heat. Sear skin side down (always skin side first, as for chicken) 1 to 2 minutes. Turn once very gently, and cook 1 to 2 minutes more to sear the underside.

4. Transfer the skillet to the center of the oven and roast 6 to 10 minutes, depending on the thickness of the fillets, until the salmon is just cooked; it is a good idea to check after 5 or 6 minutes so the salmon doesn't overcook. Remove from the oven.

5. In a medium bowl, toss the greens with a little of the vinaigrette—just enough to lightly coat the leaves. (Store remaining vinaigrette for another use.)

6. Divide the greens among individual dinner plates. Place the hot fish on the greens, with a little extra-virgin olive oil drizzled over the fillets. Serve immediately, with more oil alongside.

*TIP: Panko bread crumbs can often be found in the Asian section of your supermarket or in Asian markets. They are faintly sweet, flaked bread crumbs that keep their nice flavor and crisp texture even when cooked. While the Japanese generally use them only for rustic dishes, American chefs like the crunchy texture they give to many fried foods.

Pan-Seared Pepper-Crusted Tuna

Make a quantity of the pepper rub used in this dish and keep it on hand in a tightly closed jar or sealed plastic container for several weeks. You can use it on any cut of fish or shellfish you like. Once you have the rub in your pantry, fish for dinner becomes an even quicker option.

4 tablespoons (¼ cup) unsalted butter plus 3 tablespoons for the dressing

2 teaspoons cayenne pepper

1 tablespoon freshly ground black pepper

1 teaspoon ground white pepper

½ teaspoon garlic powder

1 teaspoon dry mustard

1 tablespoon paprika

1 tablespoon onion powder

1 teaspoon fine sea salt or regular salt

2 teaspoons dried thyme

Six 6-ounce pieces of tuna (steak or fillet), each about 1 inch thick

Vegetable oil for grill pan

1. Clarify the butter: Melt the ¼ cup butter in a small pan over low heat, skimming the foam that forms on the surface. This takes about 5 minutes. Pour off the clear yellow liquid—this is the clarified butter. Discard the white solids that have sunk to the bottom of the pan. (Alternatively, if there is time, pour the melted butter into a small bowl and refrigerate until solid. Remove the solid butter from the bowl to cook with. Discard the liquid and solids that remain in the bottom of the bowl.) *

2. Meanwhile, prepare the pepper rub: In a small bowl, stir together the cayenne pepper, black pepper, white pepper, garlic powder, dry mustard, paprika, onion powder, salt, and dried thyme.

3. Brush the tuna with the clarified butter. Sprinkle some of the rub onto each side of the tuna, pressing with your fingers to make the rub adhere well.

4. Brush a ridged grill pan with oil and heat it over medium-high heat just until it is smoking. Sear the fish 3 to 5 minutes per side, turning only once. The tuna should still be pink in the middle. *

5. While the tuna is cooking, heat the 3 tablespoons butter in a small skillet over medium heat, swirling the skillet, until the butter is dark brown, watching carefully so it does not burn. (Butter will go from golden brown to burned and unusable in a very short time.)

6. Serve immediately, with a little browned butter drizzled over each piece of tuna.

Serving Suggestion

Slice the tuna on a slant across the grain, and arrange on a bed of couscous or rice.

*TIP: Use clarified butter for cooking foods like fish over high heat. The milk solids and other impurities that burn quickly are removed for more even and efficient cooking.

*TIP: To prevent tuna from drying out, cook it until it is opaque nearly all the way through, but still with a line of pink in the middle. (Or cook for less time if you prefer the tuna more tender.)

Provençal Grilled Halibut

✓ *EASY PREPARATION*

The quick-to-make rub for the halibut can be used on any mild fish, such as sea bass or even fillet of sole. See what looks the freshest (or ask the fish vendor) at the store, then decide what will be the best fish for dinner that night.

4 tablespoons olive oil

2 tablespoons chopped fresh thyme

2 tablespoons chopped fresh basil

2 teaspoons dried lavender or herbes de Provence, lightly crushed between your palms or fingers ∗

½ teaspoon salt

¼ teaspoon freshly ground pepper

Eight 6-ounce center-cut halibut fillets

1. In a small bowl, whisk together the olive oil, thyme, basil, lavender, salt, and pepper. Spread this paste evenly on both sides of the fish fillets.

2. Preheat the outdoor grill or an indoor grill pan for 10 minutes over high heat. Grill the fish, turning once halfway through grilling time, until the flesh inside is opaque throughout and starting to flake when tested with the point of a knife, 5 to 7 minutes. Serve immediately.

SERVING SUGGESTION

Serve the fish alongside freshly steamed spinach that has been drizzled with a little extra-virgin olive oil, if you like, or with your favorite green vegetable.

∗**TIP:** When looking for **lavender** to cook with, always make sure that it is untreated dried lavender. The chemically treated lavender used in potpourri cannot be used in cooking.

CATCH OF THE DAY 111

Roasted Tilapia with Garlic and Parsley

✓ EASY PREPARATION   ✓ SOMETHING SPECIAL

This recipe is good for tilapia or any large-flake fish, including cod. It doesn't work well with more delicately textured fish like trout or sole since it may fall apart. Roasting is an easy way to cook fish because you don't have to fuss with it to get great flavor.

¾ cup panko bread crumbs or unseasoned dried bread crumbs *

¼ cup chopped fresh Italian flat-leaf parsley

3 teaspoons finely chopped garlic (from 3 medium cloves)

Salt and freshly ground pepper, to taste

Six 4-ounce tilapia fillets

1 large egg white, beaten until frothy and transferred to a flat dish

¼ cup olive oil

1. Preheat the oven to 450°F.

2. On a large, flat plate stir together the bread crumbs, parsley, garlic, salt, and pepper.

3. Dip the fillets into the egg white, then into the panko mixture. Set the coated fillets aside on a plate.

4. Heat the oil over high heat in an ovenproof skillet large enough to hold all the fillets in one layer. When the oil is hot, brown the fillets quickly on both sides, about 1 minute per side. Place the skillet in the hot oven and roast 5 to 6 minutes, just until the fish is opaque all the way through and flakes easily. Serve immediately.

SERVING SUGGESTIONS

Serve the tilapia with boiled "baby" new potatoes and steamed broccoli. Drizzle the vegetables with a little extra-virgin olive oil and sprinkle with a little Parmigiano-Reggiano cheese.

Serve the tilapia topped with browned onions and crisp bacon slices for another easy dinner.

＊TIP: Panko bread crumbs are dry flaked bread crumbs from Japan that maintain their crunch even when moistened. In this preparation, they give the final dish a delightful crunch. Panko bread crumbs are widely available in the international or Asian sections of local supermarkets.

Pan-Fried Fillets of Sole with Tartar Sauce

MAKES 6 SERVINGS

✓ *EASY PREPARATION*

This is a classic, and for good reason—it's simple and delicious. That's why I stick with the classic commercial seasonings, even though I usually prefer freshly prepared spices and herbs. You don't have to make homemade tartar sauce with all the commercial brands available, but, oh, is it good!

Tartar Sauce (below)

1 cup all-purpose flour or seasoned seafood coating, such as House Autry or Lawry's

Salt and seasoned pepper, such as Mrs. Dash, to taste

2 pounds sole fillets (6 to 12 fillets, depending on size)

3 tablespoons butter or canola oil

6 to 12 lemon wedges, for garnish (from 2 lemons)

1. Prepare the tartar sauce. Then, preheat the oven to 200°F.

2. In a large flat bowl or pie plate, combine the flour, salt, and pepper, unless using seafood coating that is already seasoned.

3. Toss the sole fillets in the seasoned flour or coating, knocking off the excess.

4. Heat the butter or oil in a heavy skillet over high heat. Fry the sole, in batches if necessary, until the fillets are browned on both sides, are opaque clear through, and flake easily, 1 to 2 minutes per side. Keep the fillets warm on a plate, uncovered, in the oven until all are ready.

5. Serve hot with lemon wedges and a bowl of tartar sauce.

SERVING SUGGESTION

Serve with Old Bay Oven-Fried Potato Chips (page 170) and cole slaw.

Tartar Sauce

MAKES ABOUT 1⅓ CUPS

✓ *EASY PREPARATION*

I like to make tartar sauce a day or two in advance so the flavors can blend and develop. Once you make your own, the commercial varieties pale in comparison.

3 tablespoons coarsely chopped green onion (from 3 whole green onions)

2 tablespoons dill pickle relish

1 teaspoon chopped capers

1 teaspoon freshly squeezed lemon juice

½ teaspoon seasoned pepper, such as Mrs. Dash

1 teaspoon Dijon mustard (optional)

1 cup mayonnaise

3 tablespoons finely chopped curly parsley

Mix together all the ingredients in a small bowl. Cover and chill at least 1 hour. ✱

✱ TIP: For a different flavor, try adding a teaspoon of grated **lemon zest** to the sauce. Use a Microplane zester to make this addition quick and easy.

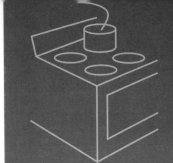

Meat Dishes
for Every Day

Even when you have limited time and energy, there are definitely days when nothing will satisfy like a good piece of beef, pork, or lamb. Steaks, chops, and roasts offer succulent, savory meal options without requiring too much effort.

Selecting good meat is key. Even if it has to be relegated to once-in-a-while status, when you buy steak, buy the best you can afford. Look for USDA Choice grade—or if you are lucky enough to be in an area that supplies it, Prime grade is even better. The higher the grade, the more flavorful the cut—due to a slightly higher fat content. Beef should be firm-textured and very red, and any exposed bone should have a slight reddish tint. No matter what the cut you choose, it should smell fresh, with not even the slightest odor or smell of ammonia. As soon as you get the meat home, take it out of the plastic package and rewrap it loosely in waxed paper. Try to cook it within two or three days.

If you are not going to be able to use the steak as quickly as you thought, wrap it in freezer paper or place it in a heavy-duty freezer bag. Press out as much air as possible and place it in the coldest part of your freezer—usually the lowest part, as cold air sinks.

Also, don't forget good-quality ground meat to make meatloaf—a great midweek crowd-pleaser. It doesn't have to be old-fashioned. I offer not only a new taste with my recipe, but also a modern twist on preparation—you bake individual servings, both to speed up cooking, and also reheating for when members of the family arrive late and want theirs hot.

The USDA also grades lamb. While Prime grade lamb is very difficult to find, high-quality Choice grade is available in most supermarkets. For the most delicate flavor and tenderness, look for lamb that is firm-textured and red in color, and has white fat around the outside. If lamb is dark red with yellowish fat, it will be strong tasting and less than tender. In the past, lamb was cooked until very well done in this country. Today lamb is best when cooked until deep pink in the middle, about 155°F to 160°F on an instant-read thermometer—that's when it is still juicy and most tender. You can freeze lamb, but plan to use it within a few weeks.

Traditionally pork has been thought of as a very fatty meat. However, today pigs are being bred leaner and leaner, and this new pork, because it is so lean, has to be treated with care when it is cooked. With little or no internal fat to naturally baste the chops and roasts, cooked pork can quickly become as dry and tasteless as sawdust and as tough as leather. Short grilling or roasting times are the key. Or if you want to ensure a succulent end result, add wine, water, or broth to the cooking pan—the added liquid will help keep the pork moist and tender. Don't be afraid if the cooked pork is very pale pink at the center. Due to new methods of feeding and raising pork in the U.S., pork no longer holds the threat of trichinosis and is fully cooked at 160°F.

When buying pork, look for pale pinkish gray meat, with white, almost translucent fat. Pork should smell fresh and clean when you buy it—put back, or take back, any that has even the slightest spoiled odor.

My most important word of advice: invest in an instant-read meat thermometer. You will find it invaluable for judging the degree of doneness whether you are cooking in the oven, on the stove, or on the grill.

Just a little forethought and some care while cooking, and you can easily serve your family and guests wonderfully flavorful and comfortably satisfying meat dishes.

Moroccan-Spiced Grilled Strip Steaks with Couscous

✓ *EASY PREPARATION*   ✓ *SOMETHING SPECIAL*

While the finished dish looks as if it has taken a great deal of effort and talent, this is really one of the easiest and quickest recipes to make. Serve it to family any time, but guests will also rave.

1 tablespoon ground cumin

1 tablespoon ground coriander

1/2 teaspoon freshly ground pepper

1 teaspoon ground cinnamon

1 teaspoon ground ginger

1/2 teaspoon salt

2 tablespoons grated onion

6 New York strip steaks,
3/4 to 1 inch thick

2 tablespoons olive oil

Couscous (below)

1. Preheat the grill or grill pan over medium-high heat for about 15 minutes.

2. Combine the cumin, coriander, pepper, cinnamon, ginger, salt, and onion. Rub each steak with olive oil and then press the herb mixture into each side. Set aside for 5 minutes before grilling. ∗

3. Prepare the couscous, then cover with foil to keep warm.

4. Grill the steaks until crusty on the outside and medium rare on the inside, 6 to 7 minutes per side.

5. Stir the cooked couscous with a fork and mound on a heated serving platter. Cut the steak on the diagonal into thick slices and arrange on the bed of couscous.

∗TIP: For enhanced flavor, **heat the spices** before using them. Combine the cumin, coriander, pepper, cinnamon, and ginger in a small skillet. Pan roast, tossing from time to time, over medium-high heat until the spices release their fragrance, about 4 to 5 minutes. Let cool and continue with the recipe.

Couscous

✓ *EASY PREPARATION*

Couscous is a versatile pasta (which looks like a grain) that can be served as an accompaniment to almost any meat or fish. I prefer to serve it simply seasoned, but there are numerous varieties of flavored instant couscous, if you would like to spice things up.

2 1/2 cups water

2 tablespoons olive oil

1/2 teaspoon salt

Freshly ground pepper, to taste

2 cups instant couscous

1/2 cup sliced green onion, white and up to 1 inch light green (from 2 whole bunches)

1/3 cup raisins, plumped in boiling water and drained ∗

1. Bring the water, oil, salt, and pepper to a boil in a medium saucepan. Remove the pan from the heat and stir in the couscous

in a steady stream. Cover and let stand 5 minutes.

2. Stir to fluff up the couscous, then stir in the green onion and raisins. Serve hot.

∗TIP: Before adding **dried fruit** such as raisins to rice or pasta, make the fruit more tender by pouring boiling water over it. Let it stand 5 to 10 minutes until plumped and juicy. Drain excess water and pat dry.

Beef Tenderloin Steaks with Tellicherry Pepper Sauce

✓ *EASY PREPARATION*   ✓ *SOMETHING SPECIAL*

While any good black peppercorns can be substituted in this recipe, the Tellicherry pepper from India has such a wonderful flavor that it makes this steak extra special. Once you try it, you will never again associate black pepper with just the spicy heat in a dish. This recipe is an excellent choice when you need to make something nice in a hurry. Look for Tellicherry peppercorns in well-stocked supermarkets and spice stores.

2 tablespoons butter

¼ cup finely chopped shallots (from 8 medium cloves)

⅓ cup brandy

1 cup low-sodium beef broth

1 cup heavy whipping cream

1 tablespoon whole Tellicherry black peppercorns, crushed *

Salt and freshly ground Tellicherry black pepper, to taste

Eight 6-ounce beef tenderloin steaks

2 tablespoons olive oil

* TIP: To crush the **peppercorns** for the sauce, place them in a heavy, resealable plastic bag. Roll a rolling pin over the peppercorns to crush them coarsely. Or, use an electric coffee grinder reserved for grinding spices. Place the peppercorns in the grinder and pulse three to four times for the desired consistency.

1. Melt the butter in a heavy medium saucepan over medium-low heat. Add the shallots and cook, stirring, until golden, about 8 minutes. Stir in the brandy, raise the heat, and bring to a boil. Add the broth and boil until the mixture is reduced to 1 cup, about 5 minutes. Whisk in the whipping cream and the crushed peppercorns. Cook over medium heat until the sauce is reduced and thickened in consistency, about 15 minutes. Taste and season with salt and pepper. Reduce the heat to low and keep the sauce warm. This sauce can be made up to 1 day ahead. Cover and chill, if making ahead.

2. While the sauce is reducing, preheat the barbecue, grill pan, or broiler for 10 minutes to medium-high heat. Brush the steaks with the olive oil. Season with salt and pepper. Grill to desired doneness, turning only once, about 6 minutes per side for medium-rare, 8 minutes or more per side depending on what degree of doneness you like.

3. Return the sauce to a simmer. Transfer steaks to plates. Spoon some sauce over each steak. Serve hot.

SERVING SUGGESTION

For fast side dishes to go with the steaks, make Polenta (page 77), and steamed green beans. Spoon the polenta onto heated plates. Arrange the steaks on top and spoon some of the sauce over them. Pass the remaining sauce and the green beans in separate dishes.

Cajun Meatloaf Patties

✓ *EASY PREPARATION*　✓ *MAKE-AHEAD*　✓ *TAKE-ALONG*

While there are somewhat similar dishes in other cultures, meatloaf seems to be a truly American concept. Variations abound and this is just my favorite. I make the meatloaf into patties so they cook more quickly. Kids find them more fun to eat, too.

¼ cup (4 tablespoons) butter

2 cups finely chopped white onion (from 2 medium)

1 cup finely chopped green bell pepper (from 1 medium)

2 teaspoons salt

1 teaspoon freshly ground pepper

1½ teaspoons cayenne pepper

1 teaspoon dried thyme, crumbled and rubbed between your fingers

½ teaspoon ground cumin

2 pounds lean ground beef

2 large eggs, lightly beaten in a small bowl, just until blended

1 cup fine dry unseasoned bread crumbs

½ cup ketchup, plus more for serving

2 teaspoons Worcestershire sauce

1. Preheat the oven to 375°F.

2. Melt the butter in a heavy medium skillet over medium-low heat. Add the onion and bell pepper and stir to combine. Season with salt, pepper, cayenne, thyme, and cumin. Cook, stirring frequently, until the onions are transparent and the vegetables are tender, about 10 minutes.

3. In a large bowl, combine the ground beef, beaten egg, bread crumbs, the ½ cup ketchup, and the Worcestershire sauce. Stir in the cooked onion and pepper and mix well. ✱

4. To cook the meatloaf, line a baking dish with foil. Shape the meatloaf mixture into 8 large hamburger-like patties. Arrange the shaped patties in the lined baking dish. Bake 15 to 20 minutes until cooked through. Drain well of any fat and serve very hot.

To cook using a muffin tin, pack the meatloaf mixture into the cups of a large 6-cup muffin tin. Bake the meat loaves for 20 to 25 minutes until cooked through. Drain fat, if any, from the tin, remove the mini-loaves, and serve very hot.

SERVING SUGGESTIONS

The patties may also be cooked on top of the stove in a preheated, ridged grill pan, over medium-high heat, for 5 minutes per side, turning only once. If some members of your family like any kind of ground beef as long as it is served on a bun, put these little meatloaves on hamburger buns, topped with a dollop of ketchup, and garnished with slices of tomato and onion.

For a traditional meatloaf, pack the meat mixture into a loaf pan and bake 50 to 60 minutes. Pour off fat from pan and let the meatloaf rest for 10 minutes before turning it out of the pan and slicing to serve.

Serve the meatloaf with Yukon Mashed Potatoes (page 79) and Green Beans with Toasted Walnuts (page 164).

✱TIP: A large wooden spoon is useful for **mixing meatloaf**, but getting your hands into the mix is the quickest way to evenly blend the ingredients. If you don't mind a little mess, it can also be a very satisfying task! Just be sure to wash your hands before and after mixing the ingredients.

Cumin-Glazed Pork Fillet with Apples and Pears

MAKES 4 TO 6 SERVINGS

Pork tenderloin can be your best friend in the kitchen. It is quick to cook—either whole or sliced—moist and tender (if you don't overcook it), and pairs very well with many sauces and accompaniments.

1/4 cup olive oil

1 teaspoon lemon zest

1 teaspoon cumin seeds

2 tablespoons chopped fresh Italian flat-leaf parsley

1 pound pork tenderloin, ends trimmed, then cut into eight 1-inch-thick fillets

2 Granny Smith or Golden Delicious apples, peeled, cored, and diced

2 Bartlett pears, peeled, cored, and diced

Juice of 1 lemon

4 tablespoons (1/4 cup) butter

2 tablespoons sugar

Salt and freshly ground pepper, to taste

1/2 cup apple cider

1/4 cup chicken broth

1/2 cup heavy cream

1. In a large resealable plastic bag, combine the olive oil, lemon zest, cumin, and parsley. Add the pork slices and seal. Shake and press the contents of the sealed bag, making sure the pork is well covered with the marinade. Set the bag aside.

2. Combine the fruit and lemon juice in a small bowl. Melt 2 tablespoons of the butter in a heavy skillet over medium-high heat. As soon as the butter begins to foam and then turn clear, add the fruit to the pan. Cook until softened, about 6 minutes, then add the sugar. Continue to cook until the fruit is soft and has turned a light golden color, about 10 minutes more. Set the mixture aside.

3. Heat the remaining butter in a large, heavy skillet over medium-high heat. Remove pork from the marinade. Season with salt and pepper and cook them in a single layer, turning once, until well browned, 2 to 3 minutes per side. The pork should still be slightly pink in the middle when you cut it with a knife. Remove to a heated plate and tent with foil.

4. Pour the cider into the pan in which the pork was cooked and cook it over medium-high heat, scraping the pan with a wooden spoon to remove any brown bits from the bottom. Bring to a boil and reduce the cider by half, 3 to 4 minutes, then add the broth and cream. Reduce again until the mixture is slightly thickened, about 2 minutes more. *

5. Return the pork and fruit to the pan. Simmer over medium heat until the mixture is hot and the pork is just cooked through, about 4 minutes more. Taste and season with salt and pepper.

6. Place the fruit mixture on a heated serving plate, and arrange the pork tenderloin on top. Serve immediately.

＊TIP: Reduction thickens a sauce slightly and intensifies the flavor. Bring the sauce to a boil and cook briskly, stirring occasionally, until the level of the liquid is half as deep as it was when you began.

Cold Roast Pork with Spicy Coconut Sauce

✓ *MAKE-AHEAD*　✓ *SOMETHING SPECIAL*　✓ *TAKE-ALONG*

Here's a crowd-pleasing Asian-style dish that you can take to a potluck, picnic, or other get-together. To transport it, pack the cold sliced pork in a sealable plastic bag or covered plastic dish. Put the sauce in a separate covered container. Once you arrive at your destination, arrange the pork slices on a serving plate and drizzle with the sauce.

1 cup coconut cream (the sweetened cream used in tropical drinks)

2 tablespoons crunchy peanut butter

2 tablespoons finely chopped onion

1 teaspoon ground ginger

2 tablespoons lime juice (from 1 lime)

1 teaspoon crushed red pepper

1 teaspoon Worcestershire sauce

1 pound pork tenderloin ✱

Salt and freshly ground pepper

4 cilantro sprigs, for garnish

1. Preheat the oven to 375°F. Heat the coconut cream in a small saucepan over low heat. Stir in the peanut butter until blended. Stir in the onion, ginger, lime juice, red pepper, and Worcestershire sauce. Simmer 2 minutes. Remove the sauce from the heat, pour into a serving bowl, and let cool completely.

2. To roast the pork: Season the tenderloin with salt and pepper. Roast 20 to 25 minutes, until an instant-read thermometer inserted in the middle reads 160°F, and the center is only slightly pink. Remove the roast from the oven and let cool completely.

3. Cut the pork into 1-inch slices. Arrange the pork on a serving platter. Beat the sauce with a fork until well combined. Drizzle the pork with a little sauce. Garnish with the cilantro. Serve with the remaining sauce on the side.

✱TIP: For a super-speedy dinner, you can buy the **pork tenderloin** already cooked in the prepared foods section of the supermarket or specialty deli, or roast it at home.

Herbed Lamb Chops with Roman Spinach

✓ *SOMETHING SPECIAL*

Lamb is delicious cooked by almost any method, but I find it most satisfying when grilled. Char it a little on the outside and leave it rosy pink inside, so it's still tender and juicy. If there are "well done" fans in the crowd, leave their chops on the grill only a minute or two longer.

2 teaspoons finely chopped garlic
(from 2 medium cloves)

2 tablespoons finely chopped shallots
(from 2 large or 3 small cloves)

3 tablespoons mixed dried herbs,
such as thyme and rosemary

2 tablespoons chopped fresh Italian
flat-leaf parsley

2 tablespoons dry red wine,
such as Cabernet Sauvignon

2 tablespoons olive oil

12 to 18 rib lamb chops, depending
upon the thickness (if ¾ inch thick,
get 12 chops; ½ inch thick, get
18 chops)

Roman Spinach (below)

2 or 3 fresh rosemary sprigs, for garnish

1. In a small bowl, mix together the garlic, shallots, dried herbs, parsley, red wine, and olive oil. Arrange the chops in one layer on a cookie sheet covered with wax paper or plastic wrap. Spread the mixture on the chops and marinate, covered with plastic wrap, for 30 minutes or up to overnight.

2. Preheat the grill. Grill the chops over hot coals until crusty on the outside and still pink on the inside, 3 to 4 minutes per side.

3. Arrange the chops on a heated platter, and tent with foil to keep warm.

4. Prepare the spinach. Then arrange a bed of the spinach on a heated platter and arrange the chops on top. Garnish with sprigs of fresh rosemary.

Roman Spinach

✓ *EASY PREPARATION*

Frozen spinach works very well when you're in a hurry but fresh spinach is preferred for flavor and nutrition. The secret to successfully cooked spinach, frozen or fresh, is minimal cooking, minimal liquid.

3 tablespoons olive oil

3 teaspoons finely chopped garlic
(from 3 medium cloves)

Two 10-ounce packages frozen chopped
spinach, thawed and squeezed as
dry as possible, or 3 pounds fresh
spinach, washed, stems removed

Salt and freshly ground pepper,
to taste

Heat the oil in a heavy skillet. Cook the garlic, stirring, for

1 minute. Toss in the spinach. Cook, tossing, until coated with oil, wilted, and heated through, about 3 minutes. Taste, season well with salt and pepper, and serve.

Fresh Crab Tacos (page 49)

Chicken Niçoise Salad with Walnuts and Blue Cheese Vinaigrette (page 100)

Chicken, Avocado, and Bacon in a Tomato Wrap (page 40)
with Spicy Pumpkin Fries (page 168)

Rotelli with Roasted Asparagus, Mushrooms, and Shaved Parmigiano (page 90)

Gorgonzola, Escarole, Garlic, and Roast Pepper Pizza (page 60)

Center: Eastern Braised Chicken over Noodle Pillows (page 127);
Inset: Cutting the noodle pillows

Herbed Lamb Chops with Roman Spinach (page 120)
over Cannellini Beans with Basil and Fresh Tomato (page 171)

Italian Meringue with Chocolate Sorbet (page 182)

Peanut Butter and Jelly Mini-Muffins (page 200)

Asian Express—
Takeout at Home

Why order in when, with just a little planning and very little time, you can make your own? This age-old cuisine presents wonderful flavors along with the ease of quick cooking. I love to cook Asian food because you can easily create unique dishes just by having the basic ingredients of the Asian pantry on hand.

Some great ingredients to have in your kitchen are soy sauce, rice wine vinegar, chili paste, pickled ginger, plum sauce, rice noodles, and fish sauce. Whether you are making a complete Asian meal, or simply want to try an Asian salad dressing for your salad or add a little chili paste (very little, because it's hot!) to a marinade, these staples will allow you to expand your repertoire of fun and flavorful (even exotic) meals.

In Asian cooking, there's usually more of an emphasis on the starch rather than on meat or fish—rice might make up nearly half of the meal. So steam up some rice, or for a fusion approach (that might please a few picky family members) try mashed potatoes or even some instant polenta for a new twist! Add cut-up vegetables (like broccoli, spinach, or asparagus) and meats or fish (like pork, beef, or shrimp) to balance the meal.

Asian food—Chinese and Thai, in particular—tends to call for a lot of ingredients. But don't be scared off; a lot of the preparation can be done ahead of time, so when dinner time comes, it may be just a matter of minutes before the finished dishes are ready to be served.

Ingredients tend to be chopped, shredded, or ground—to cook fast and pick up or blend flavors easily—so, ultimately, you get in every bite a combination of salty, sweet, and tart tastes, plus perhaps the great flavors of garlic or scallions.

I include wonton soup here because it's such a popular favorite and the preparation can be a group activity. Making wontons may take a little practice, but it doesn't take long to get the hang of it and can be fun. Get everyone involved. Call in your children or spouse, or have a wonton party with your friends. Have a contest to see who can make the best looking wontons, or the most. Then everyone can enjoy his or her own handiwork in the finished soup.

For more Asian dishes, check out the Wok Works chapter (page 74) and Hearty Pasta and Noodle Dishes (page 89).

Chinese Spiced Turkey Wonton Soup

Here's a twist on the classic wonton soup that's easier to make than you might think. With a little practice, making wontons will become easy and fun. Try getting everyone involved. Call in your children or spouse, or make it a wonton party with your friends. Have a contest to see who can make the best-looking wontons, or the most. Then everyone can enjoy his or her own handiwork in the finished soup.

You can stuff the wontons with ground turkey, ground pork, or even ground shrimp; or use them instead of fresh pasta when you want to make quick ravioli.

★ TIP: Wonton wrappers can be found in the produce section of the supermarket. Be sure to check the expiration date on the package, as the prepared wrappers can turn sour if kept too long.

½ **pound ground turkey**

¾ **cup thinly sliced green onions, white and light green (from 10 to 12 whole onions)**

½ **teaspoon chopped garlic**

1 **teaspoon rice wine vinegar**

1 **teaspoon light soy sauce, plus more for passing**

½ **teaspoon freshly grated ginger**

½ **teaspoon paprika**

½ **teaspoon salt**

30 **fresh wonton wrappers ★**

6 **cups low-sodium chicken broth**

1 **head bok choy, washed, well dried, and thinly sliced crosswise**

1. In a large bowl, combine the turkey, ½ cup of the green onion, the garlic, vinegar, soy sauce, ginger, paprika, and salt. Stir just to mix; do not overblend.

2. To make the wontons: Fill a small bowl with water and place it near your work area. Line a baking sheet with parchment or waxed paper. Prepare the wontons one at a time. For each wonton, put 2 teaspoons of the filling on a wonton wrapper just off center. (Keep the remaining wrappers covered with a damp towel to prevent them from drying out.) Brush a thin film of water all around the edge of the wrapper. Fold it in half over the filling and pinch the points tightly shut. Pinch all the edges together. Hold the filled wonton with the edges facing away from you. Bring the nearest two corners toward you and pinch them together, forming the wonton into a little cap

around the filling. Place the filled wonton on the lined baking sheet. Cover the sheet with a damp cloth to prevent the wontons from drying out. Repeat with the remaining wrappers.

3. Bring the chicken broth to a boil in a wide stockpot over medium-high heat. Add the wontons. When the broth begins to boil again, simmer until the wontons float to the surface, about 3 minutes. They are cooked when they float. Add the bok choy and the remaining green onions to the soup, and simmer 1 minute more. Remove from the heat.

4. Ladle the hot broth and wontons into heated soup bowls. Pass soy sauce for seasoning.

Broiled Teriyaki Flank Steak with Soft Yellow Onions

✓ *EASY PREPARATION*

Flank steak is one of the tastiest cuts of beef there is. Here it's broiled, but you'll love it cooked on the grill, too. Just remember to cut it on a diagonal across the grain so it will be tender and juicy. For a full meal, serve with white rice.

12 ounces flank steak

¼ cup soy sauce, plus more for passing

¼ cup dry sherry

2 tablespoons light sesame oil

1 tablespoon grated fresh ginger

1 teaspoon finely chopped garlic

1 teaspoon brown sugar

½ teaspoon freshly ground pepper

3 tablespoons butter

6 cups thinly sliced yellow onions (from about 6 medium onions)

1. Adjust the broiler rack so that it is 2 inches from the heat. Preheat the broiler. Line a broiler pan with aluminum foil.

2. With a knife, slash the steak deeply on the diagonal and cut into strips 2 inches wide.

3. In a medium bowl, combine the soy sauce, sherry, sesame oil, ginger, garlic, sugar, and pepper, and add the steak to the bowl. Stir it to coat and marinate 15 minutes or longer. (If not using it within 30 minutes, refrigerate the steak in the marinade.) *

4. While the meat is marinating, melt the butter in a heavy skillet over medium-high heat. Add the onion slices to the pan and cook, tossing with a fork from time to time, until the onions are soft and golden, still translucent but not browned, about 10 minutes. Keep warm over very low heat.

5. When ready to broil, remove the steak slices from the marinade and arrange on the broiler pan. Broil, turning once and brushing occasionally with marinade, for 10 minutes total.

6. To serve, arrange steak slices on a platter and pile the onions over the steak. Pass soy sauce for seasoning, if desired.

✱TIP: To speed up dinner **prep**, mix the marinade ingredients in the morning and pour into a resealable plastic bag. Add the steak, refrigerate, and let marinate all day.

Steamed Seafood Shumai Dumplings with Sherry Dipping Sauce

✓ EASY PREPARATION   ✓ SOMETHING SPECIAL

Shumai are Japanese steamed meat- or shellfish-filled dumplings. They are perfect as appetizers or a light main course for supper. This recipe is a classic dish at my friend Douglas Dale's restaurant, Wolfdale's, in Tahoe City, California. While Wolfdale's uses rock shrimp (a small hard-shelled shrimp that tastes more like lobster than shrimp), which can be very difficult to find, we use large shrimp here. This dish can also be made with any combination of ground meats including ground turkey or even ground pork. Serve with white rice for a more filling meal.

¼ pound scallops

¼ pound jumbo (11-15 per pound) shrimp, shelled

½ pound ground chicken

2 tablespoons white and up to 2 inches dark green, thinly sliced green onion (from 2 whole onions)

2 teaspoons finely chopped garlic (2 medium cloves)

Pinch freshly ground pepper

1 teaspoon tamari ✱

1 teaspoon pickled ginger, finely chopped, plus more pickled ginger for garnish

1½ teaspoons sea salt

1 teaspoon paprika

1 teaspoon rice wine vinegar

1 package shumai or wonton skins

½ head napa cabbage or 1 bunch fresh leaf spinach

Sherry Dipping Sauce (below)

8 to 10 large fresh lettuce leaves, for garnish

Pickled ginger (optional)

1. Combine the scallops and shrimp in a small food processor and pulse to grind into a coarse paste. Do not overprocess; the mixture should have some texture.

2. In a large bowl, combine the chicken, seafood, green onions, garlic, pepper, tamari, ginger, salt, paprika, and vinegar. Stir just to mix; do not overblend. (This filling can be made the night before and refrigerated.)

3. To make the shumai dumplings: Fill a small bowl with water and place it near your work area. Linea baking sheet with parchment or waxed paper. Prepare the dumplings one at a time. For each dumpling, put 2 teaspoons of the filling on a wrapper just off center. (Keep the remaining wrappers covered with a damp towel to prevent them from drying out.) Brush a thin film of water around the edge of the wrapper. Fold the wrapper in half over the filling and pinch it shut in the middle. Pinch-pleat the edges of dumpling shut so that it looks like a little closed drawstring pouch. Place the dumpling, pleated side up, on the lined baking sheet. Cover the sheet with a damp cloth to prevent the dumplings from drying out. Repeat with the remaining wrappers.

4. Once the dumplings are completed, they can be sealed in an airtight container and refrigerated up to several hours before steaming. Steam them immediately after removing them from the refrigerator.

✱ TIP: Tamari is a soy-based sauce that is traditionally wheat free (though check the label, as some brands do include wheat). It is darker than soy sauce and used as a seasoning with, or in place of, soy sauce.

5. Just before steaming the dumplings, bring a pot of water to a boil. Put the cabbage or spinach in the pot and boil for one minute to blanch (quick-cook) the greens. Drain. Meanwhile, make the dipping sauce.

6. Then, add about 2 inches of water to a medium pot that fits a steamer basket; bring to a boil. Meanwhile, line a steamer basket with the napa cabbage or spinach leaves. ∗

7. Place the dumplings on top of the leaves, cover, and steam them over the boiling water for 10 minutes.

8. Line a platter with crisp lettuce leaves and arrange the dumplings on the leaves. Garnish with pickled ginger, if you like. Pass the dipping sauce on the side.

∗ TIP: The **layer of greens** in the steaming basket prevents the dumplings from sticking, and if the basket is bamboo, it keeps the bamboo from flavoring the delicate dumplings.

Sherry Dipping Sauce

MAKES ABOUT 2½ CUPS

✓ *EASY PREPARATION*

This is a great dipping sauce to go with Steamed Seafood Shumai Dumplings (above)—or even with store-bought sushi. I also like to use it mixed with olive oil as a salad dressing.

2 tablespoons finely chopped garlic (from 4 to 6 large cloves)

1 bunch green onions (about 5 thin), white and up to 1 inch dark green, thinly sliced (about ⅓ cup)

1 cup tamari

1 cup water

6 tablespoons fresh lemon juice (from about 3 medium lemons)

½ cup dry sherry

2 tablespoons freshly grated ginger

¼ cup sugar

Combine all of the ingredients in a medium bowl. Stored in a sealed container, the sauce will keep in the refrigerator up to 2 days.

Thai Coconut Shrimp

Sweet and crunchy, these shrimp are especially good when served with an easy-to-make dipping sauce. If you don't have time for the sauce, use a quality bottled sweet-and-sour sauce. Packaged unsweetened coconut is a good substitute for fresh coconut. Look for it in the freezer section of the supermarket because, like any fresh product, it has a short shelf life.

Sweet and Pungent Sauce (below)

4 cups (1 quart) canola oil
or peanut oil

1 cup panko bread crumbs
or plain dried bread crumbs

1½ cups unsweetened grated
or flaked fresh coconut

3 large eggs, well beaten with a whisk

1½ pounds medium (31 to 35 per
pound) shrimp, peeled, deveined,
and butterflied *

1. Prepare the sweet and pungent sauce. Then, preheat the oven to 275°F. Line a shallow baking sheet with paper towels.

2. In a heavy 3-quart saucepan, heat the oil to 365°F, or use a deep-fat fryer if you have one.

3. On a flat dish, combine the panko bread crumbs and coconut. Pour the beaten eggs into a shallow bowl.

4. Dip the shrimp in the beaten eggs and then roll them in the coconut mixture. Deep fry in batches until crisp and well browned, 3 to 4 minutes per batch. Drain and transfer to the lined baking sheet. Keep warm in the oven. Repeat

with the remaining shrimp until all are fried. *

5. Serve the shrimp hot, mounded on a heated serving platter, along with a bowl of the sweet and pungent sauce.

SERVING SUGGESTION

These shrimp also make a delightful snack with drinks. Use small shrimp (36 to 45 per pound) for this, because the larger ones may be difficult to eat as finger food.

✱TIP: Butterflying shelled **shrimp** is easy. When you slit the back of the shelled shrimp to remove the dark vein that runs the length of the shrimp, continue the cut until the shrimp are almost but not completely sliced through. Lay the shrimp cut-side down on a board and press gently to open the shrimp (into a butterfly shape).

✱TIP: Be sure the **oil** has returned to 365°F before adding another batch of shrimp to it. When the oil is too cool, the shrimp can absorb too much and become rubbery.

Sweet and Pungent Sauce

MAKES ABOUT 1 CUP SAUCE

This easy sauce is excellent for dipping Thai Coconut Shrimp (above), but it can be used whenever you might want the combination of sweet and sour for dipping or even marinating. It can easily be doubled.

¼ cup rice wine vinegar

½ cup brown sugar

1 teaspoon soy sauce

2 tablespoons Asian chile-garlic paste

¼ cup ketchup

1 teaspoon finely chopped fresh ginger

In a small saucepan, combine the vinegar, sugar, soy sauce, and

chili-garlic paste. Simmer 2 minutes. Let cool completely, and stir in the ketchup and ginger. Let stand 1 hour before serving.

126 KITCHEN COACH: WEEKNIGHT COOKING

Eastern Braised Chicken over Noodle Pillows

MAKES 6 SERVINGS

✓ EASY PREPARATION   ✓ SOMETHING SPECIAL

In this comforting dish, shredded braised chicken is mixed with fried noodle "pillows" then set into chicken broth. For a little something different, try this dish with duck, beef, or pork.

2 pounds boneless skinless chicken breast

1 tablespoon olive oil

Salt and freshly ground pepper, to taste

Noodle Pillow (below)

2 quarts low-sodium chicken broth

¼ cup lemon zest (from 2 medium lemons)

¼ cup chopped fresh ginger

¾ cup sun-dried tomatoes packed in olive oil, drained

2 tablespoons finely chopped fresh thyme

2 tablespoons finely chopped fresh rosemary

2 tablespoons tamari

2 tablespoons bottled plum or hoisin sauce

1. Preheat the oven to 450°F. Rub the chicken with olive oil and season with salt and pepper. Place the chicken on a heavy jelly-roll pan (or other roasting pan with a lip) and roast 25 minutes or until the chicken is browned and reaches a temperature of 160°F on an instant-read thermometer when inserted into the thickest part of the breast.

2. Meanwhile, prepare the noodle pillow.

3. In a stockpot or Dutch oven, stir together the remaining ingredients and bring to a simmer.

4. When the chicken is cooked, use two forks to shred the meat, then add it to the stockpot. Warm through, about 5 minutes.

5. Break up the pillow into 6 pieces and place in the bottom of each soup bowl. Ladle the braised chicken and broth on top. Serve at once.

Noodle Pillow

MAKES 6 TO 8 SERVINGS

✓ EASY PREPARATION

Frying cooked Asian noodles makes them puff up into a deliciously crispy bundle, like a pillow.

2 bags chow mein noodles (also sold as "plain Chinese noodles")

2 tablespoons sesame oil

Salt and freshly ground pepper, to taste

¼ cup thinly sliced green onions, white and up to 1 inch dark green (from about 5 thin onions)

2 tablespoons olive oil

1. Cook noodles according to package directions; drain and cool.

2. Season the noodles with the sesame oil, salt, pepper, and green onions. Heat the olive oil in a 10-inch skillet over medium-high heat. Add the noodles all at once and cook, stirring, just until they puff up and form a crisp pillow, about 1 minute. Keep whole for a serving dish presentation, or break into pieces for individual servings.

Steamed White Rice

✓ *EASY PREPARATION*

Perfectly cooked white rice is the traditional accompaniment to countless Asian dishes. Leftover rice can be used to make fried rice, stirred into soups, or even mixed with sugar, cream, and a beaten egg and baked for a quick rice pudding.

1 cup long-grain white rice

2 cups water

1. Place the rice in a colander and rinse it well. (This step is optional with most rice.)

2. Combine the rice and water in a saucepan and bring to a boil over medium-high heat. Boil, uncovered, until almost all of the liquid has evaporated and crater-like holes appear on the surface of the rice, 6 to 7 minutes.

3. Reduce the heat to low, cover the pot, and simmer about 15 minutes, until the rice is tender. Remove the rice from the heat and allow it to stand, uncovered, for 15 minutes more. Fluff the rice with a fork and serve immediately. ＊

＊TIP: If you have trouble with **rice sticking** to the bottom of the pan, cover the pot with a clean towel while it is standing after cooking. Even if a few grains have stuck, they will release.

Flavors of the Mediterranean

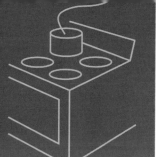

Would you like to serve a quick, flavorful, satisfying meal featuring one of the world's most favorite cuisines? In just a matter of minutes you can put together recipes such as Lemon Roasted Chicken or Fresh Tuna with Sage and White Bean Salad.

There are many pleasures associated with foods from the countries surrounding the world's largest inland sea—including the cuisines of Italy, Greece, Spain, Morocco, Tunisia, coastal France, and other neighboring countries. The aromas and flavors of the foods from this bountiful area are unforgettably enticing. And we have become more and more aware of what Mediterranean people have known for hundreds (even thousands) of years—good-tasting, hearty food can be economical and easy to prepare, and exceptionally good for us.

Mediterranean cooking means different things to different people, but it usually makes us think of the glistening sea, sunny locales, and freshly prepared, sometimes exotic, foods. The dishes are often either lightly cooked or slow-cooked—both methods maximize flavor. The foods are often freshly prepared, which helps maintain nutrients in addition to featuring the ingredients at their peak. The recipes are usually lower in saturated fats and higher in complex carbohydrates than most cuisines, with the focus on vegetables, fruits, and grains, rather than red meat. Olive oil in the dishes and wine drunk with the meals also contribute to the people of the Mediterranean living long healthy lives.

Nurtured by the gentle climate in the Mediterranean, the dishes are heavily influenced by local vegetables. Onions, garlic, and tomatoes are important parts of many of the dishes. Eggplant, squash, zucchini, artichokes, and greens are seen in most of the cuisine. Beans, lentils, and chickpeas abound. Fresh herbs flourish, including rosemary, thyme, basil, and oregano.

The Mediterranean diet also includes an abundance of fish, which may be served alone or in stews, soups, and pastas. Anchovies, fresh and cured, are widely eaten, as are various white-fleshed fish like sole, flounder, and grouper. Other seafood served in this region include swordfish, monkfish, squid, and octopus.

Small animals like lamb, goat, sheep, pig (for pork), rabbit, and domestic fowl account for most of the meat. Sheep and goats also provide milk for rich yogurts and cheeses. Beef is rarely featured in Mediterranean cuisines, because there is not enough grazing land in these countries to support herds of cattle.

Whenever I need a little inspiration in my kitchen, even without visiting these countries, I can go "on vacation" by cooking a little Mediterranean. It adds some special excitement to dinner. Try it!

Grilled Portobello Stacks

✓ *EASY PREPARATION*

This perfect weeknight hearty-but-healthful main dish is also excellent as a weekend lunch entrée, or a first course for entertaining. The meaty texture of the mushrooms makes it a surprisingly satisfying combination.

8 medium portobello caps

4 medium red bell peppers, stemmed, halved, and seeded

1 small red onion, cut across into 4 thick slices

2 tablespoons olive oil

1/2 pound fresh mozzarella cheese, cut into 4 slices

1 tablespoon dried Italian herbs

Salt and freshly ground pepper, to taste

Extra-virgin olive oil for drizzling

1. Preheat the grill on medium-high 10 to 15 minutes.

2. Brush the mushrooms, peppers, and onion slices with the 2 tablespoons olive oil. Cook on the grill until tender and slightly charred, turning each piece only once, 8 to 9 minutes total. Remove from the grill and set out on the work surface.

3. Place 1/2 pepper on each of 4 portobello caps. Top with 1 grilled onion slice and 1 slice of cheese. Sprinkle the stacks with dried herbs, and season with salt and

pepper. Finish each stack with 1/2 pepper and a mushroom cap.

4. Arrange the stacks on a vegetable grilling screen and return to the grill. Close the grill and roast the stacks about 5 minutes, until the cheese begins to melt. Drizzle with a little extra-virgin olive oil and serve hot or warm.

SERVING SUGGESTION

Before drizzling with the olive oil, arrange a few baby greens on each serving plate. Set one stack on each, drizzle with the oil, and serve.

Panzanella

✓ *EASY PREPARATION*   ✓ *SOMETHING SPECIAL*

In Italy, there are almost as many ways to make *panzanella*—refreshing and flavorful Italian bread salad—as there are cooks who prepare it. This is the hearty version I make most often at home, with a delicious blend of tomatoes, olives, and white beans, and good bread to soak up the juices. It makes one of the star attractions for an outdoor menu.

3 medium very ripe tomatoes, chopped into large pieces

1 cup very thinly sliced red onion (from about ½ medium onion)

1 cup canned cannelini beans, rinsed and drained

2 teaspoons finely chopped garlic (from 2 medium cloves)

4 ounces black brine- or oil-cured olives

3 tablespoons chopped fresh oregano

1 tablespoon white wine vinegar

⅓ to ½ cup extra-virgin olive oil, and more if needed

6 cups day-old crusty Italian or French bread cubes, crust on

¼ cup cold water

½ cup fresh basil leaves

Salt and freshly ground pepper, to taste

1. In a large bowl, toss together the tomatoes, onion, beans, garlic, and olives. Sprinkle with the oregano. Add the vinegar and 3 tablespoons olive oil. Let the mixture stand at room temperature for 1 hour to develop the flavors, and to render the juice from the tomatoes.

2. Pile the bread cubes in a large serving bowl and sprinkle with the cold water. Toss. *

3. Pour the tomato mixture over the bread, add the basil, and toss to mix well. Drizzle with the remaining olive oil and a little more if the salad seems too dry, and season well with salt and pepper.

SERVING SUGGESTION

For an easy alfresco supper, serve the salad in a big bowl with a platter of thinly sliced smoked ham, Genoa salami, and Italian cheeses, and a big loaf of crusty bread and some butter. Pass vinegar and extra olive oil on the side in case anyone wants more for the salad.

*TIP: If the **bread** is very stale and dry, drizzle with enough water to fully moisten all the cubes. Then squeeze out and discard any excess water. You can do this with your hands, or wrap all the moistened bread in a towel, roll it up, and squeeze.

Grilled Snapper with Pine Nuts and Olive Oil

✓ *EASY PREPARATION*   ✓ *SOMETHING SPECIAL*

Many of the fresh flavors of the Mediterranean are featured in this dish. The simple combination of red snapper, garlic, olive oil, and lemon juice will both refresh and satisfy you. Remember, when you are using only a few ingredients, as in this recipe, everything should be really fresh.

2½ pounds red snapper fillets

½ cup olive oil

Salt and freshly ground pepper, to taste

⅓ cup pine nuts

2 teaspoons finely chopped garlic (about 2 medium cloves)

¼ cup chopped fresh Italian flat-leaf parsley

1 tablespoon fresh lemon juice or dry white wine

1. Preheat the grill or grill pan on high heat for 10 to 15 minutes, then lower to medium-high heat.

2. Brush the snapper fillets with some of the oil and season on both sides with salt and pepper.

3. Grill the fillets, skin side down, over medium-high heat until the skin is crisp and browned, 4 to 5 minutes. Turn and grill 3 to 4 minutes more. ✱

4. While the fish is grilling, heat ¼ cup of the olive oil in a small skillet. Add the pine nuts and cook, tossing, until golden, 2 to 3 minutes. Stir in the garlic, and

cook 1 minute more. Add the parsley and lemon juice or wine. Cook 1 minute.

5. Remove the snapper fillets from the grill and arrange on a heated platter. Spoon the pine nut mixture over the fillets. Serve hot.

SERVING SUGGESTIONS

Serve pasta mixed with an oil-based sauce such as pesto alongside the fish, or serve freshly steamed rice and a tossed green salad.

✱ TIP: Try laying **sprigs of fresh rosemary** on the coals or grill grate just before putting the snapper fillets on the grill. The delicious aroma of the grilling herb adds just a hint of Provence to the finished dish.

Grilled Tuna with Sage and White Bean Salad

✓ *TAKE-ALONG*   ✓ *SOMETHING SPECIAL*

You can serve the tuna hot from the grill or warm over the room-temperature salad. Use a grill pan if the weather doesn't invite you outside to cook on the grill.

White Bean Salad (below)

2 teaspoons chopped fresh sage, plus more whole leaves for garnish

3 tablespoons chopped fresh Italian flat-leaf parsley

¼ teaspoon salt

¼ teaspoon freshly ground pepper

Six 6-ounce tuna steaks, each at least 1 inch thick

1. Prepare the bean salad. Then, preheat the grill or grill pan on medium-high 10 to 15 minutes.

2. In a small bowl, combine the chopped sage, parsley, salt, and pepper. Rub the mix all over the tuna steaks, and set aside for several minutes.

3. Grill the steaks over medium-high heat 5 to 6 minutes on each side, a little longer if you don't like tuna pink in the middle.

4. Slice the tuna steaks and arrange atop a bed of the bean salad on individual dinner plates. Garnish with whole sage leaves.

White Bean Salad

MAKES 6 SERVINGS

✓ *EASY PREPARATION*

This is one of those dishes that tastes great right after it is made, but it is even better the next day. When refrigerated overnight, the flavors develop and intensify. If you have the opportunity to plan ahead, make it the night before—dinner will be on the table even faster.

2 cups very thinly sliced red onion (from 1 medium onion)

Two 15-ounce cans cannellini or navy beans, well rinsed and drained

2 cups halved seeded and diced ripe tomatoes (from 2 medium tomatoes) *

¼ cup chopped fresh sage

2 teaspoons red wine vinegar

1 teaspoon Dijon mustard

Salt and freshly ground pepper, to taste

⅓ cup extra-virgin olive oil

½ cup crumbled feta cheese (2 ounces)

1. In a medium bowl, combine the onion, beans, tomatoes, and sage.

2. In a smaller bowl, beat together the vinegar, mustard, salt, and pepper. Add the olive oil in a slow stream, whisking constantly, until the dressing thickens. Pour the dressing over the bean mixture and toss to combine. Gently toss in the feta cheese. Serve immediately or refrigerate for 1 hour or up to overnight.

SERVING SUGGESTION

For a slightly heartier side salad, toss in 3 cups washed and dried baby greens or mesclun just before serving.

*TIP: Seeding tomatoes is easier than you think. Simply slice them in half across the middle, and gently squeeze the halves over the sink or a bowl. The seeds and some juice will fall out, leaving the solid flesh behind. The halves are ready to fill, slice, or chop.

Lemon Roasted Chicken

✓ *EASY PREPARATION*

If the mark of an excellent cook is a perfectly roasted chicken—as some have said—once you have made this, you can tell your family that they are in the presence of greatness. When they taste it, they will agree! While it takes longer than 30 minutes to cook, it requires little of your attention and is well worth the extra time—even for a weeknight.

The tang of lemon brings out the flavor of even supermarket chicken, but for best flavor, make this with a free-range bird. If you like, you can accentuate the Greek flavor of this dish by putting several sprigs of fresh oregano in the cavity of the chicken with the lemons before putting it in the oven.

¼ cup olive oil

1 teaspoon dried oregano

1 teaspoon chopped fresh rosemary

Salt and freshly ground pepper, to taste

3½-pound frying chicken

3 lemons, washed and quartered

6 cloves garlic, peeled

4 to 6 fresh oregano sprigs (optional)

1. Preheat the oven to 425°F.

2. In a small bowl, combine the oil, dried oregano, rosemary, salt, and pepper.

3. Brush the chicken all over with the flavored oil. Put 4 lemon quarters inside the cavity of the chicken. Set the chicken in a small roasting pan and scatter the garlic cloves and remaining lemon quarters around it.

4. Roast the chicken in the oven, basting with the pan juices once or twice, for 45 to 50 minutes, until the skin is crisp and the chicken reaches a temperature of 160°F on an instant-read thermometer when inserted into the thickest part of the breast. Remove the chicken from the oven and set aside, keeping it warm. ✱

5. Pour the juices out of the roasting pan, pressing the lemons before discarding them to remove as much juice as possible, and crushing the garlic into a paste. Spoon off all but 2 tablespoons of the fat that floats on top. Boil the defatted pan juices in a small saucepan until reduced by one third, about 5 minutes. Taste the sauce and add salt and pepper, if needed.

6. Cut the chicken into serving pieces. Serve warm, with the sauce on the side, and garnished with oregano.

Serving Suggestion

Accompany this perfect roast chicken with White Bean Salad (page 133).

✱ **TIP:** When **poultry** is fully cooked, the juice that runs out when you stick a sharp fork into the meaty part of one of the thighs should no longer have any tinge of pink in it; it should be clear and straw colored. (Confirm doneness with a thermometer, but avoid touching the bone, which can distort the reading.)

Comfort Food

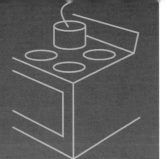

The kitchen can be a haven for a stressed and weary family, the place where you can relax and focus on the simple tasks of putting together dinner. When the sounds and smells from the kitchen waft into other rooms, your spouse or children may join you to see what's going on, to steal a taste, or possibly even to help. This can be a great opportunity for impromptu conversations about nothing in particular, or even something important.

Sometimes, though, you or someone else in your family needs something more tangibly soothing. That's when you make comfort food, food that is so simple, hearty, and satisfying, it can't help but make you happy. For inspiration, I often turn to my grandmother, who was a simple cook with a repertoire of seven dishes. Not a lot of variety, but they were practiced, perfected, and made with love.

Comfort foods usually share two qualities—they are nourishing and satisfying. They are foods we often crave in moments of sadness, or in moments of celebration. Comfort foods are the dishes we automatically think of when we want to relish the flavors from a special time in the past.

The textures and flavors of many comfort foods make them particularly appealing. The creamy, filling deliciousness of macaroni and cheese or buttery mashed potatoes make them two perennial favorites. Many people think of chicken soup as their first-choice comfort food, particularly to help counter illness. Others think of the anytime-anywhere favorite grilled cheese sandwiches, or the smooth, rich flavor of cream of tomato soup. I include all these dishes here, with some variations in case you make the dishes so often that you want a little change.

Try to build a pantry that includes ingredients for the comfort foods you and your family crave. Have pre-made chicken broth, pasta and noodles, frozen vegetables, ground meat, potatoes, cheese, and canned tomatoes in your pantry. That way you can easily take the chill off a cold night or help everyone de-stress from a busy day without a big trip to the store. This is prime feel-good food.

Spaghetti and Meatballs

✓ *MAKE-AHEAD*

What could be more satisfying than an old-fashioned plate of spaghetti and meatballs? My spicy version, modified over the years from the classic that my grandmother served, tastes like you were in the kitchen all day, but it really takes less than an hour.

★TIP: You can form the **meatballs** with clean hands or use a 1-inch ice cream scoop to make them more quickly and uniform in size. Pack the meat mixture firmly into the scoop so the meatballs will not fall apart while cooking.

MEATBALLS

1 pound ground beef chuck

1 tablespoon paprika

1/2 teaspoon cayenne pepper

1/2 teaspoon freshly ground pepper

4 tablespoons finely chopped fresh Italian flat-leaf parsley

1 teaspoon salt

3/4 cup finely chopped onion (from 1 small onion)

1 large egg, slightly beaten

2 tablespoons olive oil or peanut oil

TOMATO SAUCE

2 cups canned plum (Roma) tomatoes

2 tablespoons olive oil

2 cups chopped yellow onion (from 2 medium onions)

4 teaspoons finely chopped garlic (from 4 medium cloves)

2 teaspoons ground cumin

Pinch cayenne pepper

1/2 teaspoon freshly ground pepper, or to taste

1/2 cup chopped fresh Italian flat-leaf parsley

1/2 teaspoon dried oregano

1/2 teaspoon dried thyme

1 cup canned tomato puree (from 8-ounce can)

1 pound spaghetti

1 cup freshly grated Parmigiano-Reggiano cheese, for garnish and serving (4 ounces)

1. In a large bowl, combine the beef, paprika, cayenne, pepper, parsley, salt, onion, and egg. Using your hands, mix everything together thoroughly, but don't overwork it. Form into balls 1 inch in diameter. ★

2. Heat the oil in a large frying pan over high heat. Add the meatballs and brown on all sides, turning carefully so they do not fall apart, 8 to 10 minutes. Drain on paper towels.

3. To prepare the sauce, put the tomatoes with some of their juice in the bowl of a food processor fitted with the metal blade and process until finely chopped, but not pureed smooth. Set aside.

4. Heat the oil in a large, heavy, straight-sided skillet over medium-low heat. Add the onions and cook, stirring frequently, until tender and translucent, about 10 minutes. Add the garlic, cumin, cayenne, black pepper, parsley, oregano, and thyme, and cook, stirring, for 5 minutes more. Add the browned meatballs, the chopped tomatoes, and the tomato puree and cook for 15 minutes more.

5. While the meatballs and sauce are simmering, cook the spaghetti in 6 quarts of boiling salted water until the pasta is al dente, 6 to 9 minutes. Drain.

6. Add a small amount of sauce to moisten the spaghetti, and turn it out onto a deep serving platter. Pour the meatballs and remaining sauce down the center of the pasta, garnish with Parmigiano-Reggiano cheese, and serve hot. Pass more cheese at the table.

Quick Macaroni and Cheese

✓ *EASY PREPARATION*

This is the real, rich, old-fashioned mac-n-cheese, which can serve as a full comfort meal when accompanied by a simple green salad. It takes a bit longer than 30 minutes, but it's really worth the extra time. Children will eat it hot, warm, or even cold, and it isn't unheard of for second and even third helpings to disappear. I like to serve it alongside Cajun Meatloaf Patties (page 117).

★TIP: Undercook the pasta slightly so the finished dish will not feature mushy macaroni.

8 tablespoons butter, with 2 of the tablespoons melted (½ cup) – plus more for buttering the casserole

1 pound elbow macaroni

6 slices French (baguette) bread, crusts removed, torn into ¼-inch pieces like large bread crumbs

5½ cups whole milk

½ cup all-purpose flour

2 teaspoons salt

¼ teaspoon freshly ground pepper

¼ teaspoon nutmeg

¼ teaspoon cayenne pepper

4 cups grated medium-sharp cheddar cheese (from 1 pound)

2 cups grated Gruyère cheese (from 8 ounces)

1. Preheat the oven to 350°F. Generously butter a 4-quart oven-proof casserole. Set aside.

2. Cook the macaroni in 6 quarts of boiling salted water until the pasta is still slightly underdone and resists a little when bitten, 4 to 5 minutes. ★

3. Drain the macaroni in a large colander and rinse with cold water. Set aside.

4. Place the torn bread in a small bowl. Pour the melted butter over the bread and toss to coat.

5. Heat the milk in a medium saucepan, just until bubbles begin to form around the edges. Remove from the heat. Melt 6 tablespoons butter in a medium saucepan. Stir in the flour and cook, stirring constantly, for 1 minute. Slowly add all the hot milk, whisking all the time. Simmer, whisking, until the mixture is bubbling and thickened, about 3 minutes.

6. Remove the pan from the heat and season with the salt, pepper, nutmeg, and cayenne. Add 3 cups of the cheddar cheese and 1 cup of the Gruyère. Stir the mixture with a wooden spoon until the cheese is melted, and the sauce is smooth and golden yellow.

7. Combine the drained macaroni with the cheese sauce in a large bowl. Pour the mixture into the prepared casserole dish.

8. Spread the remaining cheese over the top of the macaroni, and sprinkle all with the buttered bread crumbs. Bake 30 minutes until heated through, bubbling, and golden brown on top.

9. Remove from the oven, let cool 5 minutes, then serve very hot.

SERVING SUGGESTION

Try baking the macaroni and cheese in 6-ounce ramekins for 20 to 25 minutes, giving everyone her or his own individual serving. This method also makes it easy to reserve for the late-arriving spouse or child who can just reheat it in the microwave.

Fried Buttermilk Chicken Drumettes

✓ *EASY PREPARATION*   ✓ *MAKE-AHEAD*   ✓ *TAKE-ALONG*

Of all the familiar dishes we make, fried chicken seems to be the one that is the biggest hit with people, no matter their age, nationality, or upbringing. Nearly everyone loves it—openly or secretly. It was definitely one of my favorite dishes that my mom made for us when we were children. She learned how to make it from her grandmother.

When I make it, I use chicken drumettes, the little upper wing joints that are available in large quantities in the supermarket. Then there are no fights over who gets what piece when the platter comes to the table.

✱ TIP: The secret to **perfectly crisp fried chicken** or anything deep fried is to allow the oil to reach the correct temperature before you add the food. Make sure that the oil comes back to the correct temperature before adding a new batch. The frying chicken or other food will absorb far more oil if it is not hot enough.

6 cups buttermilk (1½ quarts)

3 pounds chicken drumettes, rinsed and patted dry

3 cups all-purpose flour

1 tablespoon salt

1 tablespoon freshly ground pepper, or to taste

2 teaspoons cayenne pepper

1 tablespoon paprika

2 pounds vegetable shortening or 3 cups vegetable oil

1. Place the buttermilk in a large bowl with the chicken. Cover the bowl with plastic wrap. Let stand 15 minutes or longer. Drain when ready to cook.

2. In a large resealable plastic bag, combine the flour, salt, pepper, cayenne, and paprika. Shake the bag to combine.

3. Add the chicken to the bag of seasoned flour, 5 or 6 pieces at a time. Place the breaded chicken on a cookie sheet. Line another cookie sheet with paper towels and place a cooling rack on top of it.

4. Heat the vegetable shortening or oil in a skillet to 375°F on a frying thermometer. Use a pair of tongs and add the chicken to the hot fat, a few pieces at a time. Fry the chicken, turning it regularly to brown it on all sides, until dark golden brown, about 5 minutes. ✱

5. Remove the chicken from the oil and drain it on the cooling rack. Serve hot or at room temperature.

SERVING SUGGESTION

Pile the drumettes in a napkin-lined basket and serve with a mixed green salad with Simple Mustard Vinaigrette (page 16) alongside. This is a perfect meal for taking on a park picnic, an evening boat ride, a twilight trip to the beach, or any outdoor dinner occasions.

Quick-and-Easy Shepherd's Pie

✓ *MAKE-AHEAD* ✓ *TAKE-ALONG*

This wonderful layered dish of roasted meat and vegetables is popular with just about everyone. If you are going to be in a rush at dinnertime, put the shepherd's pie together in the morning (or even the night before), cover, and refrigerate until ready to bake. Put it in a cold oven so the dish heats up with the oven. If you like, try it the classic way with ground lamb.

1½ pounds Yukon Gold potatoes, peeled and cut into ½-inch pieces (about 4 cups cubed potato)

1 tablespoon olive oil

1¼ cups finely chopped white onion (from 1 large)

½ cup seeded deveined and finely chopped green bell pepper (from ½ small)

1 teaspoon finely chopped garlic

¼ cup finely chopped carrot

1 pound lean ground beef

1 teaspoon salt, plus more to taste

¼ teaspoon freshly ground pepper, or to taste, plus more to taste

One 14-ounce can Italian-style diced tomatoes, including liquid

1 tablespoon butter

½ cup whole milk

1. Preheat the oven to 375°F. Add the potatoes to a medium saucepan and cover with salted water. Bring to a boil and simmer until tender, 10 to 12 minutes.

2. Heat the olive oil in a large, heavy skillet. Add the onion and green pepper and cook, stirring, until the onion is transparent, about 5 minutes. Add the garlic and carrot and cook, stirring, 1 minute more. Stir in the ground beef, breaking up any large pieces. Cook, stirring, until browned, about 4 minutes more.

3. Pour off the excess grease. Season with salt and pepper. Pour in the tomatoes and mix well. Pour the beef mixture into a 1½-quart baking dish. Set aside. *

4. Drain the potatoes and put through a ricer, or mash well. Beat in the butter and milk and season well with salt and pepper. Spread the mashed potatoes over the beef mixture in the baking dish. Bake for 30 minutes. Serve hot, right out of the baking dish.

SERVING SUGGESTION

Set aside a portion or two in microwavable containers for late-arrivers to reheat.

*TIP: For a truly **speedy-fix version**, try using 3 to 4 cups of your favorite chili with beans in place of the seasoned beef mixture. Cover with mashed potatoes (homemade or from the refrigerated case of the grocery) and bake as usual. I make a big batch of chili and freeze it in 1-quart portions. One portion would be perfect.

Pepperoni Bread

✓ *SOMETHING SPECIAL*

While this bread is perfect as an accompaniment to meatballs and spaghetti or other Italian dishes, it has many other uses. Serve it sliced thin and lightly toasted as a snack along with a glass of crisp chilled white wine. It is also delicious for breakfast or brunch with eggs of any kind. If you would like to turn this into pizza bread, spread each piece of dough with ¼ cup pizza sauce before adding the pepperoni. Add more mozzarella if you like.

1 tablespoon olive oil

One 3-pound package frozen bread dough, thawed

½ pound pepperoni, thinly sliced, or use packaged presliced pepperoni

4 cups grated mozzarella (from 1 pound)

1 tablespoon garlic powder

1 teaspoon dried basil

1 teaspoon dried oregano

1 teaspoon dried red pepper flakes

½ cup grated Parmigiano-Reggiano cheese (2 ounces)

Salt and freshly ground pepper, to taste

1 large egg, beaten lightly with a fork

1 teaspoon sesame seeds, toasted

1. Preheat the oven to 400°F.

2. Brush three 11- × 17-inch baking sheets with olive oil. Divide the dough into 3 pieces. ✱

3. Roll 1 piece of dough out to edges of 1 prepared sheet. ✱

4. Place ⅓ of the pepperoni slices on the dough, leaving a ½-inch border at the edges. Sprinkle with ⅓ of the mozzarella cheese, garlic, basil, oregano, and dried red pepper flakes. Top with ⅓ of the Parmigiano-Reggiano cheese. Season with salt and pepper.

5. Starting at the long end, roll up the dough in a jellyroll fashion, pinching the seam to hold it closed. Then turn, seam side down, on the baking sheet. Brush with the egg. Slash shallow crosswise slits in the top of the loaf. Sprinkle with sesame seeds. Repeat the procedure with the second and third loaves.

6. Bake the loaves about 25 minutes, until golden brown. Let cool for 15 minutes. Cut into thick slices and serve.

SERVING SUGGESTION

Line a basket with a colorful dish towel and pile the bread slices inside. Cover to keep warm and pass throughout the meal.

✱ TIP: When using **frozen dough**, thaw it completely and then let it relax for 20 minutes before rolling it out so it will be easier to handle.

✱ TIP: To **roll out the dough**, first use your hands to flatten one piece into a large rectangle. Then, beginning in the middle of the flattened dough, use a rolling pin to roll the dough out toward the edges in all directions, maintaining the shape. If the dough shrinks a little, just wait a minute for the dough to relax again, and then continue.

No-Meat Nights

There are a lot of trendy diets out there but medical research still shows that your health can be compromised by eating cholesterol-rich foods (meat is a big culprit), and can be helped with the benefits of eating a high-fiber and nutrient-rich diet. Vegetables, grains, and beans fit the bill—they are high in fiber and, depending on the way you prepare them, can be cholesterol-free. When most grains and beans are eaten together they provide a complete dietary protein.

Some people become vegetarians and give up eating meat all the time, as a way of life. I haven't and you don't have to, either. As I do, you can easily incorporate healthful, satisfying, and delicious meatless dishes into your meals for variety and for nutritional balance in what you eat.

When cooking vegetarian meals, make sure that you are using fresh vegetables and quality beans, grains, and seasonings, so that you and your family won't feel you are sacrificing flavor to be "healthy." Supermarkets are dedicating more and more space to a wider range of produce and grains. If you can't find what you want in supermarkets, natural food stores and ethnic food stores, now more and more accessible across the country, are fully stocked with an amazing variety of foods for vegetarian cooking—from spices and condiments to fruits and vegetables to tofu and soy-based products. Use the recipes in this section to make complete vegetarian meals or simply to bring new variety to non-vegetarian menus.

Stir-Fried Vegetables with Tofu

✓ *EASY PREPARATION*

I have served this to many people ranging from age 7 to 70. Everyone always enjoys it! The high heat and quick cooking of stir-frying results in crisply tender, succulent vegetables. By marinating the tofu in the same ingredients as a traditional teriyaki marinade, the tofu takes on a wonderful flavor. Serve it with a bowl of steaming hot rice to absorb the sauce.

¼ cup low-sodium soy sauce

3 tablespoons dry sherry or rice wine

1 tablespoon cornstarch

1 package extra-firm tofu, well drained and cut into ½-inch cubes

3 tablespoons olive oil

1 teaspoon freshly grated ginger ✶

1 cup chopped white onion (from 1 medium)

2 cups stemmed seeded deveined and thinly sliced red bell pepper (from 1 medium pepper)

1 pound frozen green beans, run under hot water to thaw

1 cup low-sodium vegetable broth

¾ cup cashews, toasted (about 3 ounces)

1 teaspoon orange zest

1. In a large bowl, whisk together the soy sauce, sherry, and cornstarch. Add the tofu and mix gently to coat well.

2. Heat 2 tablespoons of the olive oil in a wok or large, heavy skillet over medium-high heat. When the oil is hot, add the ginger. Using a slotted spoon, remove the tofu from the marinade; set the marinade aside. Add the tofu to the pan with the ginger, raise the heat to high, and cook, stir-frying, until it is heated through, about 3 minutes. Transfer the tofu to a plate and set it aside.

3. Reduce the heat to medium and add 1 tablespoon of olive oil. Add the onion to the pan and cook, stirring, until the onion is soft and transparent, 5 to 6 minutes. Add the red bell pepper and cook, continuing to stir, until soft, 5 to 6 minutes more. Return the tofu to the pan and then add the green beans, reserved marinade, and broth. Stir the mixture constantly until it boils and thickens, 3 to 4 minutes more.

4. Remove the pan from the heat and add the cashews and the zest. Transfer to a serving dish and serve hot.

✶TIP: To preserve **ginger** you're not using right away, wrap it securely in plastic wrap and freeze it. It will then be instantly available for future use; it grates more easily when it is frozen, too.

Mozzarella in Carozza

✓ *EASY PREPARATION*

This delicious fried sandwich is made with thick, creamy slices of fresh mozzarella cheese, a mild cheese that is perfectly accented by the flavor of the garlic oil. The sandwich name means mozzarella in a carriage because of the way the bread and batter (deliciously) envelopes the cheese. The recipe can be easily doubled or tripled for a crowd.

8 thick slices white bread, crusts trimmed

4 thick slices mozzarella cheese, cut to fit the bread

1 cup all-purpose flour

2 large eggs, beaten lightly with a fork

2 tablespoons unsalted butter ✶

2 tablespoons olive oil

1 teaspoon finely chopped garlic

2 tablespoons finely chopped fresh Italian flat-leaf parsley

1. Preheat the oven to 225°F. Make 4 sandwiches with bread and cheese. Cut each sandwich in half across, not on the diagonal. Spread the flour on a flat plate and pour the beaten egg into a shallow bowl. Dip the sandwiches in flour, then in egg, then in flour again, shaking the sandwiches at each step to remove excess.

2. Heat the butter and oil in a large, heavy skillet big enough to hold all the sandwiches. Fry the sandwiches over medium heat on both sides until browned and crisp, about 2 minutes per side. Place them on paper towels as they come out of the fry pan to drain off excess fat.

3. Arrange 2 sandwich halves on each of 4 heated plates. Keep warm in the oven.

4. Add the garlic to the skillet and stir in a little more butter or olive oil, if necessary. Stir in the parsley and cook, stirring, until the garlic is lightly golden and the sauce is heated through, 3 to 4 minutes.

5. Drizzle the sauce over the sandwiches and serve very hot. ✶

SERVING SUGGESTION

For a non-vegetarian meal, add 2 tablespoons finely chopped anchovy fillets to the skillet with the garlic in Step 4 and cook until the anchovies are melted, about 5 minutes.

✶ **TIP:** Butter is a great cooking medium for fried sandwiches. The butter imparts rich flavor that no other oil or fat can. The addition of the oil to the butter in the skillet raises the burning point of the butter higher so it will reduce the chance it will burn during frying.

✶ **TIP:** If you are making a lot of these sandwiches, blot them on paper towels, then put them on a cookie sheet in the oven to keep them warm until serving.

Mushroom Tart

✓ SOMETHING SPECIAL   ✓ TAKE-ALONG

This is a recipe that is so good people won't think of it as vegetarian; it's just a delicious dish that doesn't have any meat or fish in it. Similar to a quiche, this mushroom-filled pastry tart is lightened by the addition of eggs and cream. Season very well to bring out all the flavor of the fresh mushrooms. Baking a pastry crust ahead of time (baking blind) keeps the filling from making the crust soggy.

Pastry for a 1-crust pie, frozen or refrigerated

½ cup half and half

2 large eggs, beaten lightly with a fork

2 tablespoons butter

1 large leek, well washed, white and light green parts very thinly sliced (about ½ cup)

1 pound mixed fresh mushrooms, such as cremini, portobello, shiitake, or porcini, wiped or rinsed clean, stems trimmed, caps thinly sliced (about 5 cups)

1 teaspoon finely chopped garlic (from 1 medium clove), or more to taste

1 teaspoon medium-hot curry powder, or more, to taste

Salt and freshly ground pepper, to taste

6 to 8 drops Tabasco

½ cup shredded Gruyère cheese (from 2 ounces)

1. Preheat the oven to 375°F. Blind-bake the pie crust: line the pastry-filled pie plate with parchment paper or foil. Fill with pastry weights, rice, or dried beans. Bake for 8 minutes. Remove from the oven and cool.

2. Raise the oven temperature to 400°F. In a small bowl, use a fork to beat together the half and half and the eggs.

3. Melt the butter in a heavy skillet. Cook the leek and mushrooms, stirring from time to time, over medium-low heat until tender, about 5 minutes. Stir in the garlic and curry powder. Cook 1 minute more. Season well with salt and pepper and stir lightly. Add the Tabasco and stir to blend.

4. Spread the mushroom mixture in the prepared pastry shell. Pour the egg and cream mixture over the mushrooms. Sprinkle with the Gruyère. *

5. Bake 25 to 30 minutes, until the tart is puffed and golden brown, and a knife inserted in the center comes out clean.

6. Remove from the oven; transfer to a cooling rack; let cool slightly. Cut the tart into large wedges and serve.

＊TIP: To ensure that you don't spill any filling, you can set the pie crust plate filled with mushrooms on a cookie sheet, then place it on an extended oven shelf. Pour in the cream and egg mixture and sprinkle with cheese. Carefully push the shelf back in (watch the hot oven). This trick works with quiches and custard tarts, too.

Harvest Vegetable Curry

✓ *SOMETHING SPECIAL*

I make this vegetable dish often, and serve it with a salad. The curry is made in the same pan with the vegetables for less work. For added flavor, roast the cauliflower in the oven before adding it to the pan.

1 pound tiny new potatoes

3 tablespoons olive oil

Salt and freshly ground pepper, to taste

1 tablespoon grated fresh ginger

1 teaspoon finely chopped garlic

1 teaspoon fennel seeds

2 teaspoons ground cumin

1/4 teaspoon cayenne pepper

1/2 teaspoon ground turmeric

3 cups cauliflower florets (about 1 small head)

4 tablespoons spring water (1/4 cup)

10 ounces frozen petite peas

1/2 pint (1 cup) plain low-fat yogurt

1. Preheat the oven to 425°F.

2. Scrub the potatoes, but do not peel. If the potatoes are not small enough (1 inch in diameter or less) to cook whole in 15 to 20 minutes, cut into halves or quarters. Place the potatoes in a small roasting pan; rub them with 1 tablespoon olive oil and season with salt and pepper. Roast in the oven about 20 minutes, until tender.

3. Heat the remaining oil over medium heat in a heavy, straight-sided skillet large enough to hold all the vegetables. Add the ginger, garlic, fennel, cumin, cayenne, and turmeric. Cook, stirring, for about 30 seconds. ∗

4. Stir in the cauliflower and the water. Mix thoroughly to coat the cauliflower with the spice mixture. Cover, reduce the heat to low, and cook about 5 minutes, until the cauliflower is almost tender. Stir in the peas and turn off the heat.

5. When the potatoes are tender, remove them from the oven. If they are not already quartered or halved, cut them into pieces and add to the skillet with the vegetables. Stir thoroughly to coat the vegetables with the spices and cook over medium heat just long enough to cook the peas, 2 to 3 minutes. Stir in the yogurt and heat through.

6. Spoon the curry into a large heated serving bowl. Serve hot.

SERVING SUGGESTION

Serve with freshly steamed rice and a bowl of store-bought mango chutney on the side. Hot naan bread—sold in Indian markets and some well-stocked supermarkets—is wonderful with this, but eight-inch flour tortillas work well, too. Heat them in the oven, then serve in a napkin-lined basket.

∗ TIP: To enhance the flavor of **curry powder** or other spices, heat them either in a dry skillet or in a little oil or other fat just until you can smell their special aromas. This takes only a minute or two.

Tomato-Eggplant Parmigiano

✓ MAKE-AHEAD   ✓ SOMETHING SPECIAL

Although this recipe takes about 40 minutes to cook—maybe longer than you like to spend cooking on a weeknight—it is a rich and satisfying dish and a wonderful change of pace from the standard Eggplant Parmigiano.

2 tablespoons olive oil, plus 2 tablespoons for drizzling (¼ cup total)

2 large eggplants, cut into ¼-inch rounds

Two 28-ounce cans Italian tomatoes, chopped

2 cups freshly chopped basil leaves

½ cup red wine

1 teaspoon salt, plus more to taste (optional) for sprinkling

1 teaspoon freshly ground pepper, or to taste

1 teaspoon sugar

2½ cups grated fresh mozzarella cheese (from 10 ounces)

1½ cups grated Parmigiano-Reggiano (from 6 ounces)

1. Preheat the oven to 350°F. Brush a baking sheet with 1 teaspoon olive oil and spread the eggplant slices on the baking sheet. Brush the eggplant with oil and place in the oven. Bake the eggplant for 20 minutes until soft.

2. In the meantime, in a large skillet combine the tomatoes, basil, wine, salt, pepper, and sugar. Simmer the sauce until thickened, about 20 minutes.

3. Next, cover the bottom of a 9- × 9-inch baking dish with one-quarter of the tomato sauce. Follow by arranging half the eggplant slices in the bottom of the dish. Spoon one-quarter of the sauce on top of the eggplant. Sprinkle with half of the cheeses and drizzle olive oil on top. Sprinkle a little salt over the cheese, if you like. Repeat the layers, finishing with the cheese. ✱

4. Bake for 20 minutes or until the cheese is melted. Serve hot, directly from the baking dish, or let cool and serve at room temperature.

SERVING SUGGESTION

Accompany this substantial dish with a salad of greens with vinaigrette and thick slices of hot Parsley and Herb Garlic Bread (page 87).

✱**TIP:** The dish can be **prepared up to this point**, then covered and refrigerated for several hours or up to overnight if you wish. Just remember to take the dish out of the refrigerator and turn on the oven as soon as you walk in the door. Once it is at room temperature, just pop it into the oven.

Spa Cooking

Spas are famous for their beautiful locations, luxurious treatments, fitness programs, and fresh and healthful cooking. Some spas have gardens that produce the foods that they serve guests. Others focus on maximizing the flavors of fresh and locally grown or produced ingredients, often in creative combinations. With the emphasis on healthful living and access to carefully produced foods, chefs have ample inspiration to create lighter dishes with great flavor. There truly are wonderful foods that satisfy without seeming to be light.

The dishes in this chapter are not calculated for fat content or calories, but are weighted for satisfaction. They have to taste good, not just "be good for you."

Tips for Spa Eating and Cooking

- Begin with seasonality and think creatively—foods that are fresh and in season don't need as much work. Beautiful strawberries in season can be eaten as dessert with just a dusting of sugar and a little lemon juice, or they can sweeten the greens in a salad, which would need only a dressing of quality vinegar and a little extra-virgin olive oil.

- Buy your vegetables or meats whole and prepare them yourself. Although the packages of sliced, diced, and chopped veggies or cubed meat are enticing, it is likely that they have lost flavor, moisture, and sometimes texture if they are cleaned and chopped before you buy them. But if time is a constraint, look for the freshest quality pre-cut foods available. Because they have less flavor, you may need to rinse them to be sure they are clean and add flavoring to freshen their taste.

- Choose cooking techniques that are naturally light. Grilling is one, roasting is another—so try grilling a steak or roasting a chicken breast. Or try broiling—you can have deliciously caramelized (browned) vegetables in minutes.

- Buy a heavy-duty grill pan or a nonstick pan or both. Pans that conduct heat really well require less fat for cooking. Food will also stick in a cold pan, so heat it properly. In a hot pan, foods brown without losing juice. (If food is cooking in its own juices, it is being steamed. This can leave a food like chicken breast bland, dry, and tough.)

- Try not to turn the food too much. Ideally, foods are browned on one side, turned, and browned on the other. That's only one turn. We are a nation of stirrers, flippers, and turners! My motto is, after turning once, "put your tongs down and step away from the pan." The more you turn it, the cooler the food gets, and the more juice it loses.

- Make sure the food is at room temperature before you cook it, for quicker and more even heating. Fish can be cooked cold (because it will cook so quickly), but everything else needs to be at room temperature to avoid cooling the pan when the food is added.

- Cut the fat in your recipe at the beginning, instead of at the end. Many people tend to cut the fat at the end of a recipe. I think that is exactly where you should leave it. Take mushrooms for example: Put them in a hot nonstick skillet (without any fat) and leave them alone until the mushrooms release their juices and reduce in size by half. They will brown and reduce without any butter in the pan. It will be hard to tell that the mushrooms have no fat after they have been seasoned with garlic and rosemary. But drizzling the cooked mushrooms with a little good extra-virgin olive oil will enhance the flavor dramatically. Use the fat in each recipe wisely.

- Enhance the flavors of your foods with mustards, chutneys, and vinegars. I always have several kinds of each in my pantry or refrigerator at all times. Chutneys can be heated then brushed on fish; mustards can be blended together to baste chicken. The better the vinegar, the less fat you will need in your salad dressing. I sometimes mix balsamic, mustard, and water to make a great salad dressing.

- Skip low-fat and nonfat alternative foods. In my mind they have so little flavor, I would rather just live without them. I use real foods like cheeses or butter but in smaller portions, or I substitute creatively—like a mustard-yogurt blend or chutney instead of mayonnaise—to eat lighter.

- Foods will taste better and be more satisfying if you sit down at the table and eat them. Cooking and eating provides food for the soul as well as nourishment. If you enjoy what you cook and eat, you won't feel like you're sacrificing anything.

Mustard-Crusted Chicken with a Trio of Peppers and Couscous

✓ *SOMETHING SPECIAL*

Here's a flavorful and attractive dish that's simple to make. With a hot pan you only need a little fat to get that delicious caramelized flavor when searing the chicken. The chicken cooks quickly so it stays moist and flavorful. If you can, while you are making dinner, grill some extra chicken for a great salad the next day. I've made this for some special dinners-for-two, but it can easily be doubled or tripled.

★TIP: For even **lighter results**, try grilling the chicken outdoors on the grill. You won't need the butter, and the flavor the grill creates is unbeatable.

One 8-ounce whole small boneless skinless chicken breast, halved horizontally into 2 cutlets

Salt and freshly ground pepper, to taste

1 tablespoon mustard seeds

1 tablespoon chopped fresh Italian flat-leaf parsley

¾ cup plus 1 tablespoon water

¼ teaspoon salt

½ cup instant couscous

2 teaspoons unsalted butter

1 tablespoon fresh lemon juice

1½ cups seeded deveined and very thinly sliced green bell pepper (from 1 small pepper)

1½ cups seeded deveined and very thinly sliced red bell pepper (from 1 small pepper)

1½ cups seeded deveined and very thinly sliced yellow bell pepper (from 1 small pepper)

2 tablespoons extra-virgin olive oil

2 tablespoons balsamic vinegar

1. Season the chicken on both sides with salt and pepper. Combine the mustard seeds and parsley on a plate, then press the seasoned chicken into the seed mixture, coating both sides.

2. Bring ¾ cup water and ¼ teaspoon salt to a boil in a small saucepan. Stir in the couscous; remove from the heat and let stand, covered, 5 minutes.

3. Heat the butter in a grill pan or a nonstick skillet over medium heat until the foam subsides. Grill or sear the chicken on one side until golden, about 5 minutes. Turn the cutlets and cook, covered, over medium-low heat 4 to 5 minutes more, until just cooked through. ★

4. Slice the chicken diagonally across into ¾-inch slices. Fluff the couscous with a fork and divide between 2 plates. Top couscous with chicken. Add the lemon juice and remaining tablespoon water to the skillet and simmer, scraping up brown bits on the bottom of the pan, 1 minute. Pour the sauce over the chicken.

5. Combine the peppers in a medium bowl. Toss with the olive oil and balsamic vinegar. Season with salt and pepper.

6. Serve the chicken hot with the crunchy peppers spooned on top.

Game Hens with Wild Rice and Grape Stuffing

✓ *SOMETHING SPECIAL*   ✓ *TAKE-ALONG*

This elegant recipe is simple to prepare. It takes an hour to cook the game hens, but it is worth it. (And you can do other things while you wait.) If you want to crisp their skins, broil the game hens for a few minutes just before they are done.

⅓ cup uncooked wild rice

1 cup water

Pinch salt

1 cup Madeira ✱

½ cup sliced shiitake mushrooms (about 2 ounces)

Salt and freshly ground pepper, to taste

1 cup seedless green or red grapes (about 8 ounces)

2 tablespoons olive oil

2 tablespoons chopped fresh Italian flat-leaf parsley

¼ teaspoon dried thyme leaves

2 Cornish game hens ✱

1. In a small saucepan, combine the wild rice, water, and salt. Cover tightly and simmer for 25 minutes; the rice will still be firm when you bite it. Drain well.

2. Preheat the oven to 350°F. Bring the Madeira to a boil in a small saucepan.

3. Add the shiitake mushrooms to the Madeira and boil until the liquid reduces by half, 3 to 4

minutes. Remove the pan from the heat, and set it aside. Season with salt and pepper.

4. In a mixing bowl, combine the grapes, olive oil, wild rice, parsley, and thyme and toss well.

5. Rinse the hens well and pat them dry. To split the hens, use poultry shears or scissors, and starting at the back of the hen, where the neck is, cut down both sides of the backbone from top to bottom. Discard the backbone. Carefully snip between the breasts, separating the hen into halves. Repeat with the other hen.

6. Gently loosen the skin from the meat on the breast and legs, breaking the membrane that holds the skin onto the meat. Do not tear the skin. Carefully remove any visible fat.

7. Line a jellyroll pan with aluminum foil. Place one quarter of the stuffing inside each game hen half, and gently put the

game hen halves breast side up on the pan (the stuffing will be on the jellyroll pan with the game hen on top). Brush a small amount of the Madeira-mushroom glaze under the skin and on top of the breasts.

8. Pour a small amount of the reserved Madeira-mushroom glaze into the pan around the birds, reserving at least half of the mixture for use later in the recipe. Bake the halves 50 to 60 minutes, basting occasionally. The hens are done when a meat thermometer registers 160°F when inserted in the thickest part of the breast, and the juices run clear.

9. Remove the pan from the oven. To serve, transfer the hens and stuffing to individual plates. Add the remaining Madeira and mushrooms to the roasting pan, and cook over low heat until the liquid is slightly reduced, about 5 minutes. Pour the sauce over the hens, and serve immediately.

✱ **TIP:** Madeira is a sweet, golden wine originally from Portugal. It has wonderful flavor: heat-treated and kept in motion at times during processing, the wine becomes a concentration of all the flavors of the original grapes. Madeira is found next to the sherry and port in the supermarket or liquor store.

✱ **TIP:** Real **Cornish game hens** are a cross between Cornish gamecocks and Plymouth Rock hens. They each weigh about 1 pound and are perfect split and shared for those with moderate hunger, or served whole for big appetites. In this day of tasteless chicken, game hens have a delicious, more intense flavor. Game hens, which are fully grown, are about the same size as poussins or squab, which are simply very young chickens.

Salmon Fillets with Apricot-Horseradish Glaze and Roasted Root Vegetables

✓ *EASY PREPARATION*   ✓ *SOMETHING SPECIAL*

This couldn't be easier to prepare and the unique flavors will make you feel as if you are dining at a spa resort. You can make the roasted vegetables and then begin the salmon, or cook the salmon at the end of the vegetable cooking time so they finish together.

Roasted Root Vegetables (below)

¼ cup apricot jam

2 tablespoons prepared white horseradish

2 teaspoons white wine vinegar

Four 6-ounce center-cut salmon fillets, skin removed *

2 to 3 tablespoons chopped Italian flat-leaf parsley, for garnish

1. Prepare the roasted vegetables. Then, leave the oven at 375°F.

2. In a small bowl, combine the apricot jam, horseradish, and vinegar. Spread this mixture evenly over the salmon fillets.

3. Arrange the fillets on a jellyroll pan or a baking sheet with raised

edges. Bake for 12 minutes, or until the fish is opaque in the center. *

4. Divide the roasted vegetables among the plates and top with a piece of the salmon. Sprinkle with parsley and serve.

*TIP: When buying **salmon**, make sure that you have the fish market or department give you the thick center-cut fillets (even if they try to sell you the thinner ends).

*TIP: To save time, the salmon can be put into the oven for the last 12 minutes of roasting the vegetables.

Roasted Root Vegetables

✓ *EASY PREPARATION*

Leave the skins on the vegetables so they will take on a beautiful golden color when they are roasted.

2 tablespoons unsalted butter, melted

3 tablespoons brown sugar

1 cup cleaned and very thinly sliced red potatoes (from 2 medium)

1 cup carrots, cleaned and very thinly sliced (from 2 medium)

1 cup parsnips, cleaned and very thinly sliced (from about ½ pound)

Salt and freshly ground pepper, to taste

Preheat the oven to 375°F. In a jellyroll pan or baking sheet with a raised edge, toss the butter and brown sugar with the vegetables and season with salt and pepper.

Spread the vegetables in 1 layer and roast them, tossing with a spatula several times while they are roasting, 25 to 30 minutes until they are golden and tender. Serve hot.

Linguine with Tomato-Fennel Sauce

✓ *EASY PREPARATION*

Fennel may be new to you, but try it; it adds a refreshing sweet-tart flavor to the sauce. For even more fennel flavor, add a teaspoon of dried fennel seed to the pan before you add the tomatoes. If you don't have linguine, use another long pasta. Serve with a nice loaf of Italian bread.

1½ cups chopped onion
(from 1 large)

1 cup sliced fennel (from 1 medium
bulb) ✶

2 teaspoons finely chopped garlic
(2 medium cloves)

2 cups Italian-style plum tomatoes,
crushed (from one 14½-ounce can)

1 cup canned tomato sauce

½ cup canned tomato paste

2 teaspoons dried basil

1 teaspoon dried sage

1 teaspoon salt

¼ teaspoon freshly ground pepper,
or to taste

1 pound linguine

¼ cup freshly grated Parmigiano-
Reggiano (from 1 ounce) plus more
for serving

1. Heat a large, heavy skillet over medium heat. Add the onions, fennel, and garlic. Cook until the vegetables are softened, but not browned, about 15 minutes, reducing the heat as necessary. Add the tomatoes, tomato sauce, tomato paste, basil, sage, salt, and pepper. Simmer for at least 15 minutes.

2. In the meantime, cook the linguine in 6 quarts of boiling salted water until al dente, 6 to 9 minutes. Drain the pasta, and return it to the pot. Add about 1 cup of the sauce and toss it thoroughly.

3. Pile the pasta in a bowl or on a warm platter and pour the rest of the sauce over it. Garnish with the cheese, and pass more at the table.

✶ TIP: Choose the freshest **fennel bulbs** possible. They should be plump, crisp, and white, with no tinges of yellow or brown. The stalks should also be crisp, not limp or spongy. If the stalks have been cut short, any remaining leaves should be crisp, not limp. To prepare, cut off the stalks flush with the top of the bulb. (Remove bruised or rust-colored portions if you have not found one that is perfect.) Cut a slice off the root end. Cut the bulb in half, stem to root, and thinly slice each half.

Fresh Vegetable and Noodle Lettuce Wraps with Hoisin

✓ SOMETHING SPECIAL

One of my favorite "wrappers" is a lettuce leaf. You can create a quick, light dinner with chopped raw vegetables and the fresh noodles. Or, if you have some hearty eaters, use leftovers like grilled fish or chicken to add to this delicious base.

1/2 cup peeled and very thinly sliced (julienned) carrots *

1 cup very thinly sliced (julienned) red bell pepper

1 cup shredded napa cabbage

1/2 cup enoki mushrooms, rinsed and well dried (about 2 ounces)

1 serrano chile, seeded and diced

3 ounces rice noodles, softened in water and drained (1 cup)

3 tablespoons sesame oil

2 tablespoons olive oil

1 tablespoon fresh lime juice

1/4 cup chopped fresh cilantro

Salt and freshly ground pepper, to taste

16 butter lettuce leaves (from 2 medium heads)

1/2 cup hoisin sauce, for dipping

1. In a large bowl, combine the carrots, red bell pepper, cabbage, mushrooms, chile, and noodles. Add the sesame oil, olive oil, lime juice, and cilantro to the bowl and toss to combine. Season the mixture with salt and pepper. Allow the mixture to stand 15 minutes.

2. Lay the lettuce leaves out flat, and fill each one with a spoonful of the vegetable mixture. Roll the lettuce leaves to close them slightly. (These wraps are not tightly closed like burritos and spring rolls, so the lettuce stays crisp.) Place the wraps on a platter and serve. Pass a dish of hoisin sauce for dipping.

✱ TIP: To slice the vegetables into **julienne** means to cut them into very thin strips. The carrot and the red bell pepper will need to be cut into long plank-like pieces first. Then turn and cut them lengthwise into strips about 1/8 inch wide.

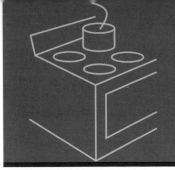

Breakfast for Dinner

Some nights you just want something to eat that's light, filling, and easy to make, and that your family will enjoy. On those nights that may just be breakfast foods like omelets, quiches, waffles, pancakes, and French toast—they are all satisfying and delicious. If it is good food, it is good any time of day. And a break with tradition is fun every now and then.

My breakfast traditions began with warm memories of great breakfasts and brunches at my grandparents' homes in Los Angeles and their cabin in Tahoe, California. The mornings had a special spirit, one they were willing to share with any friends or family that might happen to drop in to visit.

My grandfather was the self-appointed Pancake General and he manned an impressive cast-iron griddle on those weekend mornings. That griddle would show up everywhere—on camping trips, at the Tahoe cabin, and at friends' houses, too. He swore that griddle was his secret to making his buttermilk pancakes taste so good.

As the General was busy on the front line, Gram would prepare a classic brunch spread of eggs with smoked salmon, lox and bagels, sliced tomatoes, fruit, and scrumptious breads. Papa's pancakes were served with thick maple syrup and a healthy dose of berries mixed with a few dollops of sour cream. Needless to say, breakfast and brunch were greatly enjoyed in my family.

In these busy times, real breakfasts are usually enjoyed only during the day on an occasional weekend. All the more reason to take the tasty foods and good feelings to the dinner table.

You'll enjoy the simple prep work; your kids will love the idea of eating "out of order." For family members who are skeptical about eating breakfast at night, try serving an omelet with crusty bread and a tossed salad. Or add fresh fruit or potatoes to a plate of pancakes and bacon. You can also make breakfast foods more savory, such as serving unsweetened waffles with a mushroom sauce or topping French toast with cheese.

The Perfect Omelet

✓ *EASY PREPARATION*

A good omelet is hard to come by at restaurants because they are often overcooked or cold by the time they get to the table. That's why omelets are best made at home. This recipe makes one omelet. Because they are so quick to make, you can make one "to order" for each person in your family by adding fillings of choice to the simple base recipe.

2 large eggs, at room temperature

1 tablespoon whole milk

Salt and freshly ground pepper, to taste

1 tablespoon unsalted (or salted) butter

Filling of your choice ∗

1. Beat the eggs with the milk in a small bowl. Beat in the salt and pepper.

2. Heat the butter in a small nonstick skillet. The butter should foam, then the foam should begin to dissipate before the egg mixture is added.

3. Pour the egg mixture into the skillet, and stir with a rubber scraper, bringing the edges toward the middle to firm up the mixture on the bottom and to prevent it from sticking to the pan.

4. Tilt the skillet away from you at a 25° angle. Tap the handle with your fist, forcing the omelet to slide to the front edge of the skillet. Keep it there while you spread the egg that is still soft to the exposed part of the pan. Cook 3 to 6 minutes, depending on how firm you like your eggs. Repeat the process until the egg is done the way you like.

5. Add the filling that you wish, in the middle of the omelet. Using a spatula, fold half the egg over the filling to form a half-moon shape. Invert the omelet onto a plate, or hold the skillet by the handle, give the top of the handle several taps, and slide it out onto the plate. If you like, use your hands to roll the omelet into the shape of a crepe or cigar.

SERVING SUGGESTION

Serve with hot buttered toast and some roasted potatoes.

∗**TIP:** Make your fillings as simple or elaborate as you like. Try: chopped fresh herbs, chopped or cubed deli meats, chopped cooked vegetables such as spinach or summer squash, and melting cheeses such as mozzarella and cheddar, or a combination of the above fillings. Allow some extra time for the denser fillings to cook through.

Artichoke and Goat Cheese Frittata

✓ *SOMETHING SPECIAL*   ✓ *TAKE-ALONG*

I love to make frittatas because they are easy to put together and look special—it's like a pie, but you don't have to make a crust. This recipe makes two frittatas, combining the tangy-sweet taste of artichokes and the salty richness of seasoned goat cheese and Parmigiano-Reggiano. They can be put together an hour in advance and served at room temperature.

4 tablespoons unsalted butter (¼ cup)

2 cups leeks, halved lengthwise, rinsed well, and thinly sliced (from 4 medium leeks)

1 teaspoon finely chopped garlic

½ cup finely chopped white onion

2 cups canned artichokes (packed in water), quartered, drained well (from one 14-ounce can)

12 large eggs, at room temperature

1 cup half and half

1 cup grated Parmigiano-Reggiano cheese (4 ounces)

¼ cup freshly chopped basil

1 teaspoon Tabasco

1 teaspoon salt

½ teaspoon freshly ground pepper

5 ounces soft fresh goat cheese, such as Montrachet

1. Melt 2 tablespoons of the butter in a large, heavy, straight-sided skillet over medium heat. Add the leeks, garlic, and onions. Cook to soften the vegetables without browning them, about 10 minutes. Add the artichokes and cook for 3 minutes more.

2. Preheat the broiler. In a large bowl, whisk together the eggs, half and half, Parmigiano-Reggiano, basil, Tabasco, salt, and pepper.

3. Divide the vegetable mixture between two 10-inch skillets with ovenproof handles. Add 1 tablespoon of butter to each skillet. Swirl the pans over medium heat as the butter is melting to coat the bottoms. Pour half of the egg mixture into each skillet. Swirl the pans again slightly to incorporate the vegetables. Cook the frittatas over medium heat until puffed slightly and the centers are set, about 15 minutes. ✱

4. Drop pieces of the goat cheese on the top of each frittata. Cook the frittatas under the broiler until the cheese and the tops of the frittatas are golden brown. Remove from the oven, cool slightly, slice, and serve.

SERVING SUGGESTION

I like to serve this with some lightly seasoned sour cream and fresh basil. Also try it with the Pear and Cheese Salad (page 18).

If you are preparing a buffet, make individual servings: Divide the filling among muffin tins and bake at 350°F for 10 minutes.

✱TIP: If you do not have skillets with **ovenproof handles**, wrap the handles with several thicknesses of aluminum foil before adding the egg mixture.

Asparagus and White Cheddar Quiche

✓ *MAKE-AHEAD*　　✓ *SOMETHING SPECIAL*　　✓ *TAKE-ALONG*

While the unique flavors of asparagus and cheddar seem to be especially complementary, you can also substitute broccoli for the asparagus in the winter when asparagus is out of season.

1 frozen or refrigerated premade pie crust *

3 large eggs

3 tablespoons thinly sliced green onion, white and up to 1 inch dark green (3 whole onions)

1½ cups whole milk

½ teaspoon salt

¼ teaspoon freshly ground pepper

⅛ teaspoon freshly grated nutmeg

1½ cups grated white cheddar cheese (from 6 ounces)

1 cup steamed asparagus tips (from 1 pound asparagus, the rest of the stalks reserved for soup or salad) *

1. Preheat the oven to 400°F.

2. Prick the bottom and the sides of the pie crust with a fork. Line the crust with aluminum foil and poke a few holes in the foil. Fill the foil with beans, rice, or pie weights. Bake for 8 minutes. Remove the beans and foil, and bake for 4 minutes more or until the crust looks dry but not brown. Remove it from the oven and let it cool on a wire cooling rack. Reduce the oven temperature to 375°F.

3. Beat the eggs in a medium bowl until frothy. Stir in the onions, milk, salt, pepper, nutmeg, and cheese. Spread the asparagus over the cooled pie crust. Place the crust on a cookie sheet and pour the egg mixture into the shell. *

4. Bake 30 to 40 minutes, until the quiche is puffed and golden on top and the filling is set; a knife inserted in the center will come out clean. If the edges of the crust brown too quickly, cover them with aluminum foil. Transfer to a wire rack, cool 15 minutes, and serve hot, warm, or at room temperature.

SERVING SUGGESTION

Slice the quiche and serve with a bowl of sour cream that has been mixed with chopped green onions.

＊TIP: I always **prebake the pie crust** for my single-crust pies or quiches because the light browning of the bottom crust will keep it from becoming soggy when it is cooked with the filling.

＊TIP: Choose the crispest **fresh asparagus**—it should be bright green with very tight buds. The stalks should not be limp, and the tips should not be black or wet. To steam: cut the asparagus, place the tips in a steamer basket or colander over simmering water, and steam, covered, 4 to 5 minutes. Dry on a cloth kitchen towel before continuing with the recipe.

＊TIP: To ensure that you **don't spill** the filling, you can set the pie crust plate filled with mushrooms on a cookie sheet, then place it on an extended oven shelf. Pour in the cream and egg mixture and sprinkle with cheese. Carefully push the shelf back in (watch the hot oven). This trick works with custard tarts, too.

Mock Eggs Benedict

✓ *EASY PREPARATION*

Here's a simplified but similar dish to classic eggs Benedict, which requires poaching eggs and making real hollandaise sauce. While they aren't really the same, this is deliciously similar to the original and a great addition to any "breakfast-for-dinner" menu.

3 tablespoons unsalted butter

3 tablespoons all-purpose flour

1/2 teaspoon salt

3 cups milk (2% is fine)

1 1/2 cups grated Swiss cheese (6 ounces)

1 cup diced ham (from the deli is fine) (about 4 ounces)

8 drops Tabasco, or more to taste

12 large eggs, boiled until hard, peeled and quartered *

6 English muffins, split and lightly toasted

1/8 teaspoon paprika

1. Melt the butter in a large, heavy saucepan over medium heat. Whisk in the flour and salt. Cook, whisking, until smooth, 1 minute. Reduce the heat and gradually whisk in the milk. Cook, whisking constantly, until thick and bubbling, about 3 minutes.

2. Remove from the heat and stir in the cheese. When the cheese is melted and the sauce is smooth, gently stir in the ham, season with Tabasco, and then fold in the eggs.

3. If you are not serving the eggs immediately, they can be kept warm in the top of a double boiler over simmering water for 10 to 15 minutes. Stir gently from time to time.

4. Spoon the hot egg mixture over the toasted English muffins, sprinkle with paprika, and serve very hot.

★TIP: The way I **hard boil eggs** results in easy-to-shell eggs. (But don't worry if an egg is hard to shell; that often happens with very fresh eggs.) Place room-temperature eggs in a saucepan large enough to hold them all in one layer. Bring to a boil and cook for 1 minute. Remove from the heat, cover, and let stand for 12 minutes. Run eggs under cool water until cool enough to handle. Crack gently all over and peel.

Sour Cream Waffles

✓ *EASY PREPARATION*

Once you have tried these delicious waffles, you will never put another store-bought imposter in your toaster again. You can eat them hot drizzled with maple syrup, or just sprinkled with a good dusting of powdered sugar. You can throw caution to the wind (and thrill the kids) by serving dessert for dinner, spooning on sugared berries and whipped topping or going all out topping the waffles with ice cream and hot fudge sauce or caramel topping. (Of course, the other nights of the week you should serve more balanced meals!) If, by chance, there should be a waffle or two left over, freeze them for another use. See the tip if you want to make savory waffles for dinner.

Vegetable oil, such as canola, for oiling the griddle

2 cups all-purpose flour

2 teaspoons baking powder

1/2 teaspoon kosher salt, sea salt, or other salt

2 tablespoons sugar *

2 teaspoons baking soda

6 large eggs, separated, at room temperature

4 cups sour cream (2 pints or 1 quart)

1/2 cup (1 stick) unsalted butter, melted

1. Preheat the oven to 200°F. Brush the waffle iron with vegetable oil and preheat. Be sure the iron is very hot, or the first waffles will stick and separate.

2. Sift together the flour, baking powder, salt, sugar, and baking soda.

3. In a large bowl, beat the egg yolks with a fork or whisk until light yellow in color. Beat in the sour cream and melted butter.

4. Stir the flour mixture into the eggs just until all the dry ingredients are moistened. Do not overmix; a few lumps are okay.

5. With an electric mixer on medium speed, beat the egg whites until frothy. Increase the speed to high and beat the whites until stiff peaks form. (The batter will hold its shape when you lift the beaters.) Stir one-third of the egg whites into the batter to lighten it. Fold in one-third more of the whites, and then gently fold in the last of the egg whites until the batter is very light.

6. Preheat the oven to 200°F. Make sure the waffle iron is very hot. (The iron is ready when a drop or two of water skitters across the plate before turning into steam.) Pour about 1/2 cup of the batter onto the waffle iron. Close the iron and bake until steaming stops. *

7. Keep the waffles warm on a baking sheet in the oven, each wrapped in separate layers of cloth kitchen towels, so they do not steam and become soggy. Continue baking until all the batter is used up.

8. When all are made and still hot, pile the crisp waffles into a cloth-lined basket and serve.

✱TIP: If, in your house, dinner can only be a savory dish, try making these waffles savory, but **reduce the sugar** to 1 tablespoon. Then use them as a base for our Mock Eggs Benedict (page 158), or top with Coconut Chicken Curry (page 104).

✱TIP: Resist the temptation to lift the lid and peek at the **waffle** while it is baking because the batter may stick to the upper and lower plates. For waffles that are crisp on the outside and tender inside, watch for the steam coming out from between the plates of the iron. Once the steam stops you may lift the lid, then you can close it again and cook to the color you like. The timing for this changes with the type of waffle iron and the kind of batter you are using.

Banana Pancakes with Honey Butter Spread

✓ *EASY PREPARATION*

If you love the flavor of banana bread, I think you will serve these pancakes often. If you're having something else for dinner, these also make a great dessert dish, with a scoop of vanilla ice cream and a drizzle of your favorite honey.

Honey Butter Spread (below)

2 cups all-purpose flour

2 tablespoons baking powder

Pinch of salt

2 large eggs

2 cups milk (2% is fine) (1 pint)

¾ cup mashed ripe banana
(from 1 large or 2 small)

2 tablespoons unsalted butter,
melted, cooled slightly

1 tablespoon vegetable oil
or melted butter for oiling griddle

1. Preheat the pancake griddle over medium-high heat. Make the butter spread. ∗

2. In a large bowl, stir together the flour, baking powder, and salt. Beat together the eggs and milk in a small bowl until smooth. Stir the egg and milk mixture into the flour, beating just until smooth, but be careful not to overbeat. Stir in the mashed banana, and then the melted butter. Let the batter stand for 5 minutes.

3. Preheat the oven to 200°F. Lightly grease the griddle with a little oil or butter. ∗

4. Use ¼ cup of the batter for each pancake. Pour 4 to 6 pancakes onto the griddle. Do not attempt to turn them over until bubbles begin to appear on the uncooked surface and then break, leaving little holes behind. Turn the pancakes once, cooking 1 to 2 minutes more. Stack the finished pancakes and cover with a napkin to keep warm; or place them in a single layer on a baking sheet, cover with a towel, and keep in the oven while all the remaining batter is cooked.

5. Arrange the hot pancakes on a heated platter and serve with plenty of Honey Butter Spread on the side.

∗ **TIP:** If you don't own a **separate griddle**, use your largest flat frying pan for these pancakes.

∗ **TIP:** The **griddle** should be very hot, or the first pancakes will stick. With your fingertips, flick a little water onto the heated griddle. The drops should skitter across the pan, then break and evaporate into steam.

Honey Butter Spread

This spread is equally good when served with pancakes, hot muffins, toast, waffles, or even French toast.

½ cup (1 stick) unsalted butter, softened

3 tablespoons honey

½ teaspoon ground cinnamon

1. With an electric hand mixer, beat together the butter and honey until light and fluffy. Beat in the cinnamon.

2. Mound in the serving bowl. Serve at room temperature. This spread will keep up to 1 week tightly covered in the refrigerator.

SERVING SUGGESTIONS

If you are in a hurry, commercial honey butter spread found in the supermarket dairy case can be substituted (although it's not nearly as good as the homemade kind).

Try adding a tablespoon or two of crunchy peanut butter to the Honey Butter Spread for another special flavor—or spread the pancakes with warm peanut butter before adding the Honey Butter Spread. (Is Elvis in the house?)

Cream Cheese French Toast Sandwiches

✓ *EASY PREPARATION*

I love French toast, but often the bread overwhelms the dish and becomes all you taste. These excellent sandwiches are creamy on the inside, crisp and eggy on the outside. Delicious!

For a savory version of this sandwich, spread on blue cheese and add a slice of ham between the bread slices instead of the cream cheese. Dip in the egg mixture and fry the same way as the sweet version.

One 8-ounce package cream cheese (low-fat is fine, but not nonfat), softened

¼ cup plus 2 tablespoons sugar (6 tablespoons in all)

1 teaspoon ground cinnamon

Twelve ½-inch-thick slices of crusty French bread

4 large eggs

1 cup half and half, evaporated milk, or 2% milk

1 tablespoon unsalted butter for greasing the griddle

1. Preheat a griddle or a large, heavy skillet over medium-high heat for 5 minutes.

2. With an electric hand mixer, in a large bowl beat together the cream cheese, ¼ cup sugar, and ½ teaspoon cinnamon until light and fluffy.

3. Spread the flavored cream cheese thickly on one side of 6 slices of the bread. Top with the remaining bread slices. ✱

4. In a medium bowl, with a whisk, beat the eggs until light and frothy. Beat in the half and half. Beat in the 2 tablespoons sugar and ½ teaspoon cinnamon.

5. Generously grease the hot griddle with butter. Dip the sandwiches completely into the egg mixture and cook them on the griddle until well browned and slightly crisp on both sides, 3 to 4 minutes per side. Regrease the griddle, if needed, between batches. Serve hot.

SERVING SUGGESTION

At the table, pass maple syrup, cinnamon sugar, Honey Butter Spread (page 161), or your favorite preserves—warmed slightly.

✱TIP: For a change of pace, flavor the **cream cheese** with any of your favorite jams, or even with chunky peanut butter. Warm the addition to room temperature before beating it into the softened cheese.

Vegetables and Sides

"Eat your vegetables!" Vegetables have long suffered from the misperception that something that is good for you cannot possibly taste good, and coaxing is often needed for people to eat healthfully. These recipes prove otherwise. They are flavorful staples that have won over my family and will win yours too. When it comes to vegetables, first things first: Cook fresh vegetables that are in season. Modern shipping makes it easy to get just about any vegetable, anytime, but no vegetables are fresh and sweet all year long. Use seasonal vegetables and, even better, locally grown, and your side dishes will be varied and vibrantly flavored throughout the year. If you're not sure of the best season for certain vegetables, ask the produce manager of your store. Of course, if fresh vegetables aren't available, there are good frozen varieties worth cooking—corn, peas, and green beans, for starters.

The dishes that follow run from the basic steaming of different vegetables to enhance their natural goodness to the more intricate and substantial vegetable pancakes and corn cakes. The recipes call for potatoes, tomatoes, corn, and other popular vegetables, but feel free to experiment by substituting new vegetables in the dishes that your family likes.

Steaming Vegetables

There are four categories of vegetables that are often steamed or blanched:

- **Green vegetables:** Green vegetables grown above ground include broccoli, green beans, peas, and spinach. An effective way to blanch them is in a large amount of salted boiling water, uncovered. The vegetables must immediately be refreshed in cold water to stop the cooking and set the color. They can be kept at this point until you are ready to sauce, cook, or otherwise reheat them. Note that artichokes or asparagus that are blanched in cast iron or aluminum may discolor.

- **Root vegetables:** These tubers grown in the ground include potatoes, parsnips, turnips, leeks, and carrots. Root vegetables are started in cold water, covered, and then simmered gently. Covering them eliminates their strong flavor, and maintaining the water below the boiling point will keep them from breaking apart.

- **Other vegetables:** These include mushrooms, bell peppers, tomatoes, and eggplant. These can be blanched, and degree of doneness is determined by personal taste. You also need to consider whether the vegetable will be undergoing any other cooking process.

- **Legumes:** This is a family of vegetables that have double-seamed pods containing a single row of seeds, such as peas and beans. You can steam or blanch fresh beans.

Most dried beans are soaked before cooking to rehydrate them in order to reduce their cooking time. Lentils and split peas generally do not need soaking. After you soak them, beans can be simmered until soft and tender.

Tips for Cooking Vegetables

- Cook purplish-red vegetables in water containing an apple, a little vinegar, or another acid to keep them from bleeding, losing their color, or turning an unappetizing shade of gray.

- To keep white vegetables from yellowing, add a pinch of cream of tartar to the cooking water.

- Don't keep vegetables warm after blanching them. They will become mushy and lose color and texture. Cool vegetables completely and then reheat them when you are ready to serve.

Green Beans with Toasted Walnuts

MAKES ABOUT 6 SERVINGS

✓ *EASY PREPARATION*

These easy-to-prepare beans add color and crunch to a comfort meal. They taste so good, they will disappear along with favorites like meatloaf and mashed potatoes. These get an extra flavor boost from the walnut oil (available in well-stocked supermarkets). It is incredibly fragrant and is a simple way to make a big flavor difference.

2 pounds fresh green beans, ends removed ＊

2 tablespoons butter

2 tablespoons walnut oil

Salt and freshly ground pepper, to taste

1 cup chopped, lightly toasted walnuts (from 4 ounces) ＊

2 tablespoons finely chopped fresh Italian flat-leaf parsley

1. Bring a large saucepan of water to a boil. Add the green beans and boil just until crisp-tender, about 5 minutes. Drain well.

2. Line a baking sheet with a clean towel. Transfer the beans to a large bowl of iced water to cool or refresh them quickly to stop them from cooking and to retain as much of their color as possible. Drain, spread on the baking sheet, and let stand at room temperature, or refrigerate if keeping for several hours. The beans can be prepared to this point up to 12 hours ahead. ＊

3. To finish, melt the butter together with the walnut oil in a large, heavy skillet over high heat. Add the beans and toss until heated through, about 4 minutes. Season with salt and pepper.

4. Toss in the toasted walnuts and parsley, and serve very hot.

＊**TIP:** If time is really short, use **frozen green beans**. Thaw under running water, drain, and dry well.

＊**TIP:** **Nuts** absorb moisture quickly and, if not stored properly, they lose quality. Toasting restores their crispness, adds color, and brings out their flavor. You can toast nuts in several ways. No matter which method you choose, remember that nuts will burn in an instant of overcooking.

To toast nuts: Spread them evenly on a baking sheet or in a hot skillet. If you are using the oven, place them in a 350°F oven and toast, stirring from time to time, for 3 to 4 minutes. If using a skillet, toss the nuts constantly over medium-high heat for 2 to 3 minutes. Watch them carefully.

＊**TIP:** Use a pan of water large enough to allow the **beans** to move around freely while cooking. Otherwise, beans crowded in a small pan will not cook evenly, and could lose their color.

Italian Green Beans with Tomatoes

✓ *EASY PREPARATION*

This is a terrific dish when green beans and tomatoes are freshest. When fresh isn't available or if you are just short on time and want to rely on what you have in the kitchen, frozen green beans and good-quality canned tomatoes will work well. For variety, substitute yellow wax beans for the green beans, or just mix some in.

2 tablespoons olive oil

1 cup thinly sliced Vidalia onion

1 teaspoon finely chopped garlic

1 tablespoon chopped fresh oregano, or 1 teaspoon dried Italian herb mixture

4 ripe Roma tomatoes, halved lengthwise, and thinly sliced (about 2 cups)

1 pound very thin green beans, fresh or frozen and thawed *

Salt and freshly ground pepper, to taste

1. Heat the oil in a medium-sized heavy skillet over medium-low heat. Add the onion and cook, stirring, until transparent, 5 minutes. Add the garlic and oregano or Italian herbs. Cook, stirring, 1 minute. Stir in the tomatoes and beans. Season well with salt and pepper.

2. Lower the heat and cook, tossing from time to time, until beans are crisp-tender, 8 to 10 minutes. Serve hot.

SERVING SUGGESTION

Refrigerate any leftovers and then toss them with a little Lemon Vinaigrette (page 16) on another day, for an instant salad.

✶TIP: For the **green beans**, look for whole frozen haricots verts (very thin, tender French green beans), which some specialty stores (and chains) now carry.

Baby Carrots with Wine and Rosemary

✓ EASY PREPARATION   ✓ SOMETHING SPECIAL

The tiny carrots sold as "baby carrots" are not really baby carrots at all, but are regular-sized carrots that have been trimmed. Nevertheless, they are tasty and convenient to snack on raw, to cook in the oven with a pot roast, or, as they are prepared here, to simmer on top of the stove until they are fragrant and tender.

1½ pounds baby cut carrots (about 3 cups)

1 cup white wine, such as Chardonnay, or low-sodium chicken broth

2 tablespoons unsalted butter

1 teaspoon dried rosemary, crushed between your palms

Salt and freshly ground pepper, to taste

1. In a large, heavy skillet, combine the carrots, wine, and butter. Cook over medium heat until the liquid is almost all evaporated and the carrots are tender, 10 to 15 minutes.

2. Stir in the rosemary and season well with salt and pepper. Continue to cook until all the liquid has evaporated. Toss to coat the carrots with the butter that remains in the skillet. Serve very hot.

Maple-Glazed Butternut Squash

✓ *SOMETHING SPECIAL*

Butternut squash, a great vegetable for autumn and winter cooking, is sweet and flavorful in its own right. Add this luscious maple glaze and the result is almost like candy—children love it—but it's not too sweet; it's balanced with the cheese and seasonings. It is perfect with pork dishes.

2 small butternut squash

1/4 cup olive oil

1/4 cup maple syrup

2 tablespoons chopped fresh Italian flat-leaf parsley

2 tablespoons grated Parmigiano-Reggiano cheese (from 1/2 ounce)

1/2 teaspoon salt

1/8 teaspoon freshly ground pepper

1. Split the squash in half. Butternut squash has a very hard shell. If the squash is not very fresh (for instance, if it is late winter), you may want to use a heavy chef's knife or cleaver to make the first cut. Use the sharp point of a large spoon to scoop out and discard the seeds and fiber. Cut each half into several large pieces, and peel them. Cut the squash into ¾-inch cubes. You will have about 6 cups.

2. Heat the oil in a large, heavy nonstick skillet over medium-low heat. Add the squash; cover and cook, stirring occasionally, 12 to 15 minutes, until the squash is just tender and beginning to color.

3. Add the maple syrup; toss until the squash is glazed. Add the parsley, cheese, salt, and pepper. Serve hot, spooned into a heated serving bowl.

Spicy Pumpkin Fries

✓ *EASY PREPARATION*   ✓ *SOMETHING SPECIAL*

Pumpkin is not just for pies. It's a great source of nutrients and delicious cooked as fries. I like to serve these fries with grilled burgers or steaks. Slice them into very thin sticks and watch the kids down them like there's no tomorrow. You can also make these fries with butternut squash.

½ cup all-purpose flour

2 tablespoons seasoned pepper, such as Mrs. Dash

2 pounds raw pumpkin *

4 cups peanut oil for deep-frying, or more, depending on deep-fryer instructions

Salt

½ cup grated Parmigiano-Reggiano cheese (2 ounces)

1. Preheat the oven to 300°F. Combine the flour and seasoned pepper in a large plastic sealable bag.

2. Peel and cut the pumpkin into thin sticks (as thin as you like your french fries). Add the pumpkin sticks to the seasoning bag, seal, and toss to coat the fries. *

3. Cover a cookie sheet with paper towels. Heat the oil in a heavy deep saucepan or deep-fat fryer until a frying thermometer reaches 375°F. Fry the pumpkin sticks in batches until golden, 4 to 5 minutes per batch. (Make sure the oil is at 375°F before starting each batch.) Remove cooked fries with a slotted spoon and drain on paper towels.

4. Sprinkle generously with salt and cheese and keep warm in the oven until all the fries are made. Serve very hot.

＊TIP: For making fries, pies, and cookies, buy a **sugar pumpkin**, not a carving pumpkin. Much smaller and sweeter than a carving pumpkin, the sugar pumpkin is available in the fall and winter. Look for pumpkins that seem heavy for their size and have a dull rind. To cook pumpkin, cut it open and remove the seeds and stringy fiber with a large spoon. Cut it into pieces and bake it at 375°F until the pumpkin is soft. For pies, separate the flesh from the rind and puree the flesh.

＊TIP: Keep in mind that if you cut the **pumpkin** into thick fries it will take more time to cook than if you cut them matchstick thin.

Twice-Cooked Potatoes

✓ *SOMETHING SPECIAL*

These deliciously tender potatoes with a light outside crunch are so good they might just become habit forming. Try them with Beef Tenderloin Steaks with Tellicherry Pepper Sauce (page 116) or Oven-Barbecued Chicken (page 97).

2 pounds large waxy potatoes, brown- or red-skinned

2 to 3 tablespoons unsalted butter

3 teaspoons finely minced garlic (from 3 medium cloves)

Salt and freshly ground pepper, to taste

2 tablespoons finely chopped fresh Italian flat-leaf parsley

1. Peel the potatoes and cut them into ½-inch chunks.

2. Put the potato chunks into a large saucepan filled with cold water. Bring the water to a boil over medium heat, then lower the heat and simmer the potatoes just until tender but not falling apart, about 10 minutes. Drain well.

3. Melt the butter in a large, heavy skillet over medium heat.

Add the drained potatoes and cook, tossing the pan from time to time to turn the potatoes and to keep them from sticking. When the potatoes are beginning to get crisp, after about 10 minutes, add the garlic and season well with salt and pepper. Continue cooking for 5 minutes more.

4. Add the parsley and toss. Serve very hot.

Old Bay Oven-Fried Potato Chips

✓ *EASY PREPARATION*

Eggs, burgers, and fried fish fillets just wouldn't be complete without a side of potatoes. Put these spicy thin slices of potato in the oven first, so that they have a chance to crisp up before the rest of dinner is ready. While prepared spice mixes are generally never as good as those you make at home, Old Bay is in a class of its own. A mixture of peppers, salt, and spices, it is the flavor most associated with Maryland crab, and works in other dishes like this one. The mix is hot, but full of flavor and worth keeping in your pantry.

2 large russet potatoes, well washed and dried

½ cup olive oil

2 tablespoons Old Bay Seasoning, or more to taste

1. Preheat the oven to 400°F. Without peeling the potatoes, cut them into very thin slices. In a large bowl, toss the potatoes with ¼ cup olive oil. ✱

2. Spread the potatoes in a heavy roasting pan taking care to separate the slices. Sprinkle with Old Bay to taste, and toss well.

3. Roast the potatoes, tossing with a spatula several times and drizzling with a little more oil if necessary (but be very judicious)

for 25 minutes, until the chips are crisp and golden brown. Cover a cookie sheet with paper towels. Spread the finished chips on the paper-lined cookie sheet to drain. Serve hot or warm.

Serving Suggestion

To serve these chips as more of a snack, sprinkle with salt, and pass a little malt vinegar with the fries, if you like, or a bowl of Garlic Mayonnaise (page 40).

✱**TIP:** The ideal tool for creating very thinly sliced potatoes is the **mandoline**. The classic sharp French metal tool can cut vegetables into different thicknesses and shapes with ease but is expensive. (A less costly plastic version with more limited uses is also available and still makes the job of slicing easier than if using a knife.) You can use it for zucchini, squash, or even sweet potatoes to create a wide variety of chips. Just be careful; the blade is extremely sharp, so keep your fingers out of harm's way.

Cannellini Beans with Basil and Fresh Tomatoes

✓ *EASY PREPARATION* ✓ *MAKE-AHEAD* ✓ *TAKE-ALONG*

While I serve these beans warm with grilled fish or lamb, this dish is also excellent when served as a chilled salad. Try it on a summer buffet table.

1 tablespoon olive oil

1/2 cup finely chopped white onion (from 1 small)

1/2 cup seeded deveined and chopped red bell pepper (from 1/2 medium)

Two 15-ounce cans Italian cannellini beans, well rinsed and drained *

1/2 cup seeded and chopped vine-ripened tomato

1 teaspoon finely chopped garlic

1 1/2 tablespoons balsamic vinegar

1 teaspoon chopped fresh thyme

2 tablespoons extra-virgin olive oil

1/2 teaspoon salt

1/8 teaspoon freshly ground pepper

2 tablespoons freshly chopped basil, for garnish

1. Heat the olive oil in a medium-sized heavy skillet over medium-high heat. Add the onion and cook just until soft, about 3 minutes. Add the red bell pepper and cook 3 minutes more. Add the drained beans to the pan and toss to mix with the vegetables. Add the tomato, tossing for 1 minute to heat slightly. Remove from the heat.

2. In a medium bowl, combine the garlic, vinegar, and fresh thyme. Add the olive oil in a slow stream, whisking constantly, until the dressing thickens. Toss this dressing with the bean mixture. Season with salt and pepper.

3. Serve these beans hot or warm, garnished with basil.

✱ TIP: To rinse **canned beans**, pour them into a colander and rinse with cold water until the foam goes away and the water runs clear. Drain very well.

Savory Vegetable Pancakes

✓ *SOMETHING SPECIAL*

These cakes are really versatile because you can use any type of vegetables that you want or even add cooked rice to them. The eggs and the bread crumbs are just there to hold the mixture together.

3 tablespoons unsalted butter

1 cup finely chopped white onion (from 1 medium onion)

¼ cup stemmed seeded deveined and chopped green bell pepper

½ cup finely chopped celery

1½ cups coarsely grated carrots (from 2 medium carrots)

2 cups chopped fresh baby spinach (about 3 ounces)

3 large eggs, at room temperature, beaten

¾ cup dried Italian bread crumbs

1¼ teaspoons salt

Freshly ground pepper, to taste

¼ cup vegetable oil, for frying, or more as needed

1 cup sour cream

½ cup chopped tomato

2 tablespoons chopped fresh cilantro, for garnish

1. Melt the butter in a heavy medium-sized skillet. Add the onion, green pepper, celery, and carrots and cook, stirring frequently, until crisply tender, about 4 minutes. Add the spinach. Cook, stirring, for 2 minutes. Set aside to cool.

2. In a medium bowl, combine the eggs with the bread crumbs, salt, and pepper. Add to the spinach mixture, mixing well. Refrigerate the batter for 5 minutes.

3. Preheat ¼ cup oil in a large, heavy skillet. For each cake, drop ¼ cup of batter (use a clean ¼-cup measure) into the hot skillet, pressing down on the mixture if necessary to form a cake ¼ inch thick with ragged edges.

4. Cook until golden on the bottom, turn, and cook on the other side, 4 to 5 minutes total. Drain on paper towels, and serve with sour cream, tomato, and cilantro. Serve hot. ✶

SERVING SUGGESTION

Try topping these crispy pancakes with grated smoked Gouda cheese or sour cream mixed with prepared horseradish, which is in the dairy case next to the regular prepared horseradish.

✶**TIP:** These **pancakes** freeze well, so you can make them ahead, cool them, then pop them in the freezer. Reheat them in a 350°F oven when ready to serve.

Corn Cakes with Corn Salsa

✓ SOMETHING SPECIAL

To make these you will only need some frozen sweet corn on hand. That makes them the perfect pantry pancake. Make them bite-sized for a great appetizer.

Corn Salsa (below)

1½ cups fresh or thawed and drained frozen sweet corn kernels

1 large egg

½ cup milk (2% is fine)

2 tablespoons finely chopped onion

¾ cup fresh bread crumbs, made from day-old bread

¼ cup chopped fresh Italian flat-leaf parsley

Salt and freshly ground pepper, to taste

4 tablespoons (½ stick) unsalted butter (¼ cup)

1. Prepare the corn salsa.

2. Puree half the corn in a blender. Add the egg, milk, onion, and bread crumbs. Blend until smooth. Mix with the remaining corn and parsley in a large bowl. Season well with salt and pepper.

3. Melt 1 tablespoon butter in a large, heavy skillet. Drop the batter by spoonfuls to make 2-inch pancakes. Cook, turning once when golden on the bottom,

2 to 3 minutes on each side. Add butter to the skillet as necessary and continue making pancakes until all the batter is used. Serve hot or warm, topped with a little salsa. Pass the remaining salsa on the side. *

SERVING SUGGESTION

For something simpler, garnish the cakes with chopped fresh cilantro and sour cream.

★ TIP: To keep these **pancakes** warm, have the oven preheated to 225°F. Layer the cakes on a cookie sheet, separating each layer with a paper towel. Keep pancakes warm in the oven until ready to serve.

Corn Salsa

✓ EASY PREPARATION

For a great summer version of this salsa, grill whole corn on the cob that has been brushed with a little bit of olive oil. When the kernels are lightly browned, let cool, cut them from the cob, and add them to the rest of the ingredients, in place of the frozen corn.

1 cup diced Roma tomatoes (from 2 tomatoes)

1 cup frozen sweet corn, thawed

½ cup sliced green onions (from 7 to 8 whole onions)

¼ small green bell pepper, diced (about ¼ cup)

½ small jalapeño pepper, seeded and finely chopped, or use more if you like spicy heat

1 teaspoon finely chopped garlic

2 tablespoons chopped fresh cilantro

Salt and freshly ground pepper, to taste

1 tablespoon lime juice

¼ cup olive oil

Combine all ingredients in a medium bowl. Serve at room temperature. This salsa can be refrigerated, covered, for up to 2 days.

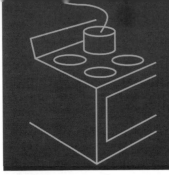

Sweet Endings

Dessert making can be culinary magic. Like nothing else you can do in the kitchen, making dessert is the transformation of a few simple ingredients into something with big impact. Even if your family regularly eats dinner without complaint, even happily at times, it's dessert that elicits cheers and smiles from the family—something I find highly motivational, which is why I love to make sweet treats. Don't worry, though; a big finish can be simple, too. All of the recipes in this chapter, for example, can fit into your weeknight cooking.

A seasoned cook can make creative dishes sometimes without much effort or advanced planning—you substitute a little of this here, you throw in a little of that there—but dessert making requires a little more patience. And unlike with savory cooking, with desserts you are usually unable to taste and correct along the way. So you need to be careful that measurements, ingredient temperatures, mixing times, pans, and oven temperature are all where they should be before starting. As you work, you will find this attention to detail will pay off. Although it all sounds like fussy work, the process of focusing on the details becomes somewhat soothing and enjoyable when you know the results will be really satisfying and will win you points with the family.

Grilled Peaches with Mascarpone and Crumbled Amaretti

✓ *EASY PREPARATION*   ✓ *SOMETHING SPECIAL*

One of my favorite ways to prepare fruit is to grill it. This recipe will work on the outdoor grill, or indoors on the grill pan or under the broiler—all succeed as long as the peaches caramelize. The creamy sweetness of mascarpone and the almond flavor of the crunchy amaretti cookies contribute to make the peaches something extra special.

4 amaretti cookies (8 halves)

2 tablespoons unsalted butter, melted

1 teaspoon sugar

1/2 teaspoon ground cinnamon

4 fresh large ripe peaches, peeled, halved, and stoned (about 1 pound) ∗

2 ounces mascarpone cheese (see Tip on page 44)

4 amaretti cookies (8 halves)

1. Put the amaretti cookies in a zippered plastic bag, squeeze out the air, and seal the bag. With a rolling pin or kitchen mallet, crush the cookies into fine crumbs.

2. In a small bowl, combine the butter, sugar, and cinnamon. Brush the peach halves on both sides with the butter mixture.

3. Arrange the peaches stone-side down on a vegetable or fish grid on a medium-hot grill. Grill 3 minutes. Turn and grill on the other side 2 to 3 minutes more. (If the grill isn't hot and you don't want to fire it up for a few peaches, use a grill pan or broil the peaches on a rack over a roasting pan, about 2 minutes per side.)

4. Arrange 2 peach halves on each plate, cut side up. Spoon some of the mascarpone into the center of each half. Sprinkle with amaretti crumbs. Serve while the peaches are still hot.

∗**TIP:** To ripen stone fruits, as well as other unripe fruits such as kiwi or avocado, place the fruit loosely in a closed paper bag at room temperature. To speed up the ripening process, add an apple to the bag. The fruit will release ethylene gas, which accelerates ripening of the other fruit.

Blueberry Sundaes

✓ *EASY PREPARATION*

This very easy dessert makes an everyday dinner into something special. Add a plate of cookies or biscotti to the table and enjoy a really festive finish.

½ cup sugar

Pinch ground cinnamon

1 pint blueberries, washed and well drained

1 pint vanilla ice cream

1 tablespoon grated lemon zest

1. In a small saucepan, heat the sugar, cinnamon, and all but ½ cup of the blueberries over medium heat just until the sugar melts and the berries begin to soften, 4 or 5 minutes. Don't let the berries collapse. Cook 1 minute more, stirring gently. Remove from the heat and let cool slightly.

2. Place a scoop of ice cream in each individual serving dish. Spoon the warm berry syrup over every serving. Garnish with the reserved whole berries and sprinkle with lemon zest.

Off-the-Shelf Mud Sundae

✓ *EASY PREPARATION*   ✓ *NO COOKING NEEDED*

I try to keep the makings of this supermarket sundae on hand all the time. No matter how simple supper might be, this assembled dessert will make it into a celebration.

One 12-ounce jar fudge sauce, microwaved on high for 60 seconds

4 large store-bought brownies

1 pint vanilla frozen yogurt or ice cream

One 12-ounce jar caramel sauce, microwaved on high for 60 seconds

¼ cup chopped pecans, toasted

Spoon a pool of fudge sauce in the middle of each dessert plate. Place a brownie in the middle of the sauce. Top each brownie with a scoop of frozen yogurt. Generously drizzle hot caramel sauce over all. Sprinkle with pecans. Serve immediately. ✱

✱**TIP:** These are even more delicious with freshly baked **brownies**. Take a few minutes to toss together a brownie mix (or brownies from scratch) to bake while the family is eating dinner. Cut into squares while they are still warm.

Toasted Pound Cake with Ice Cream and 10-Minute Fudge Sauce

✓ *EASY PREPARATION*

My rule is that if I toast or grill something then I get to take the credit for "cooking" it, even if it's store-bought. Just buy your favorite pound cake and the rest is easy.

10-Minute Fudge Sauce (below), hot

4 slices loaf pound cake, each 1 inch thick

1 tablespoon butter, melted

1 pint coffee ice cream, or your favorite flavor

1. Make the fudge sauce. Then, toast the pound cake: Brush the slices lightly with butter. Place the slices on a hot grill pan, in the broiler, or on the grill outside, if you already had it on. Grill until they are browned, 1 to 2 minutes per side.

2. Arrange the pound cake in the center of 4 dessert plates. Top each slice with a large scoop of coffee ice cream. Drizzle with the fudge sauce. Serve at once.

10-Minute Fudge Sauce

✓ *EASY PREPARATION*

Everyone needs a quick homemade chocolate sauce recipe. This one is made with everything that you could easily have on hand, and can be served as a dipping sauce for fruit and pound cake or as a topping over ice cream.

2 ounces (2 squares) unsweetened chocolate, broken up

6 ounces sweetened condensed milk (from one 14-ounce can)

¼ cup confectioner's sugar

Pinch salt

1½ teaspoons vanilla

2 tablespoons unsalted butter

1. In the top of a double boiler or in a pan set over simmering water, combine chocolate, condensed milk, sugar, and salt. Cook over simmering water until the chocolate melts, about 5 minutes, stirring from time to time. Remove from the heat and beat with a wooden spoon to combine.

2. Beat in the vanilla and butter. Serve hot.

Warm Apple Compote with Dried Fruit and Thickened Vanilla Cream

✓ *MAKE-AHEAD*   ✓ *SOMETHING SPECIAL*

Even the sophisticated folks you know will ask for seconds of this somewhat old-fashioned dessert. If you are working with what's in the kitchen and do not have any heavy cream on hand, top each serving with a scoop of vanilla ice cream.

2 cups apple cider

2 tablespoons dark brown sugar

¼ cup light corn syrup

1 teaspoon ground cinnamon

½ cup (1 stick) butter

6 Golden Delicious apples, peeled, cored, and cut into 1-inch pieces (about 8 cups)

½ cup plus 1 teaspoon sugar

2 cups golden raisins, dried blueberries, dried cherries, or dried currants, or a mixture of several small dried fruits

1 cup heavy whipping cream

½ teaspoon pure vanilla extract

Pinch freshly grated nutmeg, for garnish (optional)

1. In a small saucepan, combine the cider, brown sugar, corn syrup, and cinnamon. Bring the mixture to a boil over medium heat and cook until the liquid is reduced by half. Remove the saucepan from the heat and set aside.

2. Meanwhile, melt the butter in a large, heavy skillet over medium heat. Add the apples and cook, stirring, until the apples are slightly tender, about 10 minutes. Sprinkle with ½ cup sugar and cook until almost all of the liquid has evaporated, about 10 minutes more. Add the raisins or dried fruit and cook 3 minutes more. Toss the mixture with the apple cider reduction. Cook until the fruit is warmed through.

3. While the apples are cooking, prepare the cream: About 15 minutes minutes before you're ready to whip the cream, put the bowl and the whip of an electric mixer in the refrigerator. When ready to proceed: In the bowl of an electric mixer fitted with the whip, or in a cold metal bowl with a whisk, combine the cream, 1 teaspoon sugar, and the vanilla. Beat or whip vigorously until the mixture is the consistency of a thick milk shake.

4. Spoon the hot or warm apple compote into glasses or small bowls, and drizzle the thickened cream over it. Dust with freshly grated nutmeg. Serve immediately.

Cinnamon Noodle Pudding

✓ *EASY PREPARATION* ✓ *MAKE-AHEAD* ✓ *TAKE-ALONG*

Serve this slightly sweet dish as a dessert with a dollop of sour cream and a sprinkling of brown sugar, or serve hot alongside turkey, duck, or other poultry.

1 tablespoon unsalted butter, softened

1 tablespoon fine bread crumbs

6 ounces fine egg noodles

1/3 cup sugar

3 large eggs

1 teaspoon ground cinnamon

1/3 cup raisins

1/2 cup coarsely chopped pecans, toasted (2 ounces)

1 small Red Delicious apple, peeled, cored, and finely chopped or grated (about 1 cup)

1 teaspoon grated lemon rind

2 tablespoons butter, melted

1. Preheat the oven to 400°F. Lightly grease a 1-quart baking dish with the softened butter and dust with bread crumbs.

2. Cook the noodles in 6 quarts of boiling salted water for 6 to 9 minutes. Drain well.

3. In a medium bowl, beat together the sugar, eggs, and cinnamon. Stir in the raisins, pecans, apple, and lemon rind. Toss the noodles with the melted butter and add them to the egg mixture, blending well.

4. Turn the noodles into the prepared baking dish and bake for 45 minutes. Remove from the oven. Serve hot or at room temperature. ✱

SERVING SUGGESTION

Serve with applesauce or warmed preserves of any kind, or even with ice cream and honey.

✱ TIP: If you like casseroles or puddings with a **lighter texture**, separate the eggs and beat the whites until stiff (they hold their shape when the beater is lifted). Gently fold the whites into the noodle mixture just before turning it into the prepared baking dish. The end result will be slightly more like a soufflé than a pudding. (This also works for other dishes with eggs, such as quiches and cakes.)

Fruit Crisp

✓ SOMETHING SPECIAL

Here's a wonderful warm dessert recipe that is simple to put together. Take advantage of whatever fruit is in season for the best flavor.

1 cup all-purpose flour

1/3 cup firmly packed brown sugar

4 tablespoons plus 1/2 cup sugar

1/2 teaspoon ground cinnamon

1 tablespoon grated orange zest (from 1 medium orange) *

5 tablespoons (1/3 cup) unsalted butter, at room temperature, plus more for for the pan

1/2 cup pecan halves, toasted (2 ounces)

8 cups seasonal fruit, such as apples, pears, peaches, strawberries, blackberries, blueberries, raspberries, or plums, well washed and sliced if necessary

1 teaspoon lemon juice

1. Preheat the oven to 350°F. Lightly butter a 9- × 13-inch glass baking dish. In a large bowl, combine the flour, brown sugar, 4 tablespoons sugar, cinnamon, and zest, and cut the butter into the mixture. When the mixture resembles oatmeal, stir in the pecans and set aside. *

2. In a large bowl, mix the fruit, 1/2 cup sugar, and lemon juice. Spread the fruit in the bottom of the baking dish. Spoon the dry topping over the fruit.

3. Cover the dish with foil and bake for 20 minutes. Remove the foil and continue baking 20 minutes more, or until the top is crisp and browned. Serve hot or warm.

SERVING SUGGESTION

Serve with ice cream or lightly sweetened whipped cream spooned on top.

✱TIP: Invest in an ultra-sharp **Microplane grater**; it makes adding citrus zest to finished dishes ultra easy. Be sure to wash and dry the oranges well before zesting.

✱TIP: **Cutting butter** into dry ingredients distributes the fat evenly without melting it. A pastry cutter does the job quickly. If you don't have a pastry cutter, use two sharp knives to chop the butter into pieces about the size of very large crumbs while working it into the dry ingredients. The result will look like raw oatmeal.

Italian Meringue with Chocolate Sorbet

✓ *SOMETHING SPECIAL*

This is a simple dessert that you can enhance with presentation. You can make the simplest version— sorbet scooped into a glass, topped with meringue, and sprinkled with almonds—or take it to the "wow" level by dipping the glass rim in melted chocolate and using special glasses. Then when you serve it, you can bask in the "oohs" and "aahs."

⅓ cup water

¾ cup sugar

3 large egg whites, at room temperature ＊

⅛ teaspoon cream of tartar

⅛ teaspoon salt

¼ teaspoon pure vanilla extract

1 pint chocolate sorbet

¼ cup sliced almonds, toasted (1 ounce)

1. Combine the water and sugar in a small saucepan. Holding the pan handle, slowly swirl the saucepan over medium-high heat until the mixture begins to boil. Do not stir the mixture. Continue to swirl the pan until all the sugar is melted and the syrup is clear, 4 to 5 minutes. Cover the pan and reduce the heat to low. (If crystals form on the sides of the pan, brush them down with a pastry brush dipped in cold water.)

2. Add the egg whites to an electric mixer bowl. Beat the egg whites at a low speed; when they are foamy, increase the speed to medium. Add the cream of tartar and the salt. Increase the mixer speed to high and beat until soft peaks form. ＊

3. Remove the cover from the saucepan and bring the sugar to a boil. Place a candy thermometer in the pan. When the mixture registers 280°F, immediately remove it from the heat.

4. Set the mixer speed to medium and gradually beat the syrup into the egg whites in a slow, steady, thin stream. When all the syrup has been incorporated, add the vanilla, and increase the mixer speed to high. Beat the mixture until it has completely cooled, 7 to 8 minutes. The meringue should hold stiff peaks and be very shiny.

5. Scoop the sorbet into glasses, spoon the meringue on top, scatter some almonds over each, and serve.

SERVING SUGGESTIONS

Try any or all of these ideas to make the dessert presentation extra-special:

Make perfect scoops. About an hour before you are ready to serve dessert, scoop the sorbet into balls and place them on a cookie sheet. Put the cookie sheet in the freezer.

Serve this in wine glasses or martini glasses if you have them.

Rim the glasses with chocolate: Melt a little bittersweet or semisweet chocolate in a saucepan. Let cool slightly; dip the rim of each glass in the chocolate.

＊**TIP:** Egg whites should be at room temperature before beating so they will be as light and fluffy as possible.

＊**TIP:** Beating egg whites can become easy. If the recipe calls for soft peaks, beat just until the egg whites are lightly thickened and very opaque white. When the whisk or whip is taken out of the whites and held upside down, the tip of the peak that forms on the end of the whisk will fall over—like the tip of soft-serve ice cream. Stiff peaks form when the egg whites are beaten a little longer and the peak stands straight up—no flopping at the tip.

No-Trade Lunches

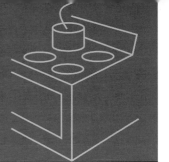

In the late summer, just as school is about to begin again, I shop for school supplies with my son, Matthew. Each year he looks forward to getting his brand-new binders and pens, maybe a new backpack, and a new lunch carrier.

He's getting older, though, and gone are the days when he wanted a lunch box covered with animated characters. Now he chooses something more sophisticated, even cool: A black insulated bag, slim, no thermos (unless it's small and stainless steel for hot tea or a cold smoothie). His sophistication doesn't end there. What goes in it is even more important. He, like most kids, can be picky.

At the same time that kids have gotten more choosy, the amount of time they have to eat has decreased; at school they may have less than 30 minutes to sit down, eat lunch, and clean up. And you know all too well you don't have time to eat a leisurely lunch either. You may leave your office for a few minutes or squeeze some time in to pick something up when running errands, or you might hit the vending machines or drive-through. All of this means that we are not eating as well as we need to in the middle of the day.

Homemade lunches, then, for you and your kids, have to meet quite a lot of requirements: They need to be efficient to eat, pack a nutritional punch, and be interesting enough that they don't get traded (or thrown) away.

The efficiency does not begin with the type of lunch you eat. It begins with the time it takes to make it.

Tips for making no-trade lunches

- Make time to make lunch. Your own outside choices for lunch are limited. If you don't bring it, you and your family have to make do with what's available that day, and more often than not, you're not really satisfied. Whatever you make at home will be healthier and more economical than that.

- Start thinking about lunches as you are planning your meals for dinner. If you are grilling chicken, grill extra to put in a sandwich later in the week. If you are making pizza, make enough to have some for lunch the next day. Most of my meal planning includes making enough for one dinner (I am not much of a leftovers person) and one lunch.

- I try to make lunch the night before. Mornings are absolutely crazy! I can barely get everyone out of bed, shower and get ready myself, make breakfast, and get out the door. Having the lunch bag filled and waiting to grab as Matt runs out the door really helps.

- Keep things on hand for emergency healthful lunches in case you don't have time to make something ahead. I always have cheese for a cheese sandwich, good mustard, bread in the freezer, dried fruit for a snack, and bottled water.

Peanut Butter, Granola, and Honey Sandwich

✓ *EASY PREPARATION*   ✓ *MAKE-AHEAD*   ✓ *NO COOKING NEEDED*

Kids love the old P, B, and J. This variation on the favorite adds some fun texture and flavor. This may also hit the spot for you. It tastes good, it's nutritious, and it's easy to eat—who says you need to dine on haute cuisine at every meal. This is feel-good food that will help you and your kids get through the day.

8 slices whole-wheat bread

1 cup chunky natural peanut butter

1 cup plain granola

¼ cup clover honey

1. Lay out the 8 slices of bread. Spread the peanut butter equally on 4 of the slices.

2. Spread ¼ cup of granola over each of the pieces of bread with peanut butter on it.

3. Drizzle 1 tablespoon of honey over each of the remaining bread slices. ✱

4. Put a slice of the honey bread over each of the peanut butter-granola pieces. These can be made up to one day ahead.

SERVING SUGGESTION

Include a small container of carrot, cucumber, and green bell pepper sticks to eat with these sandwiches.

✱ TIP: One of my favorite kitchen gadgets is a **honey wand** (probably because I use honey so much). It serves a specific but very valuable purpose. (Although it works for thick sauces, too.) The long handle keeps your hands from getting sticky, and the (often ridged) bulb at one end holds the honey well, letting it drizzle in a steady stream anywhere you want it to go.

Nutty Cream Cheese and Fruit Sandwiches

✓ *EASY PREPARATION*　　✓ *MAKE-AHEAD*　　✓ *NO COOKING NEEDED*

This sandwich is always a hit with the kids. There's just enough crunch to intrigue them and enough sweet to tempt them to finish it all. For adult lunches, try using thinly sliced artisanal raisin-nut bread. Artisanal breads are home-style rustic loaves made with quality ingredients in small batches. Unlike packaged sliced bread, the loaves are often coarsely textured and hearty, adding character to the finished sandwich. You can buy the loaves unsliced and cut them as thick or thin as you like.

★TIP: In place of the apple, try slices of **pear**, **banana**, or **peaches**.

8 slices of raisin nut bread

4 ounces (½ cup) soft spreadable cream cheese

1 Granny Smith, Fuji, or other tart-sweet apple, quartered, cored, and very thinly sliced (about 1 cup) ★

2 tablespoons fresh lemon juice

½ teaspoon ground ginger

1. Arrange the bread slices on the work surface. Spread 4 slices with a thick layer of cream cheese.

2. Toss the apple slices lightly with lemon juice. Arrange apple slices over the cream cheese. Sprinkle each sandwich with a pinch of ground ginger.

3. Cover the sandwiches with remaining bread slices.

SERVING SUGGESTIONS

To prepare in advance, cut the sandwiches in halves or thirds and wrap tightly in plastic wrap.

Send these sandwiches off in the lunch box or brown bag along with a tightly sealed container of cantaloupe slices to munch on the side.

Yogurt Chicken Pitas

✓ *MAKE-AHEAD*

Pita pockets, made with whole-wheat or white flour, make great containers for a satisfying lunchtime break. I like to pack along with this some chopped fruit and a bottle of water with lime.

2 tablespoons fresh lime juice (from 1 large or 2 small limes)

1 tablespoon olive oil

1 tablespoon fresh garlic, chopped (about 3 medium cloves)

2 teaspoons ground coriander

2 teaspoons ground cumin

Salt and freshly ground pepper, to taste

1/2 cup chopped fresh Italian flat-leaf parsley or cilantro

1 1/2 pounds boneless skinless chicken breasts

2 cups plain yogurt (1 pint)

1 cup peeled seeded and chopped cucumber

1/4 cup chopped fresh parsley, cilantro, or mint

8 pita breads

1 cup seeded and chopped vine-ripened tomato

2 cups romaine lettuce leaves, washed and well dried (from 1/2 large head)

1. Preheat the grill or grill pan 10 to 15 minutes to medium-high heat.

2. In a blender, combine the lime juice, oil, garlic, coriander, cumin, salt, pepper, and parsley or cilantro. Process until smooth.

3. Put the chicken on a large plate with an edge and pour the marinade over it. Allow the chicken to marinate 15 minutes, turning the pieces once or twice.

4. In a small bowl, stir together the yogurt, cucumber, and chopped parsley, cilantro, or mint. Reserve.

5. Drain the marinated chicken. Place the chicken breast on the grill or pan, and cook, turning once, until the chicken reaches a temperature of 160°F on an instant-read thermometer inserted into the thickest part of the breast, 8 to 10 minutes. Transfer the chicken to a plate to cool. You can grill the pita bread on the grill pan or on the grill to toast it.

6. Slice the chicken on the diagonal across the breasts. Cut the top third off each pita. Stuff the remaining large pocket with chicken slices, chopped tomatoes, and lettuce, and top with some of the yogurt dressing.

SERVING SUGGESTION

If packing for a take-away lunch, put the dressing in a small resealable container instead, to be poured over the sandwich when it's time to eat.

Fresh Dill Tuna Pitas

✓ *MAKE-AHEAD*   ✓ *NO COOKING NEEDED*

This is a great quick lunch that is so good, everyone in the family will want to brown-bag it. It only takes 15 minutes to make but, if you can, make the salad a night or two before you need it for best flavor.

2 cups solid tuna, packed in water

1 cup plain yogurt (½ pint)

½ cup mayonnaise

1 cup finely chopped celery
(from 2 large ribs)

¼ cup trimmed and chopped green
onions, white and up to 1 inch dark
green (from 4 whole onions)

3 tablespoons coarse-grained mustard

1 teaspoon chopped fresh dill

¼ teaspoon salt

½ teaspoon freshly ground pepper

6 pita breads, sliced in half

12 leaves green leaf lettuce,
washed and spun or patted dry
(from 1 small head)

2 medium tomatoes, sliced

1. In a medium bowl, combine the tuna, yogurt, mayonnaise, celery, onion, mustard, and dill. Season the mixture with salt and pepper. ✱

2. Line the pitas with lettuce and tomato and then fill with the tuna mixture.

SERVING SUGGESTION

If this is a traveling lunch, fill the pita in the morning and wrap it tightly in plastic wrap. If this lunch is going to be left at room temperature, put an ice pack in the bag to keep the sandwich cold.

For a take-away lunch, add a medley of cut crunchy vegetables to the sack with a little container of ranch dressing (for dipping), a bottle of water, and a piece of fresh fruit.

✱ TIP: Another intriguing flavor combo to try is **curry with tuna**. You can make a curry tuna pita by replacing the dill with one teaspoon of mild curry powder.

Smoked Turkey and Sprout Club

✓ *EASY PREPARATION*   ✓ *MAKE-AHEAD*   ✓ *NO COOKING NEEDED*   ✓ *TAKE-ALONG*

I love a turkey sandwich for lunch and enjoy innumerable variations. Here's one of my favorites. Don't let the sprouts make you think this is a sandwich for health fanatics. The sprouts actually add refreshing crunch, and they will keep their crispness until lunchtime. This sandwich is so flavorful, though, you may eat it before that!

¼ cup mayonnaise

2 tablespoons commercial chili sauce

8 slices wheat bread, lightly toasted

½ pound thin-sliced smoked deli turkey

¼ pound Swiss cheese, thinly sliced

8 thin slices bacon, cooked crisp, well drained on paper towels

1 medium tomato, very thinly sliced

1 cup crisp sprouts, such as garlic, alfalfa, or chive ✱

1. Beat the mayonnaise and chili sauce together in a small bowl. ✱

2. Spread the mayonnaise dressing on 1 side of each piece of toast. Divide the turkey among 4 of the toast slices. Follow with the cheese. Top with 2 slices bacon and then the tomato slices. Finish with ¼ cup sprouts on each sandwich. Cover with the remaining slices of toast, dressing side down.

Press each sandwich down a little to compact the ingredients.

3. Secure each sandwich with 2 long picks and cut in half on the diagonal between the picks.

SERVING SUGGESTION

If packing the sandwiches, wrap each sandwich in aluminum foil and keep cool with an ice pack.

✱ **TIP:** **Sprouts** of all kinds of vegetables and grains—such as mung bean, radish, broccoli, wheat, alfalfa, garlic, cress, and others—are wonderful additions to sandwiches and salads. The most common are available in supermarkets everywhere; natural food stores carry an even larger assortment. The sprouts should be rinsed and dried well before being used.

✱ **TIP:** For a spicier version of this sauce, try adding to the mayonnaise 1 tablespoon of the sauce from a jar of chipotle chiles in **adobo**. Adobo is a spicy, tangy sauce made from chiles, seasonings, and vinegar. Reserve the chiles for other uses.

Fruit Sticks with Strawberry–Cream Cheese Dip

✓ EASY PREPARATION   ✓ MAKE-AHEAD   ✓ NO COOKING NEEDED   ✓ TAKE-ALONG

My son won't eat a whole piece of fruit if I pack it for him for lunch. If I cut up the fruit and put it on sticks, it disappears.

Strawberry Cream Cheese Dip (below)

8 strawberries, washed and hulled

Eight 1½-inch melon cubes (from ½ small cantaloupe, honeydew, or Crenshaw) *

2 nectarines, halved, stoned, and quartered

2 kiwi fruit, peeled, halved across, then halved across again

Eight 8-inch wooden skewers

1 lemon half

4 to 8 sprigs fresh mint, for garnish

1. Make the cream cheese dip.

2. Arrange one piece of each fruit on each skewer. Sprinkle with lemon juice and garnish each with mint. Kebabs can be wrapped in foil or packed in a plastic bag. Pack the dip in a small plastic container.

★ TIP: For these skewers, use the **fruit** that looks fresh in the store, rather than shopping for specific fruit that may not be at its peak. Head to the market with the plan to buy at least four kinds of fruit. See what is seasonal, what looks good, and what is affordable. I don't use fruits that brown quickly on these skewers, so avoid banana unless you plan to serve them right away.

Strawberry Cream Cheese Dip

✓ EASY PREPARATION

If you are bored with just a plain piece of fruit for lunch, cut up any seasonal fruit and take it along with this fantastic dip. You can make it several days ahead.

One 8-ounce package cream cheese, at room temperature

½ cup sweetened condensed milk

¼ cup strawberry preserves, at room temperature

Milk, any kind

In a small bowl, beat together the cream cheese, condensed milk, and strawberry preserves. If necessary, dilute with just enough milk to make a dippable consistency, using 1 teaspoon at a time.

Vegetable Medley with Ranch Dipping Sauce

MAKES 4 SERVINGS

✓ EASY PREPARATION   ✓ MAKE-AHEAD   ✓ NO COOKING NEEDED   ✓ TAKE-ALONG

I always aim to use fresh foods, but sometimes a packaged product hits the spot. My mom used to make this vegetable dish with Good Seasons dressing to serve at parties (where it was a hit), or to put in our lunch box (from which it disappeared), so I maintain the tradition. I clean and slice the vegetables the night before. The dip can be made in advance, too.

½ pound carrots (about 4 medium carrots)

4 large ribs celery

1 large or 2 medium bell peppers, any color ∗

RANCH DIPPING SAUCE

2 cups low-fat sour cream (1 pint)

2 envelopes Good Seasons Zesty Italian dressing

1 teaspoon garlic powder

1 teaspoon onion powder

½ teaspoon cayenne pepper

½ teaspoon freshly ground pepper, or to taste

1. Scrape and wash the carrots. Cut into 3-inch lengths and then into sticks.

2. Wash and string the celery ribs. Cut into 3-inch lengths and then into sticks.

3. Stem, halve, and seed the peppers. Cut lengthwise into ¼-inch strips.

4. Divide the vegetables equally among 4 individual serving bags.

5. In a medium bowl, beat together the sour cream, dry Italian dressing powder, garlic powder, onion powder, cayenne, and black pepper. Spoon the dip into individual containers with tightly fitting lids. Send one bag of vegetables along with one small container of the dipping sauce.

∗**TIP:** Any assorted **vegetables** can be used for this dip. To use green beans, broccoli, or cauliflower, first steam them (separately) for a minute or two and then keep them in ice water until you are ready to use them. You can prepare the celery and carrot sticks the same way.

Frothy Orange Smoothies

✓ *EASY PREPARATION*   ✓ *MAKE-AHEAD*   ✓ *NO COOKING NEEDED*   ✓ *TAKE-ALONG*

Are you tired of the same old soda for lunch? My grandmother used to take me to a store called Orange Julius for a drink like this when I was a kid; now they call them smoothies. Why not pack it for lunch? It will fill you up on a really busy day or be a tasty supplement to a light lunch. You can add some protein powder or powdered egg white for extra vitamins and minerals, if you like.

4 cups orange juice (1 quart)

1½ cups nonfat dry milk powder

¼ cup powdered egg white (optional) *

½ cup confectioner's sugar

1½ teaspoons pure vanilla extract

1 cup ice cubes

1. Combine all the ingredients in a blender. (If the mixture fills more than half the capacity of your blender, stir everything a few times, then remove some of the mixture.) *

2. Blend until thick and frothy, 1 to 2 minutes. (If you removed some of the mixture, pour out the blended liquid into cups or a container, then blend the rest.) Serve cold.

SERVING SUGGESTION

To take it along, pour the smoothie into a chilled thermal drink container. Shake vigorously before drinking.

★TIP: Powdered egg white is often used by bakers and cake decorators especially for making icing. It is sold anywhere you buy cake decorating supplies, as well as in the baking sections of many well-stocked supermarkets. The egg powder makes this delicious drink protein-rich and extra frothy.

★TIP: A good rule of thumb is to fill your **blender** only half way, no matter what mixture you are going to puree, and no matter what size your blender is. That way, the churning action won't push the contents over the blender edge.

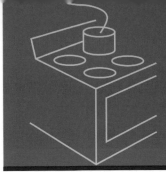

Kids in the Kitchen

When I was young, the first meal my brother and I ever tackled in the kitchen was breakfast. My brother made eggs and toast; I made the muffins. We learned by trial and error, with my mother guiding us but letting us learn the process, making mistakes as we went along.

If your kids want to help in the kitchen, you can start with breakfast or some of the simple recipes in this chapter. Many of the recipes use commercial products because the kids will first need to learn how to assemble and how to follow directions; using food or ingredients you know they like will inspire them to finish the recipe. Once your children become more confident cooks, you can have them try making some of the recipes with ingredients they create, such as fresh salsa instead of jarred salsa for the Nachos Grande. Or, have them move on to some of the other simple recipes in this book.

Have your young chefs read the following guidelines, or read them to your children if they can't yet read themselves, and describe the steps to them.

Tips for working with kids in the kitchen

- Read through the recipe. Make sure to read every word of it and understand exactly what ingredients, tools, and cooking steps are needed.

- Clear your work area. The less clutter around, the less chance of confusion or accidents.

- Get your equipment ready. Set out all the equipment you will need. Make sure your pans, bowls, spoons, spatulas, and measures are clean and dry.

- Set out all of the ingredients. If everything is ready to use and easy to reach, you won't have to race around to get something when your hands are dirty or you are working on another part of the cooking.

- Follow the recipe directions in order.

- Follow the instructions carefully.

- Clean up as you go. Put dirty dishes in the sink and wipe up spills as they occur, for safety and cleanliness.

- Use a timer. Until you can tell when food is done by the way it looks, smells, or feels, always set a timer to tell you when something is done. Set it for about 5 minutes before the end of the cooking time so you can make sure that what you are making doesn't overcook.

- Trust yourself and have fun! Because no two cooks are alike, trust your own judgment. Remember that recipes are, ultimately, just guidelines; once you understand how to make a dish, don't be afraid to make changes.

Bumps on a Log

✓ *EASY PREPARATION*   ✓ *MAKE-AHEAD*   ✓ *NO COOKING NEEDED*   ✓ *TAKE-ALONG*

This is a recipe for the young ones. Plan to have some small snacks like carrots and celery on hand for your helpers. Have them count the raisins and measure the peanut butter to introduce them to measuring and counting.

½ cup creamy or chunky peanut butter

4 large celery ribs, washed, dried, and ends trimmed

20 milk-chocolate-covered raisins or peanuts, or more if you like

1. Spoon about 2 tablespoons peanut butter along the length of each stalk of celery.

2. Press raisins or nuts at random into the peanut butter.

SERVING SUGGESTION

Add a glass of milk to the menu for a healthy snack.

Breakfast Burritos with Avocado Salsa

✓ *EASY PREPARATION*

Ordinarily my son doesn't like to eat breakfast, but the first thing I taught him to make was scrambled eggs, a dish he enjoys. When I can send him on his way with this breakfast burrito, I know that he is starting his day out right.

Avocado Salsa (below)

1 small onion

1 small green bell pepper

¼ pound spicy sausage

4 large flour tortillas

2 tablespoons unsalted butter

6 large eggs, beaten lightly with a fork

Salt and freshly ground pepper, to taste

½ cup grated cheddar or Monterey Jack flavored with hot peppers (from 2 ounces)

½ cup sour cream, for garnish

1. Preheat the oven to 200°F. Make the avocado salsa. Then, peel the onion and put it on a cutting board. With a small knife, cut a thick slice off one side. Wrap the rest of the onion in plastic wrap for another use. Lay the slice cut side down. Use the knife to cut the slice into thin strips, then cut across the strips into small pieces. Measure 2 tablespoons. ∗

2. Place a small pepper on a cutting board. Cut a large wedge out of the pepper, removing any seeds. Wrap the remaining pepper in plastic wrap for another use. Cut the pepper wedge into long, thin strips. Cut across the strips into small pieces. Measure 2 tablespoons.

3. Unwrap the sausage from its casings and break it up with your fingers. Put the sausage in a medium-heavy skillet. Fry over medium-high heat, stirring with a wooden spoon and breaking up any large pieces, until the sausage is well browned, about 6 minutes. Remove the sausage from the skillet with a slotted spoon and drain on several thicknesses of paper towels.

4. Wrap the tortillas in a damp, clean cloth towel and heat in the oven for 2 to 3 minutes.

5. Melt the butter in a heavy skillet over medium heat. Add the onion and green pepper. Cook, stirring, until the vegetables are transparent and tender, about 5 minutes.

6. Beat in the eggs and sausage. Cook, turning with a spatula, until the eggs are set but not hard, 2 to 3 minutes. Taste a little, season with salt and pepper, then taste again to be sure you like the final result. ∗

7. Fill the top half of each tortilla with one quarter of the egg mixture. Sprinkle with one quarter of the cheese. Fold the bottom of tortillas over the filling, then roll up from left to right. Serve hot with sour cream and the salsa on the side.

∗**TIP:** Whoever is **cutting the onion and pepper** should have experience using a sharp knife (or should be supervised).

∗**TIP:** If you don't have **tortillas,** try baking the eggs in a muffin tray along with the vegetables. Beat the eggs with ½ cup milk or cream. Place the chopped vegetables in the bottom of greased muffin tins; pour the egg mixture over them, and sprinkle with the cheese. Bake at 375°F for 12 minutes or until firm. Allow them to cool slightly, then turn the tray upside down to release the egg-vegetable "muffins" from the tins. Serve hot or cold, with a little sour cream for garnish.

Avocado Salsa

✓ *EASY PREPARATION*

Many children like the smooth creaminess and flavor of avocado. When my son, Matt, was young, he wouldn't eat very much, but he would eat diced ripened avocado. Make this zesty salsa with your helpers, and they won't complain about eating vegetables. (Leave out the jalapeño or onions if your kids aren't fans of strong flavors.)

1 ripe avocado, halved, stoned, peeled, and diced (about 1 cup) ✱

1 teaspoon fresh lime juice (from ½ medium lime)

2 Roma tomatoes, seeded and chopped (about 1 cup) ✱

¼ cup sliced green onions (from 4 whole onions)

1 teaspoon very thinly sliced garlic (from 1 medium clove)

½ jalapeño pepper, seeded and finely chopped

¼ cup chopped fresh cilantro

¼ cup olive oil

Salt to taste

Combine all the ingredients in a medium bowl. Let stand about 20 minutes before serving. Serve at room temperature. Covered tightly with plastic wrap, this salsa will keep in the refrigerator for 2 days.

✱ **TIP:** To keep the **avocado** from turning brown, leave the pit in the salsa until serving.

✱ **TIP:** Chop the **ingredients** for salsa evenly, so that each bite includes all the flavors.

Nachos Grande

✓ *EASY PREPARATION*

Nachos are a favorite for all ages. This easy-to-make version is just right for beginners using the stove, and they can have dinner or snacks on the table all by themselves.

1 pound ground (chuck) beef

1 package taco seasoning

¾ cup water

4 to 6 ounces tortilla chips

2 cups grated sharp cheddar cheese, or pepper jack cheese if you like things spicy (from 8 ounces)

½ cup jarred salsa

1 cup (½ pint) sour cream (optional)

1. Break up the ground beef with your fingers and put it in a large, heavy skillet over medium-high heat. ✱ Cook, stirring with a wooden spoon, breaking up any large pieces of meat, until browned, about 5 minutes.

2. Sprinkle the taco seasoning over the meat and stir. Remove the skillet from the heat and stir in the water. Return the skillet to the heat and cook on medium-low heat until the meat has absorbed most of the liquid, about 5 minutes. Cover and remove from the heat.

3. On a large microwavable platter, arrange a layer of tortilla chips. With a large spoon, spread half the meat mixture over the chips. Top with half the cheese. Repeat the layers.

4. Put the nachos in the microwave and microwave on high 1 to 2 minutes, until the cheese is melted.

5. Remove from the microwave. Wait 1 minute. Spoon the salsa on top.

6. Place the platter in the center of the table for everyone to help themselves. Pass a bowl of sour cream, if you like.

SERVING SUGGESTION

At the table, also pass around a bowl of guacamole, and/or another of pepperoncini (hot pepper pickles).

✱ TIP: When children are **using the stove**, make sure they have a stool so they are at a safe and comfortable height above the heat and pans they are working with.

✱ TIP: Children should be wearing clothing that fits tightly and doesn't have any hanging pieces that can catch on the pan or the heat.

✱ TIP: Make sure the **handle of the skillet is pointed inward** rather than outward to prevent small children from pulling it down on themselves.

✱ TIP: Stay with them at all times so they don't get hurt.

Oven Fries with Cheese

✓ *EASY PREPARATION*

Fresh French fries are real kid-pleasers. And even if you prefer fresh cheese, children really love Velveeta, which melts well, so once in a while, indulge. Help them cut the potatoes; then let them do the rest. The microwave is a simple enough kitchen appliance to handle for a child beginning to cook.

4 medium russet potatoes

2 tablespoons olive oil

Salt, to taste

4 ounces Velveeta cheese, cubed (about ¾ cup)

¼ cup whole milk

½ cup bottled pizza sauce or ketchup

1. Preheat the oven to 425°F. Scrub the potatoes well with a brush. Dry them well with paper towels. Leave the skin on. Cut the potatoes lengthwise into slices about ¼ inch thick. Cut the slices lengthwise into sticks.

2. Toss the potato sticks with oil in a large bowl. Season with salt.

3. Cover the bottom of a heavy baking sheet with foil. Spread out the potato sticks on the baking sheet. Put the baking sheet in the oven and cook the fries, turning

them from time to time with a big spatula, 25 to 30 minutes, until crisp on the outside, soft and creamy on the inside.

4. Put the cheese cubes and milk in a microwavable bowl. Microwave on high for 1 minute. Remove the bowl from the microwave and stir the cheese sauce with a spoon. Microwave for 20 seconds more.

5. Pile the fries onto a large platter and pour the cheese over all. Serve hot with pizza sauce or ketchup on the side.

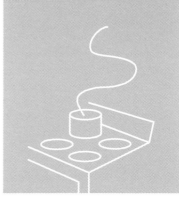

Toasted Snowballs with Honey

✓ *MAKE-AHEAD*

The best way to get ice cream ready for a gathering is to scoop it into balls in advance, then place the balls on a cookie sheet. Freeze the ice cream on the sheet, and then just lift off the scoops with a large spoon when you are ready to serve them. Try this one, with the ice cream rolled in coconut. It's so easy that kids can make it for dessert any time they want. If you don't serve the snowballs immediately after rolling them in coconut, freeze them while dinner is served and eaten.

1 pint vanilla ice cream, slightly softened

2 cups unsweetened shredded coconut

½ cup honey

1. About 30 minutes before serving, freeze scoops of ice cream shaped into balls. Scoop out 4 portions, placing each scoop on a cookie sheet with about 2 inches between them. Put the sheet of ice cream scoops in the freezer. (Make sure there's room in the freezer beforehand.)

2. Meanwhile, toast the coconut: Preheat the oven to 375°F. Place a thin layer of the coconut on a cookie sheet and toast it in the oven. Toast about 10 minutes or until it begins to turn light brown. Spread the coconut in a shallow bowl.

3. When ready to serve the ice cream, lift off the snowballs with a large spoon and roll each, one at a time, in the toasted coconut. Arrange on a small cookie sheet and freeze again about 10 minutes or more to resolidify.

4. Place 1 snowball in each serving bowl. Drizzle with honey. Serve at once.

Classroom Snacks

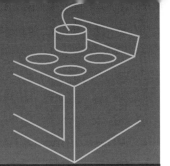

Although I love to help out in my son's classroom whenever school parties come up, it often seems to be easier to pick up food than to make it. Kids can be difficult eaters to please. But there are some foods that they are happy to eat. You just need to be sensitive to their tastes and to be creative.

In general, children are much more sensitive to the look, smell, and taste of foods than adults. Think about how spicy you make things, or how much tart mustard you use. Kids like macaroni and cheese or pasta because it is mild.

When I cooked for my son Matt's grade-school classes, I followed a checklist of kid "dos and don'ts" before I began. I paid attention to what they ate, because if they liked something, they really liked it, and it was a pleasure to see them enjoy a homemade treat. Otherwise, they were not satisfied and I wound up throwing out what I made or carting it back home.

When you know that you are going to be the one with classroom snack duty, be sure you have everything on hand the evening before the date. Get everything organized while the kitchen is being cleaned up after dinner, then set to work. If you are making a snack for the kids' class, they can be responsible for helping you or for putting things in the dishwasher, finishing their homework, and getting ready for the next day. Family cooperation makes preparing the treat even easier.

Tips for Cooking for the Classroom

- Think in advance about what the occasion is. Themes for the classes make the food special for the kids. I have made heart-shaped pizzas for Valentine's Day, Chinese pot stickers for Chinese New Year, and even sticky grilled ribs for a spring picnic.

- Take into consideration how much time you have to prepare something. For Halloween once when I had little time, I took premade pudding with whipped cream and crumbled chocolate cookies to make a graveyard of pudding pots. Another year, I baked cookies shaped like fingers for a Halloween party.

- Make different versions of the same thing; for example, variations on the tuna melt. This helps because kids usually don't all like the same things. Cupcakes can be a mix of vanilla and chocolate or of two other flavors (if you know that the kids do like other flavors).

- Keep in mind that kids prefer things that are milder in flavor—muffins with lots of nutmeg will be a real turn-off. The nutmeg will taste bitter to them. Make peanut butter and jelly muffins, a flavor combination that most kids will enjoy!

- Make foods that can travel. They will have to make it from your house to the school. The odds are that you will not have much more than a sink and a microwave in the teachers' lounge to work with. I always make things that can be completed before I leave the house or in the microwave at school.

- Keep it simple. Usually the teacher will give you only about 30 minutes to get ready for the party in the classroom. You have to have the plates unwrapped, the drinks ready to go, and the foods hot (if necessary) as soon as you arrive.

- Remember that the most important part of your effort is that you are there. My son didn't make a big fuss about what I brought; he was just happy that I was active in his life. Making something special is the icing on the cake for your child.

Peanut Butter and Jelly Mini-Muffins

✓ *EASY PREPARATION*   ✓ *MAKE-AHEAD*   ✓ *TAKE-ALONG*

Most kids love peanut butter and jelly. In these little muffins, you have their favorite flavors in one bite. Make them the night before or even two, and then take them to the classroom when you need them. They freeze well, so make more than you need for the perfect after-school snack.

1/3 cup peanut butter (smooth works best)

1/4 cup sugar

1/2 cup plain yogurt, buttermilk, or sour cream

1 large egg

1 1/2 tablespoons unsalted butter, melted

1 cup all-purpose flour

1 teaspoon baking powder

Pinch salt

1/2 cup (or more) jelly of choice, (grape is always a favorite)

1. Preheat the oven to 400°F. In a medium bowl, beat together the peanut butter, sugar, yogurt, and egg. Stir in the melted butter. In a small bowl, stir together the flour, baking powder, and salt. Combine the peanut butter mixture with the flour, stirring just until combined. ✱

2. Line mini-muffin tins with paper liners. Fill the liners half full with batter. Top each with a small spoonful of jelly. Cover with another spoonful of batter. The liners should be about three-quarters full when you are ready to put them in the oven.

3. Bake in the center of the oven for 12 to 15 minutes. Remove from the oven and transfer the muffin cups to cooling racks. Serve warm or at room temperature.

✱**TIP:** It is important to **blend muffin batter** only briefly so that it doesn't become tough when cooked. At the point when you need to add the liquid ingredients to the dry ones, combine with a wooden spoon just until all the dry ingredients are moistened. Make sure that most of the lumps are removed, but do not overblend the batter to get there! Some lumps are fine.

Mini Tuna Melts

✓ *EASY PREPARATION*   ✓ *TAKE-ALONG*

Most kids will eat tuna sandwiches, which makes this an easy snack to prepare. At the school, you just need a microwave and a sink in the teachers' lounge.

One 12-ounce can water-packed tuna, very well drained, or 12 ounces of vacuum-packed tuna that is ready to use

1 rib celery, ends trimmed, finely chopped (about 1/2 cup)

About 1/3 cup thinly sliced green onions, white and light green (from about 5 onions)

Salt and freshly ground pepper, to taste

1/2 to 2/3 cup mayonnaise

1 baguette-style French loaf, cut into 24 thin slices

8 ounces mild cheddar, cut into 24 slices

1. In a medium bowl, mix together tuna, celery, green onions, salt, pepper, and mayonnaise. Refrigerate. ✱

2. Lightly toast the bread slices.

3. Spoon the tuna salad onto toast slices. Top each with a slice of cheese. Microwave 45 to 60 seconds, until the cheese is melted and bubbling. If you are transporting these to school, pack the toasted bread, tuna salad, and cheese slices in separate containers and put the sandwiches together just before popping them into the school microwave.

SERVING SUGGESTION

Serve this along with some Bumps on a Log (page 193), and the kids will love you.

If the kids like only soft, white bread, cut the crusts off the slices of sandwich bread, make open-faced sandwiches, and when they are hot, cut them into quarters.

School aside, these little "melts" also make wonderful snacks to serve with drinks at home when friends unexpectedly drop by.

✱TIP: To satisfy a range of tastes, **make multiple versions** of the tuna sandwich. In some, add only a small amount of mayo to the tuna with no celery or green onion. If you know they won't all eat tuna, replace the tuna with finely chopped turkey, or even ham, and make some turkey or ham melts.

Chicken and Fruit Salad Cups

✓ *MAKE-AHEAD*   ✓ *TAKE-ALONG*

Kids love chicken, and this crunchy salad will have them eating something that's both good for them and fun to eat. Baked tortilla chips alongside make this wholesome as well as kid-friendly.

2 large Granny Smith apples, quartered, cored, and diced (about 2 cups)

2 teaspoons fresh lemon juice

3 pounds cooked chicken or turkey, cut into ½-inch cubes ✳

1½ cups diced celery (from 4 large ribs celery) ✳

3 large carrots, scraped and diced (about 1½ cups)

8 ounces Monterey Jack cheese, diced (about 2 cups)

½ cup salted peanuts (2 ounces)

½ cup raisins

1 cup mayonnaise

½ cup sour cream

½ teaspoon celery seed

Salt and freshly ground pepper, to taste

1. Toss the diced apple in a large bowl with the lemon juice.

2. Add the chicken, celery, carrots, cheese, peanuts, and raisins to the apples and toss well to mix.

3. In a small bowl, combine the mayonnaise, sour cream, and celery seed. Season well with salt and pepper.

4. Toss the mayonnaise mixture with the fruit and chicken, coating all the ingredients well.

5. Transfer to a large, tightly sealed refrigerator container and refrigerate overnight, or until time to take to school.

SERVING SUGGESTIONS

Transport this salad surrounded with ice packs in a cooler.

Take along a package of small paper cups—the kind you put in the bathroom—or little paper or plastic bowls from the supermarket, and a supply of plastic forks. Spoon a little salad into the cups and let the kids come back for more if they like.

✳TIP: Speed up prep by buying a fully roasted chicken from the supermarket or deli. Remove the meat from the bone and cut it up. Or, grill, bake, or poach 3 pounds of chicken breasts while dinner is cooking. Let cool and cut up.

Thumbprint Cookies

✓ *MAKE-AHEAD*   ✓ *TAKE-ALONG*

These thumbprint cookies have been a longtime favorite—at home and in the classroom. They come together quickly and without a lot of fuss.

½ cup (1 stick) unsalted butter, at room temperature ∗

2 tablespoons sugar

½ teaspoon pure vanilla extract

¼ teaspoon salt

1 cup all-purpose flour

¼ cup strawberry or grape preserves

Confectioner's sugar, for garnish

1. Preheat the oven to 400°F.

2. In the bowl of an electric mixer or with a hand electric mixer, on medium speed, beat the butter, sugar, vanilla, and salt until light and fluffy, about 3 minutes. Turn the mixer to low and add the flour. Beat the mixture until it forms a smooth dough, 2 to 3 minutes.

3. Remove the bowl from the mixer. Using a teaspoon measure, spoon mounded teaspoons of dough into your hands and roll into balls—just as if you were using modeling clay. Don't over-work the dough—you only want to form the balls, not to knead the dough. Place each ball on an un-greased cookie sheet 1 inch apart. Make an indentation in the cen-ter of each ball with your thumb or the round tip of a wooden spoon handle. Spoon a little of the preserves into the indentations.

4. Bake the cookies for 10 min-utes, or just until they begin to brown. Let the cookies cool on the cookie sheet on top of the stove for a few minutes. Then transfer the cookies with a spatula to a wire cooling rack. If the cookies begin to stick to the cookie sheet, pop the whole sheet back into the oven for 30 seconds, then remove and continue to transfer them to the rack. Cool com-pletely on the rack. ∗

5. To serve: Arrange the cookies on a platter and loosely wrap them in plastic wrap. Once you get to school, dust the cookies with confectioner's sugar.

SERVING SUGGESTION

Use a variety of preserves to make the cookies, for colorful effect and so everyone can have his or her first choice.

∗**TIP:** To tell if the **butter** is at the right temperature for baking these, take the stick and hold each end in your hands. Bend the stick. You should be able just to bend it into a wide "U." It will take about 45 minutes out of the refrigerator to come to 70°F to 75°F. This is the perfect temperature to mix the butter. If it breaks when you bend it, the butter is too cold to beat. If when you bend the stick, the butter squishes through the wrapper, it is too soft. (Put it back in the fridge for a few minutes.)

∗**TIP:** If you have only one **cookie sheet**, rinse it with cold water and dry thoroughly between batches, or the dough will begin to melt before you even get it into the oven, affect-ing its shape and texture.

Mom's Peanut Butter Cookies

✓ EASY PREPARATION   ✓ MAKE-AHEAD

My mom makes the best peanut butter cookies I have ever tasted. The key to these is to allow them to bake long enough to get crisp, but not so long that they brown too much and taste burned. You can make these cookies up to several weeks ahead and then freeze them.

1 cup super chunky peanut butter, at room temperature

1 cup (2 sticks) unsalted butter, at room temperature

1 cup loosely packed light brown sugar

1 cup sugar, plus ¼ cup for rolling the cookies

2 large eggs, at room temperature

2 teaspoons pure vanilla extract

3 cups all-purpose flour

1½ teaspoons baking soda

½ teaspoon baking powder

½ teaspoon salt

1. Preheat the oven to 375°F. In a large bowl, cream the peanut butter, butter, and sugars together with a wooden spoon until smooth. Add the eggs and vanilla and beat well to incorporate the ingredients.

2. Place the flour, baking soda, baking powder, and salt together in a sifter. Sift into a small bowl. ✷

3. Add the dry mixture to the creamed ingredients in thirds, mixing well after each addition. Using a tablespoon measure, spoon mounded tablespoons of dough into your hands and roll into balls about the size of a walnut—as if you were using modeling clay. Don't overwork the dough; you only want to form the balls, not to knead the dough. Transfer to a plate.

4. Place the ¼ cup sugar in a shallow bowl, then roll each ball of dough in the sugar, knocking off the excess so there is only a light coating of sugar. Place the sugared balls of dough on an ungreased cookie sheet.

5. Press each cookie with the tines of a fork to flatten it to about a ⅓-inch thickness. Make one press horizontally and one vertically to create a crisscross pattern. Dip the fork in flour, if necessary, to keep it from sticking.

6. Bake the cookies about 10 minutes, or until they begin to puff and are golden. ✷ Let the cookies cool on the cookie sheet on top of the stove for 3 minutes, then transfer them to a wire cooling rack to cool completely. ✷

SERVING SUGGESTION

Turn the cookies into scrumptious ice cream sandwiches. Place a small scoop of cold, firm vanilla or chocolate ice cream in the middle of half of the cookies, then press the remaining cookies on top of the ice cream to form sandwiches. (If you like, roll the sides of each cookie in finely chopped nuts or sprinkles.) Wrap the ice cream sandwiches with plastic wrap and put them in the freezer to set. If taking them to class, surround them with dry ice in an insulated carrier.

✷ **TIP:** If you do not have a **sifter**, place a large fine-mesh strainer over a bowl. Spoon the dry ingredients into the strainer. Shake and tap the side of the strainer until all the flour mixture has sifted into the bowl. If you don't have either tool, use a fork and vigorously stir all the ingredients together in a bowl to fluff them up.

✷ **TIP:** These **cookies** will puff up when baking, and then fall. Be sure to bake until they have puffed. These cookies benefit from baking to a slightly darker color than, say, Jennifer's Chocolate Chip Cookies (page 205). It gives the peanut butter a deeper flavor.

✷ **TIP:** If you have only one **cookie sheet**, rinse it with cold water and dry thoroughly between batches, or the dough will begin to melt before you get it in the oven.

Jennifer's Chocolate Chip Cookies

✓ *MAKE-AHEAD*   ✓ *TAKE-ALONG*

These are the cookies that started it all. After years of baking with my grandmother and mother, it was natural to make these cookies when I needed extra money in college. My soft, chewy chocolate chip cookies seemed to be just what students needed when they were slaving over term papers or cramming for exams. That early enterprise was the beginning of my culinary career. I have made thousands of cookies using Fleischman's margarine and Nestlé's chocolate chips, but you can use your favorite brands.

3¼ cups all-purpose flour

1 teaspoon baking soda

1 teaspoon sea salt

1 cup margarine (Fleischman's preferred) at room temperature ★

¾ cup granulated sugar

¾ cup lightly packed dark brown sugar

1 teaspoon pure vanilla extract, Madagascar if possible ★

2 large eggs, at room temperature

2½ cups semisweet chocolate chips (Nestlé preferred) ★

1. Preheat the oven to 375°F. In a small bowl, use a fork to combine the flour, baking soda, and salt.

2. In a large bowl, cream the margarine, granulated and brown sugars, and vanilla together with a wooden spoon until very smooth, light, and fluffy. ★

3. Add the eggs to the margarine mixture and beat until well combined.

4. Stir one-third of the flour mixture into the margarine mixture, taking care to incorporate the flour well. Repeat two more times until all the flour has been added.

5. At this point, test the cookie dough with your fingers. You should be able to roll it into balls in the palms of your hands without any of the dough sticking to your fingers. If the dough is sticking, add more flour, 2 tablespoons at a time, until the dough no longer adheres to your hands.

6. Stir in the chocolate chips, just to blend.

7. Use a tablespoon measure or larger spoon to gather the dough. Form the dough into balls using about 1 tablespoon dough or more for each cookie, or into balls of whatever size you choose. Roll the dough between your palms as if you were forming

balls of modeling clay. Do not overwork the dough. The larger the ball of dough, the larger the finished cookie will be. ★

8. Arrange 9 to 12 of the dough balls on each of 3 or 4 ungreased cookie sheets. Bake, one sheet at a time, in the oven, about 10 minutes. Begin checking at 8 minutes. Do not overbake. The cookies will flatten and spread out during baking. They are done when they begin to brown around the edges. Remember, the larger the cookie, the longer the baking time—but keep checking.

9. Remove the cookie sheets from the oven and cool on top of the stove on the pan for about 1 minute. Use a flat spatula to transfer the finished cookies to a wire cooling rack to cool completely. Store fully cooled cookies in an airtight container until ready to serve.

★**TIP:** To me, margarine provides the best **cookie texture**. You can use butter, but to get them soft and cake-like, add ¹/₂ cup more flour.

★**TIP:** **Madagascar vanilla** is the best, with a rich, full flavor. It is available in many specialty stores and some well-stocked supermarkets. If you can't find it, use the best pure vanilla extract available, never imitation vanilla.

★**TIP:** **Cream fat and sugars together** by beating briskly with a wooden spoon, fork, or electric mixer, until they are thoroughly combined, light in color, very smooth, and greater in volume. The volume increases because beating introduces air into the mixture.

★**TIP:** **Ice cream scoops** are ideal for forming cookies of equal size and they are quick and easy to use. There are scoops available in sizes ranging from 1 teaspoon to several tablespoons.

Index

Metric Conversion Guide

Weight

U.S. Units	Canadian Metric	Australian Metric
1 ounce	30 grams	30 grams
2 ounces	55 grams	60 grams
3 ounces	85 grams	90 grams
4 ounces (1/4 pound)	115 grams	125 grams
8 ounces (1/2 pound)	225 grams	225 grams
16 ounces (1 pound)	455 grams	500 grams (1/2 kilogram)

Volume

U.S. Units	Canadian Metric	Australian Metric
1/4 teaspoon	1 mL	1 ml
1/2 teaspoon	2 mL	2 ml
1 teaspoon	5 mL	5 ml
1 tablespoon	15 mL	20 ml
1/4 cup	50 mL	60 ml
1/3 cup	75 mL	80 ml
1/2 cup	125 mL	125 ml
2/3 cup	150 mL	170 ml
3/4 cup	175 mL	190 ml
1 cup	250 mL	250 ml
1 quart	1 liter	1 liter
2 quarts	2 liters	2 liters
3 quarts	3 liters	3 liters
4 quarts	4 liters	4 liters

Note: The recipes in this cookbook have not been developed or tested using metric measures.

Temperatures

Fahrenheit	Celsius
32°	0°
212°	100°
250°	120°
275°	140°
300°	150°
325°	160°
350°	180°
375°	190°
400°	200°
425°	220°
450°	230°
475°	240°
500°	260°

Measurements

Inches	Centimeters
1	2.5
2	5.0
3	7.5
4	10.0
5	12.5
6	15.0
7	17.5
8	20.5
9	23.0
10	25.5
11	28.0
12	30.5